thinking
and
speaking

a guide to intelligent oral communication

Otis M. Walter

Professor of Rhetorical Theory
University of Pittsburgh

Robert L. Scott

Professor and Chair,
Department of Speech Communication
University of Minnesota

Macmillan Publishing Co., Inc.
NEW YORK

Collier Macmillan Publishers
LONDON

Earlier editions © 1962 and copyright © 1968 and 1973 by Macmillan Publishing Co., Inc.

Macmillan Publishing Co., Inc.
866 Third Avenue, New York, New York 10022

Collier Macmillan Canada, Ltd.

Library of Congress Cataloging in Publication Data

Walter, Otis M.
  Thinking and speaking.

  Includes index.
  1. Public speaking. I. Scott, Robert Lee, (date)
joint author. II. Title.
[PN4121.W325 1979]   808.5'1   77-28651
ISBN 0-02-424320-5

Printing: 1 2 3 4 5 6 7 8   Year: 9 0 1 2 3 4 5

preface

Neither misery nor folly seems to me any part of the inevitable lot of
man. And I am convinced that intelligence, patience and eloquence
can, sooner or later, lead the human race out of its self-imposed
tortures provided it does not exterminate itself meanwhile.

BERTRAND RUSSELL

We have written this book first of all because we believe that speech
should be taught more as a liberal art than as a technical skill. Emerson
remarked that speech was the greatest of the liberal arts. But what is a liberal art?

The term dates from ancient Rome when only freemen (*liberi*) were permitted to study that which was not immediately and solely applicable to job
tasks. By association with freedom, the liberal arts have become the sign of
a free person. These arts are, moreover, that which makes freedom possible and meaningful. Speech belongs among them because it helps people

do more than adjust to their environment; it enables people to change their environment or to recognize when change should be resisted. Clearly, speaking belongs among the arts of free people because speech can influence human destiny and human purposes. We have, accordingly, tried to emphasize those principles of speaking most important in societies that are striving to be more free. Hence, we have emphasized the rhetorical problems involved in designing speeches about the forces that enfeeble and brutalize humankind. We have emphasized the analysis of the causes of these forces, the development of solutions to them, and the place of values in establishing humane goals.

We have written this book, secondly, because of the changing nature of students in the past three or four decades. Students have become less proficient in the traditional skills of mathematics and grammar. Yet more than ever, we believe that the best students want to learn to speak well, and, especially, want to learn how to recognize, understand, and solve the problems we face. These problems cannot be solved without a careful study of problem solving. Our students need a course in speech that will exercise their abilities vigorously. While so many courses have become denuded of significance and rigor, we believe speech courses should have these important qualities. We have, therefore, selected those skills of rhetoric that will require the most careful thought, the greatest amount of study, the most incisive imagination, and the greatest powers of analysis.

We owe much to others. We can never repay our own professors, colleagues, and students in ten universities who have stimulated us. We are indebted to disciplines outside our own since many philosophers, psychologists, and sociologists have been concerned with the same kinds of problems that produced this book. Especially do we owe a heavy debt to the great rhetoricians of the past 2,500 years, whose visions we hope we have correctly caught. If the book has merit, that merit is traceable to sources such as these. If it lacks merit, the fault belongs to us rather than to those who taught us so well and who saw so much so clearly.

In the specific preparation of this book, throughout its various editions, we would like to extend our appreciation to the following at the University of Pittsburgh: Professor Trevor Melia; especially to Professors Robert and Dale Newman, who prepared a careful critique of much of the book; Professor William S. Tacey, who carefully read the entire manuscript and offered many significant comments; Professor Terry Pickett, who prepared a computer retrieval of over 15,000 items pertinent to the book, mostly from works in psychology, and Professor Nancy Metzger for many items.

Others have helped: Professor Donald K. Smith of the University of Wisconsin, Professor Bradlee Karen of The College of Wooster, Professor Franklyn Karns of the Cincinnati Seminary, Professor William K. Price of the University of Massachusetts, Karen Garvin of the University of Minnesota.

The help of such people as these produced an edition thought desirable to have in Spanish and in 1975, the *Compañia Editorial Continental*, SA, prepared the first edition available throughout the Spanish and Portuguese speaking world, adding, we hope, a bit of help to societies struggling to become more free. We are justly proud of our work, but with such help we must be modest, for the achievement is the achievement made possible by help as diverse as ancient Athenian rhetoricians and contemporary computers. In this fourth edition, the primary responsibility for writing chapters 1, 2, 3, 4, 5, 6, 8, 9, and 15 was Robert L. Scott's; the primary responsibility for writing chapters 7, 10, 11, 12, 13, and 14 was Otis M. Walter's. The preface was composed jointly.

O. M. W.
R. L. S.

contents

1

our rhetorical world

> Yet, in holding scientific research and discovery in respect, as we should, we must also be alert to the equal and opposite danger that public policy could itself become the captive of a scientific-technological elite.
>
> Dwight D. Eisenhower

You are undertaking the study of speech either because you thought it was a good idea to do so or because someone else thought so and either advised or required you to enroll in the course. But why study speech? This is a legitimate question for you to ask or for someone to ask you. Many answers can be given to that question. We hope that you will examine your own answers and expect you to find reason to recognize additional ones, not just in this course but throughout your life. We shall make some suggestions for you to weigh in considering the essential question: "Why study speech?"

In what has become known as his "Farewell Address," Dwight D. Eisenhower gave an answer to the question, although that is not what he set out to do. Then President Eisenhower, at the end of his second term, having acted firmly for eight years to counter the power of the Soviet Union in foreign affairs, seemed to discover suddenly that our welfare was being threatened internally by forces we created, ironically, to assure our security.[1]

---

[1] The speech, broadcast from the President's office in the White House on the evening of January 17, 1961, is readily available in a large number of sources. It is well worth examining against the backdrop of the events that have filled the years since.

Most people remember his warning against the "military-industrial complex" but few remember the words quoted as an epigraph to this chapter. The key to the meaning of democracy lies in the ability of its citizens to participate in its processes. Eisenhower observed the growing power of special segments of our society and a diminishing ability of most to play effective roles in governing themselves.

As the date made famous by George Orwell, 1984, approaches, the spector Eisenhower raised is by no means exorcized. We are still more than a little inclined to see our problems as mainly questions demanding technical solutions, ones that can be referred to specialists while the rest of us remain passive.

Of course we should respect science and technology. Clearly, however, what we shall do to assure ourselves of the energy necessary to survive, of decent health care for all citizens—regardless of wealth or age—of housing, of a humane environment, and a myriad of other elements that we may take as essential or as merely pleasant, depends on our values and our will.

Even if all our problems could be solved by specialists, would our lives then be those of free men and women? Would persons accepting such solutions as the entire fabric of their lives not have lost something vital to being fully human? In point of fact, not all our problems *can* be solved for us; we must participate.

As textbook authors, we do not pretend that speech-making is in and of itself the sole constituent of a participatory and free mode of life. We do argue that traditionally expressing oneself in the ongoing public dialogue is tightly bound up with the values of freedom. In this first chapter we shall examine that tradition briefly as a backdrop for studying thinking and speaking in our immediate worlds.

SPEAKING IN RESPONSE TO PROBLEMS

The fact that people live together in social bodies generates problems that threaten the well-being of individuals and of the groups with which they identify. Speechmaking is a chief instrument people use in grasping, examining, and settling their problems. The decision to speak may be a critical one for a person and for the group of which he or she is a part. Let us illustrate this assertion by glancing briefly at the life of one of the most famous speakers in American history.

A little more than a hundred years ago, a man no longer young turned from a relatively comfortable professional life to politics, a career from which he had retired some years before in disillusion, having had so little success as to justify the epithet *failure*. But he had come to believe that his country was adopting policies that would be tragic. The proposal of popular sovereignty embodied in the Nebraska Bill and a movement to repeal the principles of the Missouri Compromise threatened to guarantee the growth of slavery. To prevent the growth of an institution that he believed to be only legally sufferable in limited circumstances, he plunged actively into the campaign for the re-election of the United States Representative from his district who had been fighting the legislation he feared. "Stand with anybody that stands right. Stand with him while he is right, and part from him when he goes wrong," he told an audience.

As Abraham Lincoln spoke to audiences, he felt reactions in himself and among his listeners that he had never felt before, although he had always been a crowd pleaser.[2] He began traveling farther from Springfield to speak, although he was not a candidate for an office. People quickly identified him with the opposition to the Nebraska Bill and those who shared his position turned to him for leadership. He spoke and was elected to the Illinois legislature in which he had served years before. He spoke and was nominated a candidate for the United States Senate. During his campaign for the Senate he engaged in that unprecedented series of debates with Stephen Douglas. Although the Republicans polled more votes than the Douglas Democrats, he was defeated for the office in the election held in the Illinois legislature. But he continued to speak and in 1860 he was nominated for the Presidency.

From 1854 to 1861 Lincoln spoke in order to bring about a just settlement of the issues that divided the nation. He sought a peaceful means to his end; but the forces of division, for a multitude of reasons the relative influences of which are still undetermined, were too strong. As President in a nation torn by war, he put the ideals of democratic liberty into words that still live.

Other persons arose to speak during these times. The names of many mark the pages of history—Stephen Douglas, John C. Calhoun, Wendell Phillips, Frederick Douglass, Charles Sumner. There were many others whose names we have never heard, persons who spoke in mass meetings, in frontier churches, in lecture halls, and in polite parlors. They also lived with the issues of the time and felt compelled to speak, to exert what persuasive influence they could, and to give expression to the feelings that moved within them.

In the debate at Alton, Illinois, Lincoln said, "That is the real issue. That is the issue that will continue in this country, when these poor tongues of Judge Douglas and myself shall be silent. It is the eternal struggle between two principles—right and wrong—throughout the world. They are the two principles that have stood face to face from the beginning of time and will ever continue to struggle."[3] Lincoln spoke of the will to oppress and the will to be free. People have oppressed others, do oppress others, and will continue to oppress others, but the issues that have united and divided are much more complex than this simple statement indicates. We cannot recount all of them, but in general people have dealt with them in two ways—by force and by persuasive discourse. Perhaps Cicero overstated the case

[2] See the editor's introduction to *Created Equal? The Complete Lincoln–Douglas Debates of 1858*, ed. Paul M. Angle, Chicago, University of Chicago Press, 1958, p. x.

[3] Ibid., p. 393.

when he claimed that persuasion is the very spring from which civilization flows,[4] *but the history of humankind's attempts to live together seems to indicate that forbearance and persuasion are the alternatives to terror and force.*

The lessons that we have drawn from the brief examination of Abraham Lincoln's speaking are scarcely unique to him or to his times. Consider for a moment one more historical example.

After a revolution had driven the tyrants out of the Greek city of Syracuse in the fifth century B.C., the citizens had to lay the basis for a renewed civil life. One of the most perplexing questions was the ownership of land. Much of the land had been seized and held by the ruling clique for years. How was the land to be restored to its rightful owners? Claims, often conflicting ones, arose. The city could easily have disintegrated into a chaos of grab-and-hold with killings, reprisals, and counter-reprisals. Instead the citizens established courts into which claims could be brought orally and decided by juries. Effective speaking had been useful undoubtedly in many places at many times, but this historical instance is unique because it was at this time, as far as we know, that people first tried to develop a systematic art of speaking that could be taught and learned.

The ancient Greeks studied this art—the art of *rhetoric,* a word that now has taken on much more limited meaning and for which consequently no satisfactory modern equivalent exists. Rhetoric was the art of prose composition, and in those times almost all prose was communicated orally. The ancient Greeks had uses for their art in the democratic assemblies, in which at least hypothetically any citizen could speak. They also spoke in the law courts, in which any citizen could bring a charge against another; the person who brought the charge had to prosecute and the person against whom it was brought, to defend himself. They spoke in great gatherings to commemorate occasions of public interest. *The principles and teachings of rhetoric* (today often known under other names) *have persisted because the conditions that make ours a rhetorical world are the innate results of the need to communicate.* Recognizing the sort of world in which he lived, Aristotle asked in effect, "Why should we be ashamed to defend ourselves physically but not of being able to defend ourselves in rational debate? Is not the use of intelligent speech more distinctive of human beings than the use of our fists?"[5]

OUR RHETORICAL WORLD

Our world is much different from that which the Greeks of Syracuse knew. Even if we were to agree that we face civil war and revolutions, and many believe that we are so faced today, we would probably also agree that the

[4] See *De Inventione,* Bk. I, ch. 1, sec. 2 and *De Oratore,* Bk I, ch. VIII, l. 33.

[5] *Rhetoric,* Bk. I, ch. 1. Paraphrased.

twentieth century is radically different from Lincoln's or Samuel Adams' centuries.

Still, as the old wisdom has it, the more things change the more they remain the same. Our general historical claim concerning forbearance and persuasion as the alternatives to terror and force has been vividly put by Malcolm X as the choice between the ballot and the bullet.[6]

The problem to which Malcolm X addressed himself is in one sense unique to our time and place: Can blacks and whites in America find the means of living decently together? In another sense, the problem is the timeless one of human freedom. Freedom, war, poverty, health, knowledge, and individual values—all of these words give rise to a twisted skein of particular issues that are both private and public.

The fact that we think and feel as individuals but recognize that we share with others the world in which we think and feel brings us to search for ways in which we can act in harmony. Questions such as these find our interests mingled with those of others: Are our conceptions of male and female roles consistent with fulfillment as unique individuals? Can we justify material affluence with the existence of poverty and privation at home and abroad? Is war the price of our material affluence? Does the goal of self-determination for all peoples mean that nonintervention must govern our foreign affairs? Is the family obsolete? Has universal, public education in America become stultifying rather than liberating? Under present conditions can the individual make meaningful political choices?

THE LIMITS OF A POINT OF VIEW

In raising the question "Why study speech?" we have inevitably developed a point of view. Looking at anything from one angle precludes looking at it from another—at least momentarily. In labeling ours a rhetorical world, we have made one statement that we believe is important and descriptive. Accepting the validity of such a statement does not preclude making other statements that may be equally, or even more, important about the way humans live in a world and relate to one another. But even in our sense of rhetorical there are further limitations that shape what will follow in the remainder of this book. It may be helpful to consider two of these now.

The approach we took in the first three editions of this book and maintain in this one has been labeled "problem-oriented" by many who have chosen to use the book and some who have not. Such an orientation is scarcely peculiar to this book or to speaking, but when one finds it, what one finds is highly relative. Things are simply what things are. Nothing is a problem unless someone finds it so. Some state of affairs that one person calls a problem, which suggests that one is hurt or upset and desires to change

[6] *Malcolm X Speaks*, ed. George Breitman, New York, Grove Press, Inc., 1966, pp. 23–44.

things, may strike another as being benign or even delightful. Often such persons can shrug their shoulders and pass each other by, but inevitably as we set about to redress those circumstances we call problems, we find others involved, and our problems become those of human relations.

Although we believe that human beings often need to focus on problems in order to create decent social environments for those concerned, not all communicative behavior is problem-oriented. A good deal of our talking together may be quite routine, which is not to say unimportant; we could scarcely get along without such communication. Furthermore, much of our speaking may be designed, consciously or unconsciously, to share feelings, perhaps affirming the legitimacy of those feelings and identifying ourselves with our fellows.

Although it is not sensible to apply a problem-orientation to all communication, such an orientation may often be unavoidable. Since people who study at all must sort out segments of the world in which they live and, further, must sort out their responses to these segments, beginning with problem-oriented communication strikes us as being useful for speech students. Undoubtedly many, we hope most, students will wish to expand the scope of their study of communication beyond problem-oriented speaking. Other sorts of beginnings are possible, but any will involve some sort of limitation.

Not only do we take problem-oriented communication as an important focus, but we focus even more narrowly on the making of speeches. Surely we feel the pressures that make ours a rhetorical world, and we respond to these pressures in a multitude of ways that are not speech-making. Again our emphasis is one among many possible emphases. Not only do we believe that the making of speeches is a persistent human activity worth study in and of itself, but we are convinced that students will discover in their study a number of concepts and will develop skills that will be useful in understanding other forms of communication and in undertaking that most subtle and difficult task—understanding communication generally.

Making speeches, then, is not the only way, and perhaps not the most important way of influencing the opinion and action of others. The mass media of communication not only transmit and report speeches but are used to carry a myriad of messages in forms quite different from the typical public speech. Furthermore, even in these days of the staggering importance of publicity, no one should discount the fundamental influence of informal, everyday, face-to-face communication.[7]

---

[7] The research of Paul Lazarsfeld and Elihu Katz indicates that in the forming of opinion the personal influence of someone the man or woman feels close to is vital. Even in absorbing information and ideas that are disseminated through the mass media, word-of-mouth repetition, to reinforce or reinterpret, and especially to validate, the information and ideas seems crucial. Thus there are opinion leaders, not only in government, education, business, and labor in obvious leadership roles, but in the neighborhood, family, on the job, and on the street. See, for example, Katz and Lazarsfeld, *Personal Influence*, New York, The Free Press, 1955; and Katz,

There is no scarcity of important forms of communication nor important problems and concepts for the student to study. There is only the question of where one might start. We believe that studying speechmaking gives ordinary persons an opportunity to concentrate on something that is distinct enough in their ordinary activities for them to become conscious of the principles and problems involved and yet is simple enough for them to exercise a decent control over the complexities that face humans in any communication situation.

THE CIRCLE OF INFLUENCE

When we begin to think about all the forces that are influential in forming our opinions and actions, we may become discouraged. We are especially likely to become discouraged if we concentrate on the bewildering complexity of our world. At such moments, it is easy to say that the issues that face us are too perilous for ordinary hands. The examples of great speakers, verbal geniuses from Cicero to Churchill, may discourage rather than encourage us. We may think, "Let the geniuses speak." To take this attitude, however, is to have too narrow a view of speaking and, much more important, of ourselves and our society. Moreover, we invite those who are only too ready to step forward saying, "I'm just the sort of Caesar the moment requires."

Every person using this book will inevitably associate himself or herself with a number of groups, both informal and formal. Many of these groups—social, religious, educational, labor, business, and political—conduct themselves through speaking. Members speak and listen to speakers. In these groups we inevitably come to grips in some way with the issues that face our times. In these circles we may be influential; and no matter how small the circle or how limited our influence, it is important. Our society—economic, political, and religious—is composed of a tangle of interwoven circles within which men and women talk and exert influence. The influences exerted have a way of transmitting themselves back and forth throughout the skein. Take as an example: How shall industrial wastes be disposed of? To what extent shall citizens through governmental bodies exercise control of disposal? Who shall pay the costs? How? At what levels shall the pollution of our environment bring us to stop certain production and do without the products? These and more questions are not beyond our reach. They will be decided; and they have too long been decided by default. No matter when or how they are decided in the future, the climates of opinion within which the decisions are made will be vital. Many of the relevant questions will be decided in governmental bodies, but even in these we should be able to make our influence felt. For example, what sorts of men and women will be elected? What environments will influence them? What will influence their values? All

"The Two-Step Flow of Communication: An Up-to-Date Report on an Hypothesis," *Public Opinion Quarterly*, XXI (Spring 1957), 61–78.

these questions and more will be determined by the circles of influence that will inevitably operate and of which we shall be a part. The way in which they operate, how openly and freely they operate, will also be determined by ourselves—how we think, what we say, and what we do.

Our problems are manifested on many different levels. We tend to see the obviously great manifestations of our problems and sometimes overlook the manifestations in which we may be more intimately involved. Take human conflict as an example. In living together human beings come into conflict. What shall be done? We may tend to think first of global conflicts, but we find human conflict in the home, in the neighborhood, in the school, and in the community. We must deal with human conflict in thousands of cases and in many different ways, and we shall often want to speak.

THE EXPRESSIVE VALUE OF SPEECH

We have been emphasizing the communicative function of speaking. This emphasis is altogether proper and is, indeed, primarily important. Too often, however, we are led to be unsympathetic with speakers and fail to recognize another important possible value of speaking. Our impatience is sometimes indicated with statements such as, "There's altogether too much useless talk in the world." "People should talk less and listen more." "He has nothing to say that I haven't heard. It's all been said a thousand times." No doubt some of this complaining is justified and may be healthful to the degree that it stimulates speakers to make worthwhile demands on themselves. Ralph Waldo Emerson put the criticism neatly in a single phrase; we do hear too much of the "small-pot-soon-hot style" of speaking.[8] Still the criticism is too easily made and may well lead us to turn quickly toward allegedly great leaders, failing to see our potential roles in our own circles of influence. Moreover we may fail to recognize an important value of speaking.

We should emphasize, especially as students and teachers, the value speaking has not only as communication but as expression. People live together in societies and share problems, but each of us is a unique human individual. The lessons we learn may be ancient ones; the answers we find may be common ones. But we must learn lessons and find answers ourselves; we must appropriate them to make them ours. We may listen; we may read; we may experience in a hundred different ways multitudes of forces that communicate meaning to us. But do we *know* unless we ourselves express the ideas that we find moving within us as a result of our varied experiences?

When we say that we must express for ourselves the lessons we learn from books and from experiences, we are saying more than simply that we must recite. We must commit ourselves to ideas—to understanding, to analyzing, to solving—and stand responsible for recommending those ideas as good in-

[8] "Of Eloquence."

formation or opinions to others. Although students may be modest in the presence of what others have accomplished, although we may feel grateful for the advantage of studying what others have left for us, we must make knowledge for ourselves. If our concept of what knowledge can and should be does not include the responsibility to make it active, then we have a stunted concept of what it is *to know*.

To put the matter another way, expression is an innately human need. This need will create tensions that seek resolution just as do the commonly recognized physiological needs. Speaking, of course, is only one means of expression. Some may manipulate lines, colors, or musical notes meaningfully, but most of us must depend primarily upon the use of verbal symbols to fulfill our expressive needs.

When Cervantes wrote, "Make it thy business to know thyself," he echoed a lesson more than 2,000 years old, but in over 400 years more it is still, as we know, "the most difficult lesson in the world."[9] Speaking is one road we may take in our search for knowledge of ourselves. In confronting others we may come face to face with ourselves. We may choose to speak or not; we may choose to speak on trivial matters or try to grasp important problems; we may choose to search for important meaning that we sense in what seems trivial to others and so lift ourselves a trifle and, perhaps, them; or we may make anything we touch trivial. But we shall choose, and by our choices we shall form ourselves.

SPEECH AS A HUMANE STUDY

In discussing the expressive value of speech, we indicated that speaking is one way of learning about oneself. In speaking one must face problems—problems that have a history and a relationship to other people, groups, and traditions we have formed for living together. If we take this point of view, we cannot be satisfied with looking at speech simply as a skill. We are not arguing that skill is in no way involved in good speaking; we do argue that speech has little meaning if taken as something wholly apart from the matrix of human involvement, which has given rise to a fascinating skein of studies all of which are, from their own particular angles, the study of being human. We conclude that the study of speech belongs in that area of the liberal arts traditionally designated the humanities.

Speech is commonly called a *tool*. Whether or not this label is healthful depends on one's attitude in applying it. Human tools are nothing to be taken lightly. In order to help determine whether or not certain fossils should be designated as human, archeologists seek in the strata where they find the remains for tools that might be associated with the fossils. Truly humans are tool-using animals. But we must step beyond this simple observation.

[9]*Don Quixote*, Part II, Bk. 4.

Arguing along lines similar to those we have taken, Michael Polanyi has written:

Every time we assimilate a tool to our body our identity undergoes some change; our person expands into new modes of being. I have shown before that the whole realm of human intelligence is grounded on the use of language. We can reformulate this now by saying that all material life by which we surpass the animals is evoked in us as we assimilate the articulate framework of our culture.[10]

This book, and the course in which you are involved, are modest efforts in the enterprise Polanyi has identified.

From another point of view, speech is a humane study. We are surrounded by phenomena. Education is largely a matter of coming to understand these phenomena. A part of our world is composed of speakers and speeches. If we are interested in understanding our world, we ought to be interested in what is a uniquely human product. Certainly a speech is a work representative of humanity. If it is important to study the art, the music, and the literature that humans have produced as representative of the characteristics of human potentialities, it is important to study speeches. If we are to understand the forces within and outside ourselves that urge us to expression, we must be interested in the efforts of others to communicate. To become a student of speech is to develop an intellectual disposition that will help make a person humane.

Speech has a history, many theories, and a body of literature. You could study speech as history, as theory, or as literature without speaking. This book, however, emphasizes your role as a speaker. In studying the chapters that follow, you should gain a deeper understanding of what a speech is, of how speeches are made, of the problems that speakers face. In so doing, you will come to understand better a pervasive part of your human environment.

This understanding is an end in itself and also a tool. This understanding may be viewed as a foundation for the further study of speech, study that may range from the theories of persuasion in ancient cultures through the outstanding speeches produced by the leaders who have built our nation to contemporary theories of communication. Frankly we believe that these studies will be more meaningful to students who have themselves struggled with the commitment to ideas that have led to attempts to gain the understanding or belief of others.

WHY STUDY SPEECH?

We have tried to answer the question with which the chapter began by discussing three general purposes:

---

[10] *The Study of Man*, Chicago, Phoenix Books, 1963, p. 31.

1. *To serve the needs of public communication.* Fundamentally our argument is that people in living together face common problems. If those problems are to be resolved cooperatively, individuals must develop the skills required to participate intelligently in the public arena. Even though that participation will often be frustrating and difficult, we must find ways to be effective or give up more and more control over our own lives.

Of course speech-making is only a fragment of the compendium of skills that free citizens need, but it seems to us an especially important fragment because it is one readily available to ordinary persons. Further, the habits and insights gained in studying a problem-oriented approach to speaking ought to serve individuals well in participating in other forms of expression.

2. *To serve personal needs of expression.* Again, speech-making is but one means of self-expression, but each of us has very real needs to find out what our creative capacities are. Speaking should help us learn about ourselves and the lessons we learn should transfer to nonspeaking situations. Many of our personal needs and our personal problems will be pursued quite privately. Nonetheless, our private selves live public existences; most problems are simultaneously private and public. The student of speech has an opportunity to understand some of the tensions people feel in balancing the pulls of self and the pulls of the communities of which they are a part.

3. *To build a basis for understanding the traditional values of a humane culture.* Again, these values transcend the study of speech. Moreover, we often feel that the simple fact that values are *traditional* does not make them good. That feeling should be all the more motivation for trying to meet those values firsthand and intensively. Making choices about presenting information and beliefs to others in speeches should give most persons an experiential basis for understanding their own culture and, perhaps, rejecting aspects of it. Often we will decide that what we need is more understanding, and students of speech should be motivated to seek that understanding in diverse paths.

We introduce these purposes here for your thought. You should evaluate the skills recommended in the first part of this book in the light of these purposes. The second part of the book is designed to unfold a process of thinking applicable to speeches and, for that matter, to facing problems in almost any circumstance.

Throughout this book, we try to suggest that human beings constantly face ethical questions. Again, we would argue that the process of making speeches gives persons realistic experience in clarifying for themselves their ethical orientations. Rather than leaving all discussion of such responsibilities to latter chapters, although we trust that much that students find later in this book will be highly relevant to making ethical decisions, we shall add one more preliminary discussion to this introductory chapter.

THE RESPONSIBILITIES OF A SPEAKER

Speakers exercise rights, but these rights carry contingent responsibilities. Speakers have a right to communicate thought and feeling; they have the right to give expression to the needs of their own personalities. On the other hand, these rights are assured only by the cooperation of a society in which they are valued. In our particular society we have been assured rights as a part of a political system. Many of our citizens hold strong opinions concerning the disparities between the promises of that system and the practices they observe daily. In short, clarifying ideal values and taking actions that will assure the exercise of these values are vivid problems for us. We do not pretend that we have a formulary answer for the problems, but we do believe that the concept of responsible speaking may give students a way of approaching them.

Speakers, basically, may speak freely, but they must speak in such a way as to protect and extend this right. Any action that weakens the right of free speech is irresponsible. Putting such a general proposition into practice is not simple. Consider three personal responsibilities as guidelines: [11]

1. To speak with the best knowledge possible.
2. To seek and respect the responses of others.
3. To reveal openly one's own commitments.

As we speak, we must realize that for the moment we are the source of knowledge for our audience about ideas and occurrences. We have a right to our opinions, but we have the responsibility for stating openly and as clearly as possible those opinions and the grounds upon which they are based. To mislead an audience concerning our ideas or to distort the facts relevant to them is irresponsible.

We have, then, the responsibility to understand the subjects about which we speak as completely as possible. This burden is not an easy one to bear. Often extremely conscientious persons are nearly paralyzed, refusing to take action on the grounds that they do not know enough. This sort of person is more to be respected than the person who is ready to give an opinion on anything with scarcely a second thought. But our argument is that being human and finite we cannot expect perfect insight nor can we wait indefinitely if we are to fulfill our obligations to ourselves and our fellows. The situations that demand our participation come and go. We can fail in two ways—by not preparing sufficiently to meet them as well as we can be expected to and by refusing to act at all.

Recognizing our right to our own opinions, as good speakers we should respect the right of our listeners to form their own opinions. We will then shun

[11] Our analysis here is similar to that of Karl R. Wallace, "An Ethical Basis of Communication," *Speech Teacher*, IV (Jan. 1955), 1–9.

any opportunity to foist our views upon others. We will try to foster those circumstances in which ideas and the speakers who hold them may be freely confronted by other speakers and questioned by listeners. "In the end," Walter Lippmann has written, "what men will most ardently desire is to suppress those who disagree with them and, therefore, stand in the way of their desires."[12] Lippmann sees this desire as the outcome of the right of speaking freely unattended by the concomitant responsibility to entertain direct confrontation of contrary opinions.

We have discussed briefly two responsibilities: to act with the best knowledge one can obtain in the circumstances and to act in such a way as to encourage the freedom of response, the more direct the response, the better. There is a third we would mention: to act openly in one's self-interest.

As speakers we will inevitably have our own interests in subjects with which we are concerned. We have a right to be committed to ideas, to persons, to groups; but in speaking to others we must be responsible for these commitments. We must, in short, be willing to disclose our own interests. Although it is not easy to gauge the motives out of which we act, willful distortion of these motives in speaking to others is irresponsible.

Some social scientists see the lack of this responsibility to be a serious threat to the soundness of the social fabric in mid-twentieth-century America. For example, in his study of the Kate Smith war bond radio marathon during World War II, sociologist Robert K. Merton was struck by the way men and women emphasized Kate Smith's integrity. He commented:

> The emphasis on this theme reflects a social disorder . . . in which common values have been submerged in a welter of private interests seeking satisfaction by virtually any means which are effective. It is a product of a society in which "salesmanship"—in the sense of selling through deft pretense of concern with the other fellow—has run riot.[13]

Unfortunately the widespread feeling that "everyone's out to get you" was not a momentary phenomenon of the Second World War. Everyone knows only too well the tendency to joke cynically about the motivation of politicians, labor leaders, businessmen, students, college professors, and everyone else.

We can respond in one of two ways, we can use "everyone else" to rationalize our own disposition to distort for public consumption our own motivation, or we can act as openly as we are truly able.

As you gain experience in speaking, weigh the good sense of these three responsibilities. We ask you to consider one test—effects. A speaker is accountable for the effects at which he or she aims and for the means used to gain these ends. To answer the question, "What are good means and good

---

[12] *The Public Philosophy*, New York, Mentor Books, 1956, p. 100.

[13] *Mass Persuasion: The Social Psychology of a War Bond Drive*, New York, Harper and Brothers (now Harper & Row, Publishers, Inc.), 1946. p. 10.

ends?" is no simple matter that we can settle with finality for each reader. This is a question that you will constantly meet in many different contexts and applications—many of these will not directly involve speaking but the insights you gain will be relevant to your problems as a speaker.

As a speaker you must be concerned with the effects of your speech. John Dewey has argued compellingly, "Certainly nothing can justify or condemn means except results. But we must include consequences impartially. . . . It is willful folly to fasten upon some single end or consequence which is liked, and permit the view of that to blot from perception all other undesired, and undesirable consequences."[14]

The person who says, "He gets good effects, but his methods are bad," speaks nonsense. Methods are bad because they have bad results. Often these bad results will be long range and difficult to predict. This fact does not relieve one of his responsibility for them. For example, I may get you to take good actions immediately by keeping you ignorant, but I shall be responsible, at least in part, for both your immediate desirable action and for the ignorance out of which other undesirable action may grow. Often the bad results will be the weakening of some societal values; for example, if one in speaking attains a laudable goal in such a way as to lessen an audience's ability to make free decisions, both effects must be weighed, and the speaker is responsible for both.

Speakers must make commitments to the groups within which they act. As speakers we benefit from the institution of free speech and abuse our rights only at the peril of the value that we enjoy. A person who jeopardizes the rights of others in speaking is no less immoral than one who steals from others or injures them physically.

SUMMARY

We have discussed briefly the forces that make ours a rhetorical world. We have mentioned some advantages to be gained by speaking and some responsibilities of the speaker. In undertaking the study of speech you are helping to prepare yourself to live effectively in a world of human, verbal interaction; you will gain insight into the advantages and responsibilities of speaking by your own experience. You may come to disagree in some ways with our interpretation of speech and the situation of the speaker. These are complex issues as are most of the issues we face as individuals and as groups. But we must struggle with these issues if we are to deserve the advantages of a materially rich society that has provided the instruments and the freedom necessary to participate in working out our own goals and the directions to be taken in reaching these goals.

In undertaking the study of speech you will be gaining increased ability

---

[14] *Human Nature and Conduct*, New York, Henry Holt and Company (now Holt, Rinehart and Winston), 1922, pp. 228–29.

and opportunity to express yourself. "An idea," says the Swedish film maker Ingmar Bergman, "is a brightly colored thread sticking out of the dark sack of the unconscious. If I begin to wind up this thread, and do it carefully, a complete film will emerge."[15] We may not be artists and the film may not be our medium of expression; we may never become the speakers that Lincoln or Churchill were, nor be moved by the circumstances that moved them. But we too must find ideas and express them for ourselves, making them *our* ideas.

In undertaking the study of speech, you should expect a deep pleasure. It will be the pleasure that comes from acquiring important knowledge, from learning to speak with increased skill, and from committing yourself to meaningful social values.

[15] Hollis Alpert, "Bergman as a Writer," *Saturday Review* (Aug. 27, 1960), p. 23.

2 *forming ideas*

To ask at what time a man has first any ideas is to ask when he begins to perceive; having ideas and perception being the same thing.

JOHN LOCKE

Every idea is an incitement. It offers itself for belief and if believed it is acted on unless some other belief outweighs it or some failure of energy stifles the movement at its birth.

JUSTICE OLIVER WENDELL HOLMES
(Dissenting Opinion in Gitlow vs. People of New York, 1924)

Somehow most people harbor the notion that great ideas lie indistinct in the future and must be waited on with varying degrees of patience. Perhaps so. But if so, we suggest that the student be a little impatient. We are struck with Ingmar Bergman's suggestion that an idea "is a brightly colored thread sticking out of the dark sack of the unconscious." We must "wind it carefully" as he says, but we must *wind* if the idea is to take form.

Too often the lament, "if I only had a subject . . ." is simply an excuse for inactivity, human enough to be sure, but eventually debilitating. Finding a subject may at times seem troublesome, but don't make too much of the difficulty. Although the *right subject* is important, one should not expect sudden, immense revelations more than once or twice in a lifetime. Our advice is no secret formula; almost every creative artist has attested to it: *Start!* You may start with vague notions or less, but start. Start reading, start conversing, start making notes. Ideas form slowly. Even those that seem to burst in sudden flashes of insight come to persons who at the moment are resting or engaged in other tasks but who have been working on problems to which the "inspiration" is related. Everything else may come to the person who waits, but inspiration comes to the person who works.

The beginner may agree with what we have said, but still want more specific instruction. We shall try to comply with this quite proper desire. But we must warn, as we shall repeatedly do, that if the general suggestions we shall make are to be at all meaningful, they must become so as individuals apply them in specific, personal efforts to compose speeches.

It is common to hear statements like these: "The speaker needs a good idea." "Good ideas make good speeches." "If I only had a good idea. . . ." But these statements raise a question: *What makes an idea a good idea for a speech?* To approach an answer, let us consider two other questions, the first of which we have already dealt with generally: "Where does one find ideas for speeches?" and "How should one state ideas for speeches?" Both of these questions should be understood in the sense of the title we have chosen for this chapter. The problem is not so much *finding* and *stating* ideas that are somehow just there waiting to be picked up and polished as it is a problem of *forming* ideas for speeches. The answer, then, is not once-and-for-all sort of matter; it is a continuous process. What we set forth in this chapter will be nothing more than a few suggestions for grasping and beginning to wind those bright threads of thought.

FINDING IDEAS FOR SPEECHES

Let us imagine a conversation. Two friends leave speech class after having been assigned a speech. The instructor has not assigned specific subjects. The students are free to choose their own "as long as you choose something you feel quite strongly about. Something you *want* to talk about. You should choose something significant." The two friends walk across campus.

FIRST: That's the trouble. I don't *want* to talk about anything.
SECOND: *You* don't want to talk? That I've never noticed.
FIRST: Well, who knows what'll strike him as significant.
SECOND: Strike who?
FIRST: The instructor, that's who.
SECOND: What difference does that make? It's what you think is significant.
FIRST: Don't be silly. You know who counts in there and it's not us.
SECOND: Getting a little paranoid? People picking on you?
FIRST: You know what I mean. He just sees things differently than we do.
SECOND: The point is to make him see them your way.
FIRST: No way. There's just a big barrier. You know.
SECOND: You sound as if you take the cliché about the generation gap seriously.
FIRST: It may be a cliché, but it's there.
SECOND: I'm not so sure. What makes you think so?

We'll take the hypothetical conversation no further. But it is clear that so many people think that there is something *there* that the "generation gap" has become a cliché. Should it be a cliché? What are the feelings, the experiences, the points of view that give the concept some reality? How might someone who senses the importance of the differences make others who do not sense those differences begin to understand them? Questions such as these might be starting points for several speeches.

It is also worthwhile to notice that in this hypothetical case the students are interacting. You should not simply form ideas; you should form ideas for an audience. The concept of "speaker" is not sensible in isolation from "listener." The relationships among people, and how people perceive and act in a common environment, are what should fascinate the speaker. We shall discuss "adjusting ideas to people" in Chapter Six, but the notion of others responding should permeate the preparation process from the outset.

Personal experiences

Beginning speakers too often neglect what they have seen, what they have done, what they have thought. There is not a freshman college student who has not played, worked, and studied with some degree of intensity. The beginner should ask himself questions like these: "What hobbies or leisure activities do I enjoy?" "What jobs have I held?" "What subjects have I studied?"

Often personal experience will only start beginners toward subjects. They are not yet experts who can bring to bear immense knowledge and understanding. But at the same time the beginners ought not underestimate what they have done. Some useful beginnings are indicated in these remarks: "I met a Buddhist yesterday. I knew a little about Buddhism and would like to know more. . . ." "I used to help make ice cream in a little plant in my home town. I wonder where ice cream got started anyway. What I mean is. . . ." "I visited Quebec last summer and this separatist movement is. . . ." You could multiply the list endlessly.

We shall discuss material, what we shall call supporting material, in Chapter 3. We might remark in anticipation of that chapter that the beginner should not fail to search his or her own experience for the material that goes with ideas. A near traffic accident may lead a student to want to talk about problems of safe driving. At the same time the story of the experience may well be useful in communicating the idea to an audience.

Although most students underestimate the worth of their own experience, a few overestimate the sufficiency of what they have seen, done, and thought. "I know all about the attitude of Canadians toward the United States. After all, I spent all last summer there." This example may seem too patently absurd, but a number of speakers, not all of them beginners, display similar attitudes toward their subjects. Most of the men and women we have met who deserve to be called "experts" are just those who seem the quickest to express their limitations and seek even more information.

Conversation

What do you talk about ordinarily? Much that is frivolous without doubt; we all do. But on the other hand, not everything that you and your friends discuss is of no potential concern to audiences you might address. The very student who in the morning says, "I have nothing to talk about. How can I make a speech?" will probably, before the day is over, discuss with his friends at least two or three subjects that potentially might be the bases of speeches.

People talk about clothes. Clothes have history, utility, and meaning. On one level, talk about clothes might be the sheerest sort of trivia; on other levels, the same people might discover ideas that would be well worth communicating. Clothing as a social symbol, for example, is illustrated in the fascinating progress of blue jeans from what was nearly a uniform for campus radicals in the late 60s to the most fashionable boutiques of the early 70s. Clothing involves color and, necessarily, theories about the psychological effects of color.

Students of speech may well wish to sharpen their conversations by pointing them more directly toward ideas that they are considering using in speeches. There is no better way to work some of the vagueness out of the early ideas for speeches than to try them in conversation. Speakers may find themselves becoming more and more interested in their subjects and developing stronger desires to learn more about them. On the other hand, conversation may be discouraging. Some speakers discover that their great ideas (almost all untried ideas are *great*) when scrutinized are rather flat. But in such cases, they may be challenged to learn more. At any rate, it is better to become disillusioned about the merit of an idea before one uses it in a speech rather than during or after the use of it.

Conversation, of course, is one means of gathering ideas and materials from one's friends. Often speakers will want to formalize the process, will want to talk to an expert or two; in other words, they may find interviews to be valuable. Students are usually surprised at how readily businessmen, labor leaders, politicians, college professors, experts of all sorts will take time to talk with them. The student, of course, should make a definite appointment, telling the person from whom the interview is sought the purpose of the request. It is extremely important that the student prepare for the interview carefully. One should formulate his own thoughts as definitely as possible, preparing specific questions to ask. The student speaker who "wants to know something about the purposes and techniques of interviewing persons applying for employment" and asks a personnel manager to "just tell me everything you know about interviewing applicants," will be met with either disgust or a deluge of information that will sweep him or her hopelessly adrift.

Reading

The first impulse of many beginning speakers is to run to the library to collect material. And, if the beginner is not unaware of the potential profit of assessing past experience and using conversation in preparation, this impulse is excellent. For most of us, no general source will be as profitable as our reading. We should do two kinds of reading to help us form initial, tentative ideas for speech and to help us gather the material to refine our ideas and support them: general, daily reading and specialized reading to find data on whatever particular topics we tentatively think we might pursue.

The speech student who suffers from a paucity of ideas probably reads neither regularly nor from substantial sources. There is no "program" that everyone should follow to be well informed, but there are some general recommendations that might be made. Read a newspaper daily, and read it carefully. The columns and editorials may especially stimulate ideas for speeches, but the news sections will not prove barren to a good mind. Often students complain that they live in communities in which the daily newspaper is inadequate. Although we ought not be too quick to despise our local newspapers, the thorough, inquisitive student (in or out of college) may want to make use of library facilities to read one of the well-known metropolitan newspapers. *The New York Times* and *The Christian Science Monitor* probably come to your mind, but there are other fine newspapers—*The Washington Post*, the *St. Louis Post-Dispatch*, and the *Atlanta Constitution*, to mention a few. The student may, and probably should, read one of the popular news magazines regularly, although it might be wiser to rotate one's reading among them. The alert student probably already reads at least one magazine of the *Harper's, Atlantic Monthly, Fortune* sort rather regularly. A person with a mind that is at all active will probably read several nonfiction books each year. If there are too many people, in college classes and out, with too few ideas, our reading habits may give at least a partial explanation. The student who reads only when forced to and who says, "I don't know what to talk about," deserves no sympathy.

There is another grave weakness in our reading habits. Most of us, when we do read about controversial problems, select material written from points of view that match our own predilections precisely. We make certain that our minds are not exposed to new ideas. If for no reason other than to find out what the devils on the other side are up to, we should read from sources with which we differ, and, if we intend to speak to audiences composed of people other than enthusiastic mirror-images of ourselves, nothing could be wiser.

The complaint that one can only get one point of view in commercial newspapers and magazines is becoming more and more common. Whether or not one agrees, the sudden birth, and often as sudden death, of scores of "underground newspapers" must be accounted a significant phenomenon indicating fundamental dissatisfaction with ordinary sources. One may suspect that devotees of *The Berkeley Barb* or *Rat* are as apt to read uncritically their favorite sources as do the readers of *National Review* or even *The American Legion Magazine,* such suspicions should not blind anyone to the fact that materials of a greatly varied nature are available to the person who is inquisitive and who may be motivated to seek varied points of view.

Many experienced speakers keep notebooks or files of ideas and materials. The beginning speech student would be well advised to keep an idea notebook. Buy a notebook that is handy to carry with you. Then assess your past experience, your ordinary conversation, your past reading for potential ideas. Jot down any ideas that occur to you; do not hesitate because they may seem vague or wild or stale. You can make them grow. A good idea that occurs to you now and goes unrecorded may be unrecallable later. Add to your notebook day by day. If you are in the least conscientious in the enterprise, you will not need to complain later, "I just don't have anything to talk about."

Once you have a tentative idea for a speech, one perhaps that you have tested in conversation, you will want to dig out some relevant materials to help you refine and support it. This desire may lead you to the library. Undertaking special reading and making notes are two topics relevant to our discussion at this juncture, but these matters are also relevant to the subject of our next chapter. We shall discuss them, then, in a special appendix to this chapter where they will stand as a transition to the chapter on supporting materials that follows.

FORMING IDEAS

It is impossible to separate getting ideas from stating ideas. In practice the two are inseparable. In phrasing ideas the speaker should turn to his or her own past experience, to conversations, and to reading, and in so doing hold in mind that one seeks to communicate to an audience possessing knowledge, abilities, needs, and attitudes. One should begin to jot down any idea that stumbles in. Most beginners make the mistake of wanting to wait until the idea seems fully formed and satisfactory before attempting to write it down as the beginning for working out a speech. The experienced speaker knows that every start, no matter how faltering, can be the basis of a fresh start.

Using topics

Most ideas for speeches begin as what we call *topics* but ought not to remain long in that form. A topic represents a more or less vague center of interest. "I'm interested in ecology," would not be a surprising statement to hear someone make. But just what would that someone be interested in? The person would probably be worried about the fragile balance of living beings, but the more one knows about the topic, the more one realizes that like the forms of life, a nearly infinite variety of speeches are possible "on ecology." The United Nations, personnel practices, George Bernard Shaw, world law, pornography, population, mutual funds, urban sprawl, ping pong, Christianity, participatory democracy, and so on all represent topics.

Given any one of these topics, a prospective speaker might be soon inclined to add words: George Bernard Shaw's theory of humor, world peace through world law, personnel practices that dehumanize, the influence of mutual funds on the stock market, the Christian underground. These are still topics, but each indicates a narrowing focus of thought. The speaker should seek progressively to narrow his topics, realizing that like the small, unattended child in a cafeteria, one is apt to take more than one can handle.

All too often we hear speakers, in the classroom and out, who undertake to talk about "problems in the Near East," "maps, mapmakers, and mapreaders," "reviewing election procedures," and the like; but we are never quite sure just what they are talking about. Whereas topics make good places to begin and might serve well as titles for printed programs or announcements, the speaker must have a much more precise statement of his ideas. A speaker who cannot state the subject with precision and clarity, can scarcely expect an audience to be able to do so.

A good speech should be unified; it should be governed by a single idea toward which all other ideas and materials in the speech should point. This central idea can be indicated by a number of different labels, but for the sake of convenience we shall use only one and that is a very common one— *thesis*. The thesis should be stated as a single declarative sentence. It may take many attempts to phrase the thesis in such a way that the speaker feels it expresses the idea properly. Starting with topics and narrowing them will be useful, but the speaker should not be satisfied with less than a careful, complete statement of this thesis. Before discussing the statement of thesis further, another point should be considered. In arriving at a position where one can view a subject in relationship to an audience in such a way as to make a satisfactory statement of the thesis possible, the speaker should consider quite carefully the purpose with which he or she speaks.

Stating the purpose

The speaker speaks to communicate, true; but that is the most general statement of purpose. One must communicate something to someone. The best way to think of the purpose is in terms of the *response* that you want from your audience. What do you want them to think, to understand, to say, to feel, to know, to do, to value, to despise? The audience will respond in some way, if only to decide (although the decision is not always a highly conscious one) that the speaker is not worth listening to and that dozing or staring out the window will be more pleasurable. You must realize that an audience will respond and you must seek to guide those responses. *The way to start is by deciding what response to the speech you want the audience to have.*

Traditionally, purposes are classified generally by three infinitives: to entertain, to inform, and to persuade. A speech "to entertain" may be thought of as one in which the speaker desires to keep the audience pleasurably engaged in listening for five, ten, twenty minutes or so. Beyond the recollection of having enjoyed listening, the speaker does not care how the listeners respond.

A speech "to inform" may be thought of as one in which the speaker has some body of knowledge that the audience does not possess or at least does not understand fully. The purpose that engages the speaker is to help listeners to comprehend more fully and to remember the more salient aspects of the material.

A speech "to persuade" may be thought of as one in which the speaker undertakes to change the attitudes of an audience or to urge them toward some action. Traditionally, the speech "to persuade" is subdivided into speeches "to stimulate," "to convince," and "to actuate." The speech "to stimulate" operates on the assumption that the speaker's attitudes and those of the audience are highly similar (they, too, believe in the doctrine, the candidate, the program, the principle), but that the attitudes need to be sharpened, to be made more immediate and important to the listeners. The speech "to convince" is one in which the speaker assumes that the listeners possess attitudes that differ in some important respects from his or her own and speaks to modify those attitudes. In the speech "to actuate" the speaker aims at getting an audience to take some action either immediately or in the future.

The speaker may state a purpose for a specific speech by extending the infinitive to make a phrase. This sort of statement may be called "the specific purpose." Some examples of specific purposes are indicated in these infinitive phrases:

1. *To entertain* my listeners with a series of anecdotes concerning a child's difficulty in communicating with adults.
2. *To inform* my listeners of the common methods of merchandising best sellers in paperbacks.
3. *To convince* my listeners that the federal government must operate on a balanced budget this year.

Although viewing purpose in speaking as taking three general forms and using one of these general forms to state a specific purpose for a speech may be useful procedures, they are limited and too often misleading. For your own use you should try to state your purpose in terms that seem to you uniquely proper for expressing your particular subject in terms of the desired response of your listeners. In doing so, the infinitive form will probably occur. Further, the traditional forms of "to entertain," "to inform," and "to convince," may be useful if they are viewed as points of departure rather than as necessary categories into which all speeches will fit neatly.

When you examine a specific speech to determine purpose, you rarely find a clean example of a speech to entertain or to inform. Almost inevitably speeches that seem at first to fit into these categories take on persuasive colorations, sometimes quite strong ones. "Pure" speeches to entertain are rare.

This is not to say that a speaker who may aim only to relieve the tensions of daily living by amusing an audience is not performing a legitimate speech purpose, although such distraction may be better served by means other than speeches. Most speeches that are highly amusing attempt to change attitudes, values, and behavior. The speech to entertain an audience with a series of anecdotes concerning a child's difficulty in communicating to the adult world may bring the audience to be more sympathetic with the attempts of children to communicate and to be more sensitive to the nature of the problems children face. "Pure" speeches to inform are also rare. Many speeches to inform may demand that the audience listen because the information is important if not vital to its interests. If indeed the information is important, it will probably have some effects upon the attitudes of the audience. For the speaker to say, "I don't care about these possible effects," is blind at best and dishonest at worst. It may be that you will not want to make evaluations or demands explicit, but you ought to examine clearly the implications of the material and take into account what effects these may have in planning your purpose.

Every speech will be at once a speech to entertain (in that the audience will find pleasure in listening or probably won't listen at all), to inform (in that even a conscious effort to give no information will probably fail, you ought to recognize that you will be dealing with information of some sort), and to persuade (in that at least you will want the audience to value what is done and at most will want to direct specific beliefs or actions). It is possible in a well-unified speech to serve several rather distinct purposes if you work carefully; ordinarily, however, one purpose will tend to be dominant.

We feel that it is quite useful for you to write a paragraph, or even more, setting out the purpose for which you speak—the response or group of interrelated responses you desire from the audience. This paragraph will not be part of the speech as such but will be a preliminary step in composition. There is a danger in this procedure. Speakers are apt to be too indefinite in their aims, and indefiniteness may arise in writing at length about purpose just as it may in the most terse statement of a topic. However, if you also state a thesis quite carefully, you can avoid this danger.

Let us consider an example of the statement of a speech purpose adapted from the work of a speech student.

My audience expects a speech to entertain, and I hope not to disappoint them; however, I have a rather specific attitude that I hope to communicate to my listeners and perhaps at least shake their predispositions to respond heartily to the subject with which I shall deal, the so-called "adult TV westerns." In my opinion adult westerns are adult only in superficialities—the heroes sometimes drink, smoke and carry on romantic relationships but in the end, "good" triumphs. The emphasis is mainly on the distractions of physical violence, but, in addition, violence is enthroned as a means to an end.

Basically "adult westerns" are not much different from old-fashioned "children's westerns." I shall, therefore, advocate the return to "children's westerns" which are at least morally superior in that the heroes do not drink, smoke nor consort with women. I hope in so doing to make it clear that westerns are childish. Making my point of view clear will be difficult, but I shall aim at convincing my audience, or at least upsetting them a little, and to do so in a way that will entertain them.[1]

This statement is not perfect nor was the speech perfect. But the speaker did have rather clear ideas of the sort of response he wanted from his audience. Full statements of purpose are likely to bring speakers to the clearest possible understanding of what it is that they are attempting.

In working out a statement of purpose, whether you simply think one through making few notes, or whether you write out a paragraph or two discussing your purpose, try to hold in mind these suggestions.

1. In speaking you are seeking a *response* from your audience. The familiar infinitives, to entertain, to inform, or to persuade, may be useful starting points, but you should try to indicate the unique response you seek from your particular audience.
2. In speaking you stand in some *relationship* to your audience. Ask yourself what sort of function you can serve. You will be an agent of some sort. What sort of responsibilities do you want to take as an agent?
3. In speaking you seek to make some ideas *relevant* to your audience. Whatever the subject matter may be that you draw from, for the moment at least, you are its advocate. If part of your sensitivity in forming ideas must be to the audience, part must be to the subject. The speaker is an intermediary. In seeking a purpose, you must think in terms of the connections possible between people and ideas.

Stating the thesis

The thesis should be stated as a complete declarative sentence and as precisely and vividly as possible. Sometimes the statement of a thesis will come quickly; often you will find it difficult to state and will revise your phraseology time and again. The more carefully you have worked out the purpose of your speech, the more confidently you will be able to state the thesis.

Try to think of the thesis as an assertion. We make assertions constantly: we ought to go to work earlier; nutritious lunches can be inexpensive, tasty, and easy to prepare; this dictionary is better than that one. Let your assertion represent the subject with which you want to deal and reflect your consideration of the particular audience to whom you will speak. Here are some samples.

Final examinations are designed to stimulate students to learn, to help them evaluate their accomplishments, and to provide the instructor with a basis for assigning a grade.

Final examinations are absurd.

Final examinations should be abolished.

[1] Adapted from an outline prepared by Donald Marti, University of Minnesota student, 1959.

Any one of these three examples might serve as the thesis for a speech. The first will probably be basically a speech "to inform"; the other two, speeches "to persuade." The second, however, might be the basis of a quite entertaining speech. You will notice that each succeeding example is broader. The second might be included as a part of a speech for which the third example stood as the thesis.

One difficulty that speakers often face is in making some idea dominant. Usually a person truly caught up by a subject will discover that one idea leads to another. Soon one will want to talk about this, this, this, and this. That impulse is quite normal, but, if one wishes to leave an audience with a coherent impression of what has been said, one will need to form a thesis. For example, the speaker interested in adult TV westerns discussed his purpose usefully, but the statement of a thesis is needed for a clear focus. Consider these two possibilities:

TV westerns are nothing but childish diversions.
Since TV westerns generally suggest that individuals use violence to gain their goals, they inculcate a childish morality.

These two statements are different. A speaker might be interested in either, but if he or she seems to support both, the result may confuse the audience or at least distract the listeners from the purpose the speaker would most like to accomplish. The first thesis would probably enable the speaker to make a lighter, more entertaining speech. But material that is highly amusing would probably detract from the impact of the second thesis. Perhaps the second thesis would require more time to develop adequately than the first, but in reading the discussion of the speaker's purpose, you might conclude that it is the latter thesis that the speaker is the more interested in.

At any rate, if the speaker simply says, "Well, I want to talk about TV westerns," he or she is not likely to focus sharply on either thesis or to realize the advantages that either may hold for an audience.

You may have noticed that the student whose work is cited here spoke about television two decades ago. Much has changed; currently "cop shows" are popular and westerns have waned. But the attitudes expressed by the student are still common. Perhaps they match your own; perhaps they do not. Such a dominant aspect of our culture as television needs constant assessment. For example, the *topic* of violence on television is one that is addressed again and again. Unfortunately, we find all too few examples in which speakers or writers seem to have taken stock clearly of their purposes. And if they have not, a thesis is either notable by its generality, or is not present at all.

Most experienced speakers know that they have to state a thesis carefully, and, further, that as they develop materials for the speech they may be wise to reconsider and perhaps to restate the thesis to make it match more closely the dominant thought they are developing. In phrasing and rephrasing the thesis, a speaker should constantly ask, "Does my thesis reflect well the purpose I have for addressing my audience?"

WHAT ARE GOOD IDEAS FOR SPEECHES?

Good ideas for speeches are those that you have drawn from your own experience—either your personal activities, or from your reading, or, preferably, both—and that you have tested in conversation. Good ideas for speeches must be chosen and limited in terms of the listeners for whom they are intended. Good ideas for speeches must be well stated. You should consider your purpose carefully and state it fully; you should state the thesis as a single declarative sentence.

Good ideas are those that you want to talk about. You should not, however, feel that a strong desire to speak must fasten on you unbidden and with a terrible swiftness. A strong desire to speak will probably grow as you consider your own experiences, values, and convictions, as you think through and talk through your vague ideas, and as you relate these ideas to your audience's knowledge, needs, and attitudes. That your ideas may be vague at the outset should not concern you. Most persons need to work with specific materials in order to bring their ideas the specificity necessary to make good thesis statements.

For class discussion

1. Come to class with a topic that you feel has the potential to become a good subject for a speech.
2. Working as a class, or in smaller groups, try to phrase different purposes upon which speeches might be made selecting from among the topics individuals suggest.
3. Discuss the merits of the statements of purpose. Select those that seem to be most interesting to the group.
4. Try to phrase a thesis for each statement of purpose selected.
5. To supplement this exercise, choose one thesis. Go to the library to find relevant material. Make an annotated bibliography of not less than five items. (By *annotated* we mean add to the bibliographical citation of the source a paragraph or more in which you summarize the material presented in whatever source you cite. Strive to be concise.)

APPENDIX ON READING AND MAKING NOTES

Reading

Once you have a tentative idea for a speech, one perhaps that you have tested in conversation, you will want to dig out some relevant materials to help refine and support it. This desire will carry you to the library. We could at this point add highly detailed information on finding material in the library, but we shall not. It is our opinion that many students reading this book will not need such information, and those who do will profit little from such explanations. We shall give the latter only a brief introduction.

One should not assume too readily that one knows all about library resources. The only way to discover what sorts of materials are available and learn how to use them is by visiting the library repeatedly with specific projects and the object in mind of discovering as much as possible about what's there. Most libraries can furnish printed guides, but for the person who has had no opportunity to use a library, personal help may well be advisable. Library personnel are usually among the world's most helpful people. Your speech instructor is able and willing to give you guidance; you will find some helpful exercises at the end of this chapter. As you use library facilities time after time, you will become quite at home and be amazed at the amount of material available and at the different ways you can track down the necessary material.

Books.   Most students are fully aware that a library lists its book holdings in a card catalog. Ordinarily each book has three cards appearing in different places in the alphabetical file: an author card, a title card, and subject matter card. If you know either the author or title of a book, you can find it easily. If you are interested in discovering all the books in the library on some given subject matter, you can look for the general heading, e.g., League of Nations. Because the cataloger may not have used the topical headings you think of, you may have to look under various associated headings. Usually the subject matter cards will list other headings used in the catalog for related subjects.

If you have a book related to the ideas you are interested in exploring, check the author's bibliography and footnotes for references to other books (periodicals, reports, pamphlets, and so on), which you might find useful. Most students report that this simple expedient usually yields a helpful list of sources quite quickly.

By glancing through the table of contents and index, you can often locate specific discussions in which you may be interested. You may well miss some important matter in so doing, but this is a risk all must run. For the sake of conscience one can recall Francis Bacon's famous remark: "Some books are to be tasted, others to be swallowed, and some few to be chewed and digested." Unfortunately, Bacon did not state once and for all which are which.

Periodicals.   In their regular reading, students of speech should locate a number of articles relevant to ideas they wish to develop. But as you begin to work on your ideas you will find quickly that your store of information has obvious lacunas, and that you want to compare your ideas and materials with other views.

Most students have used *The Reader's Guide to Periodical Literature.* Ordinarily you will be checking subject matter headings in this source and must, as when you use the card catalog, do a good deal of cross referencing.

Occasionally you will have the name of a specific writer and can check the alphabetical listing by his name.

Quite often you should not be satisfied with the popular periodicals indexed in *The Reader's Guide*. As good as many of these sources may be, you will often want to check more technical or professional work. *The American Psychologist* or *The Economics Quarterly* may contain articles that will give you the ideas and materials to carry your analysis beyond what your audience might typically be faced with.

You should become acquainted with special indexes. *The Social Sciences and Humanities Index* (before June 1965, *The International Index*) is useful for speech students. You should certainly become acquainted with indexes to materials in areas in which you are especially interested. Education students should be familiar with *The Education Index;* engineering students, with *The Engineering Index.*

Newspapers. Students with good reading habits long ago may have begun to keep a clipping file. If you have, you may discover that you have a rough sort of index to help you find information in newspapers. If you have clipped newspaper articles relevant to some idea you'd like to develop in a speech, you probably can find similar reports in other newspapers of about the same date. Checking different newspaper versions of events is sometimes highly informative. Major libraries will subscribe to a wide variety of newspapers.

The New York Times Index lists its articles by subject matter and by author, if the article is by-lined. It is the only indexed newspaper in the United States. Again, the date on which an event is reported or discussed will be an excellent clue to tracing down similar items in other newspapers.

Pamphlets. Pamphlets are usually more difficult to use in most libraries than are books or periodicals, but often they will yield specific information that you will find useful. *The Vertical File Service Catalog* lists pamphlets issued by a wide variety of organizations. Publications of the various departments, agencies, and bureaus of the federal government are listed in *The Monthly Catalog—United States Government Publications.* Most major libraries have special reference rooms and a reference librarian who can assist you in using the available resources.

Other sources. The speaker may need all sorts of special information and may have recourse to many more sources than we shall discuss here. For example, one of the authors recalled the quotation from Francis Bacon used earlier and needed to check to see that he had it accurately. He turned to H. L. Mencken's *A New Dictionary of Quotations* [2] a more familiar book of the same sort is *Bartlett's Familiar Quotations.*

Almanacs (*The World Almanac, Information Please Almanac,* and so on)

---

[2] New York, Alfred A. Knopf, Inc., 1962.

will yield all sorts of statistical and other factual information. The *Statistical Abstract of the United States,* published yearly, is an even richer source of statistical information. Sources such as these are usually held in the reference room of large libraries; in looking for them, a student may find *The Statesman's Yearbook: Statistical and Historical Annual of the States of the World.* Quite often encyclopaedias will be well worth consulting for specific, factual information.

In looking for information about the authors of information, speakers may consult such sources as *Who's Who in America* (or one of the regional versions of this reference book), *Current Biography, The Directory of American Scholars,* or *International Who's Who.*

Making notes

As you read, you will want to make notes. What should you note? You will want specific pieces of information (Chapter 3 should help indicate what sorts); you will refine your ideas and, perhaps, begin to build outlines (Chapter 4, as well as the rest of this chapter, should help indicate how you may proceed).

In making notes of specific pieces of information, the speaker will be wise to arm himself with a good supply of index cards, either $4'' \times 6''$ or $3'' \times 5''$. Learning to jot separate bits of information on separate cards will prove to be advantageous. It is easy to sort cards, to classify and reclassify, to put aside those that turn out not to be directly useful, and to rearrange those that are.

You should put three things on each card: (1) a heading indicating what's on the card so that you can sort and rearrange easily, (2) the information itself, and (3) the source. There are various formats you might follow, but a common one looks like those on the following page.

Notice that an indication of the author's position is included with the source in the second example. Some note takers like to indicate the author's name, and often a few words indicating who he or she is, at the top of the card as we have done, but they put the source, the magazine or book or whatever, at the bottom of the card after they have recorded the information itself. But, as we said, the placement of the details involves arbitrary choices; it is important to have the details clearly at hand.

Some note takers, to avoid the labor of copying the complete source several times on different cards, use a code number that matches a bibliography list. This method may save time *if* the note taker is an orderly person who never misplaces lists.

It is often wise to delay affixing headings to notecards until a later rereading. At that time, you may have a clearer idea of the shape that your ideas are likely to take in the speech and, therefore, be able to label your information in a more useful fashion.

Library assignments

Note: In making bibliographical citations of sources, use these forms.

1→	Human experience evokes a sense of self.
2→	Robert J. Lifton, *The Life of the Self: Toward a New Psychology,* New York, Simon & Schuster, Inc., 1976, pp. 50–51.
3→	Central to human experience is the struggle to evoke and preserve the sense of the self as alive, and avoid the sense of the self as dead. All living beings share the struggle to remain alive. But the urge to retain and enlarge the *feeling* of being alive—of vitality—is specifically human, an evolutionary trait of symbolizing mentation that stands at the border of biology and culture.

1→	A dilemma in government regulation.
2→	Charles L. Schultze, Chairman of President Carter's Council of Economic Advisers, "The Public Use of Private Interest," *Harper's,* May 1977, p. 50.
3→	The benefits of potentially superior information that a regulator can bring to bear have to be balanced against the inability of monolithic regulatory judgments to match the diverse preferences of individuals and by the inevitable sluggishness with which regulators adapt to changing circumstances. Where the potential harms from a product feature are great and where the technical difficulty of evaluating information is very high, then regulation may be the best alternative, despite its inefficiencies. But in all cases we should compare an imperfect market with an imperfect regulatory scheme, not with some idea and omniscient abstraction.

For books

Percy, Walker. *The Message in the Bottle.* New York: Farrar, Straus & Giroux, Inc., 1975.

Blankenship, Jane, and Hermann G. Stelzner (eds.) *Rhetoric and Communication.* Urbana, Ill. University of Illinois Press, 1976.

For periodicals

Trilling, Diana. "Daughters of the Middle Class," *Harper's,* Apr. 1977, pp. 31–38, 92.

For periodical articles with no listed author

"Plain Talk about America's Global Role." *Time,* June 6, 1977, pp. 8–10.

1. Using *Reader's Guide to Periodical Literature,* look up "television violence" (or some other topic assigned by your instructor).
   a. What cross references are given?
   b. What magazines are cited with which you are not familiar?
   c. List articles from at least three magazines, preferably from magazines unfamiliar to you. Browse through several issues of each of these magazines just to get acquainted with them.

2. Using *The Social Sciences and Humanities Index,* repeat the steps for number one. What is the difference between these two indexes?
3. What other indexes to periodical literature can you find in your library?
4. Using the card catalog
   a. Look up either *pacifism* or *guerrilla warfare.*
      (1) What cross references are given?
      (2) List at least three books on one of these topics.
   b. Does your library have a copy of the Percy book listed on page 31? If so, note its subtitle. Does it have a copy of Tom Wolfe's *Mauve Gloves & Madmen, Clutter & Vine?* If so, note the information given about the book on the catalog card. Of Carl Belz's *The Story of Rock?* If so, what edition or editions? Note the dates.
5. Using Saul Bellow (or some other major author assigned by your instructor.)
   a. What books *by* the author does your library have?
   b. What books *about* the author does your library have?
   c. What periodical articles published during the last four years about the person or the person's work can you find through the use of relevant indexes?
6. Compare articles on the same subject from at least three encyclopedias.
   a. Which article do you consider best?
   b. Why?

3

supporting ideas

They do not understand me; I am not the mouth for these ears.
NIETZSCHE

True beauty and usefulness always go hand in hand.
QUINTILIAN

As you formulate ideas in relationship to an audience and your own purposes, you will assert these ideas for your own analysis and ultimately you will either assert or imply them in the speech itself. One of the primary tasks in your speech will be to make the ideas clear, interesting, and acceptable to your listeners. All of us can sympathize with Nietzsche's Zarathustra. Like him we may wish to withdraw to the mountains. But Nietzsche makes Zarathustra come down from the heights repeatedly to preach in the town and to the passersby.

The tendencies to rail at listeners for being obtuse or to stand haughtily aloof are all too familiar. Rather than turning away from audiences it may be wiser to turn toward our *truths* and our development of them. Consider, for example, these assertions: "When the Russians use the word *détente*, they do not mean by it what we Americans are likely to assume." "The principles upon which the slide rule is constructed are simple ones that can be readily understood and applied by anyone." "If we are to fulfill our responsibilities toward ourselves and others, we must be governed by the concept of self-determination." "Norman Mailer's *The Prisoner of Sex* is a bad book." How many of these assertions are clear, interesting, and acceptable? The speaker cannot, of course, answer this question without first modifying it by asking another: *To whom?* But assume yourself to be the audience to whom the assertions are addressed. What ones meet all three criteria? Imagine yourself making these assertions to any audience. What kind of responses might you get? "What do you mean 'bad book'?" "Slide rules! I never could understand math." "Another moralist is about to tell me how I should behave."

The point should be clear. Whereas some assertions may be instantly clear, interesting, and acceptable to audiences and then may be used to help support other assertions, most assertions cannot stand alone; and most ideas, asserted or implied without support, deserve the application of the often-heard *mere assertion* with all the negative evaluations that phrase implies.

If an intelligent person who had never studied theories of speech-making were to listen carefully to a large number of speeches or were to read the best speeches of the ages, that person would soon discover that good speakers tend to make use of recognizable means of making assertions clear, interesting, and acceptable. These means have traditionally been isolated and discussed in speech textbooks usually under the heading of *supporting materials.*

The term *supporting materials* is a good one. Think for a moment about the function of *supporting;* think in a physical sense of things that need supporting and of what supports. You and the chairs you sit in have legs; houses have foundations; battles have supporting actions; he who is destitute has "no means of support." Think for a moment about the word *material.* "That which gives substance" is material. "We can't build a bookcase. We just don't have the material." Football coaches are often heard to make similar statements. Too often speakers "just don't have the material" necessary to build ideas—clearly, interestingly, and acceptably.

The person who would become a speaker must take responsibility for answering three questions. *What sorts of supporting materials are there? Where can I discover supporting materials for my speeches? How can I distinguish good material from poor or just passable material?* We have dealt with the second question in Chapter 2 and reviewing that chapter when you have completed this one should prove useful. We shall now give some terms and suggestions that may help speakers answer the other two questions. But you must remember that these are not the sorts of questions that can be answered "once and for all." You must continually endeavor to increase your understanding of the answers, and to find fresh answers as well, as you deal with specific subjects and specific audiences. Our answers will be somewhat arbitrary. With the third question especially, one might well work endlessly, and we shall make only a beginning in answering it.

What sorts of supporting materials are there? An answer to this question must be arbitrary and artificial. In the first place, many different divisions and labels are possible. We shall choose a list of categories that we believe is simple and useful. In the second place, a given passage may be composed of the intertwined elements of several different kinds of supporting materials. A good speaker, for example, may make simultaneous use of testimony, statistics, and visual aids. The student ought not to be misled by any textbook's categorization of materials into believing that the types necessarily stand neatly apart. But in general, supporting materials may be classified as

1. Examples.
2. Statistics.
3. Testimony.
4. Analogies.
5. Visual Aids.

Examples

In Alberto Moravia's novel *The Lie*, the protagonist, an intellectual, undertakes to explain an idea to his wife, a shrewd, complex woman, but no intellectual. He says to her:

"Ah, yes, there may be some truth in that. I was looking . . . I was looking for something which I then called 'genuineness' and which it seemed to me I had found in you."
"Genuineness?"
"Yes."
"What does 'genuine' mean?"
"Genuine, in the sense in which I use it, means 'sincere.' "
"Sincere?"
"Yes—that is, real, authentic, not false, not a parody."
"A parody?"
"A parody—that is, an ironical imitation."
"Well, tell me something that's genuine, give me an example."

If this conversation makes you smile slightly, your amusement may result partly from its familiarity. All of us have demanded of someone, "Give me an example of that." And we have all had similar demands made on us. Listen carefully today to see how many times you hear the words *for example* used. In trying to make ideas clear and compelling in conversation, we all use examples and often label them as such.

In trying to understand an idea or to get another to accept an idea, a critical question is, "Has the thing happened?" If so, when? Where? How? Many speakers bewailing the moral decay they purport to see among their contemporaries and wishing to stress the danger may point to the oft-used example of Imperial Rome. Speakers desiring to make viable the idea of patient, persistent commitment to a goal in spite of staggering obstacles may tell us in some detail about the work of Marie and Pierre Curie. An entire speech may be composed of a single example. Although rare, such speeches can be impelling, as Wendell Phillips' famous "Toussaint L'Ouverture" demonstrates.[1]

A contemporary counterpart of Phillips' "Toussaint L'Overture" is Paul Ehrlich's "Eco-Catastrophe!" Like Phillips', Ehrlich's work takes the shape of a single, long example, although, unlike Phillips', Ehrlich's is fundamentally hypothetical. He set the hypothetical scene in 1979, for him ten years in the future, and projected what would occur to our natural environment given certain assumptions. Dramatically, he announced near his conclusion, "A pretty grim scenario. Unfortunately, we're a long way into it already. Everything mentioned as happening before 1970 has actually occurred. . . ."[2] The whole, although basically a detailed, hypothetical example is formed of a mixture of specific instances and detailed examples. The work is fascinating from several points of view; for the student of speech, it is a complex and rich set of intertwined examples.

A speaker who knows what examples are, who is continually looking for examples, is likely to find them. The more examples you find, evaluate, and use the more you learn about examples. Some elementary classifications of examples may prove useful. Examples are either detailed or undetailed, factual or hypothetical.

Undetailed examples

Opinion polls are such an overpowering feature of our existence that even more than three decades after the event we are still likely to hear someone say with a touch of relish, "The pollsters can be wrong. Look what Harry Truman did in 1948." His election to the presidency took the flavor of the victory of the underdog because the leading opinion polls had predicted that Thomas Dewey would be elected.

Almost everyone has heard some speaker or another say, in effect, "Great handicaps can be overcome, as Helen Keller's life proves." Other undetailed examples to the same effect can be easily and quickly cited. And therein lies the advantage of this sort of supporting material.

Probably any example could be detailed, but there is an advantage in using undetailed examples: The speaker assumes that the examples are well known to the audience and simply need to be mentioned; the result, if well-chosen instances are used, is a sense of sharing experiences. In a sense, the listeners help to make the speech.

Although undetailed examples may stand singly, it is common and highly effective to compound them. Notice how Lee Loevinger, a former member of the Federal Communications Commission, piles example upon example in

---

[1] This rather long address is an excellent one for the serious student of speech to study. See Wendell Phillips, *Speeches, Lectures, and Letters*, Boston, Lothrop, Lee & Shepard Company, 1893, pp. 468–94. The speech may also be found in W. M. Parrish and Marie Hochmuth (eds.), *American Speeches*, New York, Longman, Green and Company (now Longman, Inc.) 1954, pp. 311–22.

[2] For a complete text see Karlyn Kohrs Campbell, *Critiques of Contemporary Rhetoric*, Belmont, Calif., Wadsworth Publishing Co., Inc., 1972, pp. 111–23.

this excerpt from a speech, "Is There Intelligent Life in Washington?" given to an audience of professional broadcasters.

Shortly after World War II, Hollywood stopped making movies for entertainment and devoted itself to significant social and political messages. Broadcasting since then has concentrated on commercials and crime reports—fictional, clinical and statistical. Publishing has eliminated virtually all topics except religion, personal gossip and reports of sociological investigations into the sexual customs of American natives. This has left the country with a gigantic Entertainment Gap.

Always responsive to the wishes of the people, the residents of Washington are making it the entertainment capital of the world. The name of the game in Washington today is not politics and power, it is publicity. Local celebrities are those who get publicity like Barbara Howar, Woodward and Bernstein, Barbara Walters, Shirley Temple Black, Walter Cronkite and Eric Sevareid.

Some of you may recall the good old days when professional comedians were people who lived on the West Coast like Buster Keaton, Charlie Chaplin, the Marx Brothers, Laurel and Hardy, Abbott and Costello, the Ritz Brothers and the Keystone Cops. Where have they all gone? It is simple. The contemporary comedians have all gone to Congress. Those who used to pass themselves off as actors are now appearing before the public as politicians. Time permits mentioning only a few such as Ronald Reagan, George Murphy, Cary Grant, Jane Fonda and Paul Newman.

On the other hand, clearly the entertainers are in Congress. On a normal day in Congress someone gets up to speak and says nothing. Nobody listens. Then everybody disagrees. Among recent Congressional acts, Congress repealed the corporation income tax by mistake, then instructed IRS to collect it anyway. Congress also held a lively debate on a bill to promote General George Washington from a three-star to a four-star general.[3]

Here you notice the names. Each has been connected with an event or two that should be familiar to the speaker's audience. But some of them may miss you completely. The important lessons to notice here are two: (1) the opportunity to pack a good many details into a short compass of time, and (2) the assumptions about listeners that make all materials, but especially undetailed examples, effective, or not effective.

Undetailed examples may be especially useful in answering the question, "What is there in my immediate experience that makes me think, feel, or act as I do?" Assuming that our listeners will often be persons like ourselves in many respects, such examples will also be useful in sharing our experiences with others, that is, in reminding others that they have thought, felt, and acted as we have. In speaking of the influence of the incessant commercial messages echoing through a consumption-oriented society, one student speaker said:

---

[3] *Vital Speeches of the Day*, Jan. 1, 1977, pp. 173–74. This speech is an interesting example to study from the angle of the speaker's purpose. Clearly it is a speech to entertain; but equally clearly, it is not only that: it is a persuasive speech. To be more specific, one must consider carefully the nature of and the direction of Loevinger's numerous humorous barbs.

We are what we own. We find our personalities, make identities for our very souls, from our possessions. Our cars, our clothes, our stereos with their stacks of records— these are more than things for us. Think of the name-brands that go with them. Think of the slogans. What do these say of our personalities?[4]

Often examples are so undetailed that they may be referred to as "allusions." Allusions have long been a part of the skilled speaker's art, especially useful because they do depend heavily on the participation of listeners.

Detailed examples

Having invited her audience to participate by supplying details from their own lives, for that is what undetailed examples should do, the student speaker just cited chose to analyze in some detail several advertisements for well-known cosmetics. The details helped clarify and intensify the interpretations she wished to share with the audience.

The detailed example should have the characteristic of good story telling. Speaking on a highly controversial subject—the effects of television on children—Elton H. Rule, President of the American Broadcasting Companies, argued that parents must share viewing experiences with children; he used this example:

A given television program may inform a child—or it may confuse him. It may delight a child—or it may disturb him. The difference is the degree of his parents' involvement. Eda LeShan, a noted expert in the field of child psychology, tells the story of a mother whose marriage was collapsing. She thought she and her husband had shielded their problems from their 11-year-old son, until the day she and her son watched an ABC Afterschool Special dealing with divorce.

The mother reported that "as the program went on, Andy kept inching closer and closer to me. I put my arm around him and suddenly realized his whole body was trembling. It was a terrible shock. I realized that he had known all along what was going on, was terrified, and that my husband and I should have discussed it with him a long time before. That program kicked off the most honest and important conversation I'd ever had with my child." We can all wonder what effect the program would have had on the child if his mother hadn't been there.

That's an extreme example, but a revealing one. Let me offer a different one. . . .[5]

If the speaker has chosen well, the details will help the audience identify with the ideas the speaker believes are bound up with the example. But, of course, the speaker *interprets* the example. The very notion of *choosing* an example indicates that the speaker interprets. Rule seems to recognize that the audience may see things differently and immediately introduces another example to help fix the ideas he wishes to stress.

[4] Adapted from a speech by Susan Bradley, University of Minnesota student, 1970.

[5] "Children's Television Viewing," *Vital Speeches of the Day*, Sept. 15, 1976, pp. 25–26.

Consider the way in which John R. Silber interprets an experience to create a detailed example:

Recently, I had occasion to evaluate a lecture on the language of fish. It included a stunning movie with fish swimming by, making a babel of fishy noises. Some sang from their swimbladders, little bubbling, gurgling sounds like a coffee pot; others swam by with snaps and clicks, tiny aggressive sounds, little tap, tap, taps; still others made amorous noises too subtle for description. Eighth-and ninth-grade students watched the film. But on its sound track was also the noise of a rock band! (The imposition of Schubert's *Serenade* would have been equally distracting.) When I asked why rock had been added and why students were expected to distinguish fish sounds from all the implausible noises of the band, I was told that rock music would increase the children's interest![6]

Certainly the details are imaginative: "sounds like a coffee pot"? "amorous noises"? Probably the details will raise no quibbles, and they do add interest. The most pointed interpretation, however, follows the speaker's account of what he saw and heard:

The assumptions were clear. So was the condescension toward children. Without distracting gimmicks, no eighth- or ninth-grade child could be interested in the possibility that fish use sounds in order to communicate. No normal children would want to watch the fascinating movements of the fish or hear their entrancing sounds. It was assumed, in short, that the young have no intellectual curiosity, no interest in organized and meaningful data; that instantaneous, non-meaningful education is not merely acceptable, but ideal.[7]

In being inaugurated as a university president, Silber criticized much that he thought current in education; detailed examples were a principal vehicle for that critique.

Hypothetical examples

The categories of examples we have listed overlap. For the most part the examples referred to in the previous discussion of detailed and undetailed examples are also factual. Whereas the meaning of *factual* should be clear enough in this context, a few words concerning *hypothetical* examples may prove useful.

In fighting for the Compromise of 1850, Henry Clay stated the issues that threatened to lead to disunion, and then argued, "Well, now, let us suppose that the Union has been dissolved. What remedy does it furnish for the grievances complained of in its united condition?" Twenty years earlier in his famous reply to Hayne, Daniel Webster used the hypothetical mode of dealing with the threat of disunion by imagining in some detail the circum-

---

[6] The example is from Silber's inaugural address as President of Boston University, "The Pollution of Time," *Boston University Alumni Magazine*, Sept. 1971, p. 5.

[7] Ibid.

stances—the actions of the states and of the representatives of the federal government—that would probably occur in order to emphasize the impossibility of peaceful secession.

The hypothetical example, the "supposed" case, is an ancient device, but too often the beginning speaker overlooks the possibilities. The speaker with vigor and imagination can often invent hypothetical examples to make his ideas clear, interesting, and acceptable. Russell W. Peterson, President of New Directions, a citizens' action group, creatively extends possibilities to make a hypothetical example:

India extracted from the wastes of a commercial power reactor the plutonium it used to set off the atomic explosion that shattered the world's confidence that the proliferation of nuclear weapons could be prevented.

Less than 20 pounds of material can be fabricated into a terribly potent suitcase-size weapon. The technical know-how to do it is obtainable from school libraries and public government papers, as was demonstrated by the young Princeton Graduate Student, John Phillips, last year.

The Hanafi Muslim terrorists, who held over a hundred hostages in Washington, D.C., had guns and machetes in their guitar-shaped cases. Suppose that it had been a nuclear bomb made from stolen plutonium—with the explosive power comparable to the bomb dropped on Hiroshima? The possibilities for terrorist power and blackmail boggle the mind.[8]

Quite often speakers are warned against the use of hypothetical examples. Even though most authorities grant that such examples may be useful for making ideas clear and interesting, "they don't prove anything." Making ideas clear and interesting are no mean achievements, but we would argue that the hypothetical examples may help listeners structure their thoughts in ways resembling the speaker's. In such cases, the speakers will come closer to gaining acceptance than they probably would otherwise. Peterson, you noted, bound up his hypothetical example with two that were factual. The entire group makes a tight pattern that his listeners probably found compelling. Of course that effect depends on the listeners familiarity with the details mentioned.

Roy W. Menninger, of the famous Menninger clinic in Topeka, Kansas, works hypothetically to arouse responses in an audience:

I would start by asking if each of you, at one time or another has not had some experiences like this—maybe drinking a little more than usual, maybe laughing a little louder at jokes that are not that funny, maybe working a little longer, maybe playing a little harder, maybe making love a little less often. Perhaps on top of this you have experienced a few of those restless feelings that are hard to name. A sense of disquietude, not exactly depression; a feeling that you have not got much to look forward to, as you think you should. . . . If you have experienced any of these—and there are

8"We Citizens Cannot Sit Back and Relax," *Vital Speeches of the Day*, June 1, 1977, pp. 490–91.

many more symptoms like this I could note—I suggest that you are experiencing symptoms of what I would call the mid-life transition, the mid-life crisis.[9]

Like most good speakers, Menninger seeks to enlist his audience's aid in creating meaning. Hypothetical examples work well to make the effort a joint one.

Selecting and using examples

The alert speaker will continually search for examples—undetailed and detailed, factual and hypothetical. He or she will search for examples to support specific ideas in order to make them clear, interesting, and acceptable to prospective listeners. Finding examples, in turn, may bring the speaker to new insights. In composing a speech, the speaker will constantly ask, "What is a good example? Is this example phrased as it should be? Which of these examples should I use?" Although there are no criteria that can be applied as set, unchanging rules, the beginning speaker will raise these questions:

1. Is the example clearly relevant to the idea?
2. Is the example appropriate to the audience?
3. Is the example typical?
4. Is the example properly detailed?

We must emphasize that these suggested questions are not iron rules. Take, for example, the third question. When will an audience accept an example as being typical? Often this question will depend on the number of examples used and the context in which the example or examples are used. A speaker might, by citing examples of dishonest police in a given city, charge that "Our police force needs reform." How many examples would warrant such a generalization? Surely we would not have to wait until 50 per cent of the force were shown to be dishonest; the assertion is a limited one and in this case even a few examples would constitute cause for concern. The rule must, therefore, be applied sensibly, not rigidly—a statement that applies to any of the other "rules" presented in this and in any other book about speaking. On the other hand, if the idea the speaker were making is that "Our police officers are corrupt," one or two examples would in no way establish the generalization.

How many examples should a speaker use? In general it is safe to say that one should use as many as possible. It is often useful to demonstrate that the examples are typical either by producing enough of them to satisfy one's listeners or by demonstrating statistically that the examples used fit the average for the sort of example. We shall discuss statistics in more detail later, but statistics and examples tend to have offsetting advantages and disadvantages: examples can be fascinating and easy to identify with whereas statistics are

[9] "Mid-Life Crisis: Assessments and Opportunities," Address to the Indian Hills Homes Association Annual Meeting, Kansas City, Mo., Nov. 21, 1974, Menninger Clinic, mimeograph, p. 2.

often dull and difficult; but examples lack scope whereas statistics supply scope concisely. One often finds statistics and examples mingled.

Attention to detail should help listeners relate what is said to their own experience.

On the use of humor in examples

"May I use humor in my speech?" a student will often ask. Of course the question may involve plans to use material other than examples, but it most often arises when a speaker believes that he or she has a "funny story" to tell. The question is a most difficult one to answer; any reply must be prefaced with "yes, if. . . ."

There are few occasions upon which humor would not be appropriate, but very few. The speaker should not equate a long face with serious purpose. The person who has never learned to smile at adversity, who has never sensed the absurdity that permeates so much of human conduct, may be the most frivolous thinker of all. When one thinks of the coupling of humor with serious intent one almost inevitably remembers the great dramatists from Aristophanes to Molière to Shaw who certainly caught the attention of their contemporaries and whose work remains an important part of the accumulation of human thought. Speakers have been no less aware of the utility of humor than have the dramatists. The reports of the Lincoln–Douglas debates in 1858 are heavily interspersed with the reporters' notes of "laughter."

"The theory of comedy in general is perhaps the most elusive and tenuous among all theories in polite learning," Marvin T. Herrick has observed, "and certainly the theory of what makes people laugh is the most baffling element in comedy."[10] Although we cannot analyze at length the theory of the laughable, we ought to look for humor in incongruity; any statement, situation, or action that upon closer examination is not what it seems at first to be is potentially humorous.[11] George Bernard Shaw claimed that humor lies in the discrepancy between what people are and what they pretend to be, in their attempt to romanticize fallible human institutions.[12] At any rate, the speaker who is alert to problems will see manifestations of them, which present opportunities to make use of examples that are humorous.

We recognize, however, that although humor can be useful in gaining the attention of an audience and making others remember an idea presented,

[10] "The Theory of the Laughable in the Sixteenth Century," *Quarterly Journal of Speech*, XXV (Feb. 1949), p. 1.

[11] For classical discussions of humor see Aristotle, *De Poetica*, chapter 5, and Cicero, *De Oratore*, Book II. Aristotle defined the ridiculous as "a mistake or deformity, not productive of pain or harm to others . . ." (1449^a 34–35). Although it is difficult sometimes to determine what produces pain or harm, the speaker should take care that his humor is not at the expense of others. Many successful speakers have learned that it is often wise to make oneself the butt of one's jokes.

[12] See the preface to *Plays Pleasant in Prefaces by Bernard Shaw*, London, Constable and Company, 1934, pp. 701–702.

many speakers err badly in making use of humor. The wise speaker will keep an eye squarely upon the subject, for material that he believes humorous, no less than any other material, must be relevant to the matter at hand. The most common mistake the beginner makes (and many others who should know better from experience) is to tell an allegedly funny story for its own sake. Resist that temptation. If the ideas are worthwhile, they deserve the speaker's effort to make them clear and interesting; by no means should one distract the audience's attention with irrelevant though humorous examples. The best humor is that which grows out of the ideas and the situation in which the speaker is engaged.

By no means should a speaker adopt a "stop me if you've heard this" attitude. One must determine in advance whether or not the material is relevant. If it is, perhaps, it will bear retelling even though some of the audience may have heard it, but the speaker should be cautious, knowing that retelling wears a story thin quickly. There is no easy way to tell whether or not material will really be humorous. Actual trial is best; practice before listeners whom one respects may help the speaker decide upon the appropriateness of his material.

Unfortunately many speakers, not only college students, need to be cautioned concerning the propriety of some sorts of humor. Too many speakers learn to their chagrin that the embarrassment level of an audience is much more quickly reached than that of the individuals who may compose it. What may well be appropriate in an informal gathering even of "mixed company" may not be responded to at all well in a public speaking situation. As a student once put it, "When in doubt, leave it out."

The answer to the student's question, "May I use humor in my speech?" is yes, *if* . . . if it is relevant to the ideas of the speech, if it really is humorous, and if it is appropriate for the audience to whom one speaks.

STATISTICS

Statistics are closely related to examples. Suppose you wished to impress an audience with the poverty of a given geographical section of the country. You might use detailed factual examples of several families residing there; but probably because of the inevitable demand, "Typical?" you might add, "Only 10 per cent of the families live on incomes of more than $12,000 a year, while more than 50 per cent live on incomes of less than $7,000 yearly." Statistics serve to give an orderly summary of many examples.

Technically, the term *figures* may be used to indicate numbers referring to simple quantity: "There are twenty students present." *Statistics* may be used to refer to a statement of ratio or proportion: "Only half of the students were present." For ordinary purposes, however, the terms may be interchanged which is fortunate for the many speakers who find *statistics* a difficult combination of sounds to utter.

Call them *figures* or *statistics* but use them. In speaking about the economic progress of black Americans, Martin Luther King, Jr., once said:

I mentioned economic justice and I gave a big figure, $30,000,000,000 as the figure that tells us about the annual income and buying power of the Negro, but when we look at the other side it tells us that we still have a great deal of work to do. But that other side reminds us that 42% of the Negro families of our country still earn less than $2,000 a year, while just 17% of the white families earn less than $2,000 a year; 21% of the Negro families of our country earn less than $1,000 a year, while just 5% of the white families earn less than $1,000 a year. 88% of the Negro families of our country still earn less than $5,000 a year while just 58% of the white families earn less than $5,000 a year. This reveals to us that we have a long, long way to go.[13]

As King knew, the simple weight of figures may make an idea dramatic, especially when some contrast of one thing to another is made evident.

Just as are examples, statistics are open to interpretation; in fact, a more accurate statement would be that statistics *are* interpretations. Economist G. C. Wiegand makes use of that fact in a speech keynoting a conference on monetary policy:

The New Zealand government recently announced—with some alarm—that there were 5000–6000 unemployed in the country. Local economists promptly placed the figure at "about 25,000—if Wellington were to use the same statistical methods as Washington." Yet according to the AFL-CIO, the U.S. Department of Labor statistics actually understates the number of unemployed in the U.S. Instead 7½ million unemployed there are, according to the AFL-CIO, some 11–12 million Americans in need of jobs, because the government statistics do not take into account those who have become "discouraged" and dropped out of the labor force, and those who work part-time but would like to have full-time jobs.

A 4½ percent rate of unemployment in the U.S. as a rule corresponds to a 2–2½ percent rate in Europe, where only those actually seeking work are regarded as unemployed. Who is right: the Europeans and New Zealanders, the Bureau of Labor Statistics, or the AFL-CIO?[14]

Out of context, Wiegand's question is misleading. The question is not what is the actual percentage of unemployed persons but rather what does it mean to be "unemployed"? Given the answer to the second question, the first can be resolved. The answer to the second question, however, is highly controversial, and that is what Wiegand's speech was about. Statistics are useful, but they need to be related clearly to the fabric of ideas on which they depend for their meaning.

[13] "A Long Way to Go," in *The Voice of Black Rhetoric*, eds. Arthur L. Smith and Stephen Robb, Boston, Allyn & Bacon, Inc., 1971, p. 194.

[14] "Thirty Years of 'Full Employment' Policies and Growing Unemployment," *Vital Speeches of the Day*, June 1, 1977, p. 506.

Some complexities of statistics

A good speaker should understand something about the nature of statistics. Various professional fields require special courses in statistics. With the increasing use of statistical statements, any citizen who desires to act intelligently will need some knowledge of statistics. Disraeli is supposed to have quipped, "There are three categories of liars: plain liars, damned liars, and statisticians." Unfortunately, in this chapter we can say little more than, "Take care," and offer a few general remarks for the speaker's guidance.

Central tendencies.   Many statistics that speakers use are statements of central tendency. The most common statement of central tendency is the mean, or arithmetical average. Averages may be misleading. Take this hypothetical example: "These persons have an average salary of $14,000. This figure is very close to the national average." If "these persons" are five, two of whom earn $6,000; one, $10,000; one, $14,000; and one, $34,000, the average is quite misleading.

Two other common sorts of statements of central tendency are the mode and the median. The mode is that item of those in the range that appears most frequently. The medium is the middle item. In the hypothetical example of incomes, the mode is $6,000; the median, $10,000. In this case, both are considerably lower than the mean.

Often, to be meaningful, statements of central tendency should be accompanied with some information about the distribution of the data. What is the top; what is the bottom? What per cent of the total falls between different intervals on the scale? A normal distribution is one in which most cases fall near the average (the mean) with about an equal number above and below. If the distribution is near normal, the mean, median, and mode will be about the same. To present some statistical statements clearly may necessitate using visual aids.

A critical question that the speaker (or listener) should ask is, "Just what is involved?" Suppose that a speaker says, "The average salary paid by University X is Y dollars." The average *faculty* salary? Or does the average represent custodians and typists as well? If he means faculty salary, are part-time faculty included? The careful speaker, of course, will say that "the average full-time faculty salary at University X is Y dollars."

Samples.   The question "Just what is involved?" is important when one is dealing with statistics based on samples. "Four out of five students at our University favor the administration's policy controlling the rights of student groups to sponsor public meetings," may not be a meaningful statement if the speaker queried the first five students he or she met among the 25,000 in residence. Most professional polling services employ dependable sampling techniques, but even so, sampling will give at best an *approximation*. The margin of error for the famous 1948 polls that indicated Thomas Dewey's election over Truman was small but significant. The problem was that communicators of the results of the polls were not careful in pointing out the *margin of error* and its meaning. In this case the margin of error was about 2 per cent, which means that the prediction was not that the vote would fall at a certain point but within a narrow range. Inasmuch as the difference between the two candidates indicated by the poll was slight, no confident prediction as to which would poll the more votes could be made.

Recently a "straw vote" taken at a state fair indicated that one candidate for governor of the state was favored by a large margin over the other candidates. This phenomenon was less perplexing after a newspaper reporter pointed out that the booth of the organization taking the "straw vote" was next to a booth sponsored by one of the major political parties and a considerable distance from the one sponsored by the other major party.

Sources. The problems the speaker will encounter in evaluating the sources of statistics will be quite like those of evaluating testimony generally, a topic to which we shall turn immediately. Often speakers and listeners will have to depend upon what appears to them to be reputable sources for statistical statements, although this fact does not relieve anyone of the responsibility for knowing something about the use of such statements. Both the speaker and listener should be especially wary of unidentified sources. Vague references to "figures indicate that . . ." or "statisticians tell us . . ." and their variants are usually the signs at best of uncritical mouthings of whatever the speaker may have stumbled across.

Selecting and using statistics

The alert speaker will raise the same sort of questions about statistics that he raised about examples. Is this material *relevant, appropriate, typical,* and *properly detailed?* But the speaker will want to raise some special questions about statistics.

1. Are the statistics dependable?
2. Are the statistics clear?
3. Are the statistics interesting?

In discussing the nature of statistics, we have touched on the problem of dependability. It should be apparent that this problem is a complex one that you will have to struggle with. You should be prepared to defend the objectivity of agencies upon whom you depend for your statistics. If a current claim is made, the statistics should be current.

It may seem surprising that statistics, which like other supporting materials may be used to make ideas clear and interesting, should themselves be examined for clarity and interest. But statistics tend to be dull and are often anything but clear. Some figures are so large or small as to carry little meaning to an audience. This is why we may hear a speaker in addition to the number of feet say, "The wingspan of that plane is as great as the length of this building in which we are sitting." The explosive power of modern nuclear bombs is sometimes given in multiples of "Hiroshima bombs." Often a speaker will (and should) round off a number if exactness is not a critical question, thus "nearly 50,000 people rallied in the square" has more immediate clarity and impact than "49,450." To bring his figures home clearly and interestingly to his radio audience, Billy Graham said, "Alcoholics are being produced in the U.S. at the rate of more than twelve hundred a day—over fifty an hour—around the clock." [15]

Finally, when using statistics, the speaker should ask:

1. Can I simplify the statistics in any way?
2. Am I using so many statistics without relief that I'll lose my audience's interest?
3. Can I use these statistics in conjunction with other supporting materials, particularly with visual aids or analogies, to increase clarity or interest? Will the use of statistics closely related to examples help establish the reliability of my basic claim?

TESTIMONY

In our complex society we are becoming increasingly dependent upon testimony. Our small world is filled with incidents that we are unable to observe or which, if we could observe, we are unable to interpret intelligently for ourselves. Therefore we must listen to the scientist describe the effects of radiation; we must weigh the opinions of military experts as to the efficacy of so-called "nuclear deterents"; we seek out the reports of journalists on political demonstrations in other countries. But the dependence upon testimony is no modern phenomenon; our history ranges from ancient testimony of the efficacy of the worship of the Sun or a Tree-God to modern testimony that certain toiletries transform ordinary men into objects highly desired by women.

Although we have heard all too often speakers who claim that their points are "proved" simply because they have cited several opinions that seem to agree with them we should not be too quick to dismiss the utility of quotations. Data provided by authoritative sources may give us more confidence in the accuracy of the material and should help us check the material against other sources. Opinions from authoritative sources are, of course, opinions still, but quotations are useful because they give the weight of authority to an opinion (which accounts for the myriad times George Washington's advice to steer clear of permanent alliances with any part of the foreign world has been quoted by American politicians), or because they phrase an idea in a particu-

[15] *Alcoholism*, The Billy Graham Evangelistic Association, Minneapolis, Minn., 1959, p. 1.

larly striking manner (which accounts for the frequent use of Shakespeare's words), or both (which accounts for the frequent use of that most-quoted book, the Bible). You may wish, then, to use testimony to lend your statements particularly apt phrasing or authority.

Consider the copious use of testimony in this passage from a speech given by a college student:

One may be prompted to ask at this point what it is about the man of high education which discourages certainty, creates doubt, and thus "causes him to lose the name of action"? Hamlet said that "conscience makes cowards of us all," that "the native hue of resolution is sicklied o'er with the pale cast of thought." What Hamlet called conscience we recognize as the product of intelligence. Coleridge tells us that "conscience is but the pulse of intellect." Hamlet refused to take the word of an apparition, even though it assumed his father's shape and confirmed his own suspicions. He preferred to put his trust in reason. "The play's the thing," he said, "wherein I'll catch the conscience of the king." In this manner he sought to remove his doubts. Schiller spoke of "the constraint intellect imposes upon the imagination"; he also might have mentioned the constraint intellect imposes upon a man's actions.[16]

This passage also indicates the tendency for types of supporting materials to become intermingled in use, for more than testimony is involved. In a sense, Hamlet is used as an example.

In building an argument defending the role of the United States in Vietnam, Senator Gale W. McGee of Wyoming, speaking before his colleagues in the Senate, drew mainly from testimony of two sorts: first, from American leaders whom his colleagues, and especially the critics of the policy, would be likely to respect, and, second, from Asian Communists, whose statements were used to suggest that force must be met with force:

But unfortunately mainland China is still in the hands of men who believe—as Mao Tse-Tung has said again and again—that "all political power grows out of the barrel of a gun." And his disciples have turned to a new form of aggression which they offer to the world behind a false face called "wars of national liberation."

Quotations of the first tended to be lengthy:

It is well worthwhile to recall here today the key passage of that historical proposal which came to be known as the Truman doctrine. The President pointed out that the survival of Greece was threatened by terrorists led by Communists—that Greece must have our assistance—that there was no other place to turn except the United States—that the future of Turkey as an independent state likewise was threatened. And then the President enunciated the policy he was recommending to the Congress and the people in these words:

"I am fully aware of the broad implications involved. We shall not realize our objectives, however, unless we are willing to help free peoples to maintain their free insti-

---

[16] From a speech prepared by Frank Louis Greenagel, University of Minnesota student, 1961.

tutions and their national integrity against aggressive movements that seek to impose upon them totalitarian regimes."[17]

McGee went on to argue the similarity of this situation and others to that in question. A number of questions could be raised concerning this material. We shall suggest a few lines for inquiring into the use of testimony.

In considering these suggestions for using testimony, you may want to compare to Senator McGee's defense of Vietnam policy with an attack on that policy by M. S. Arnoni. Like many of the speakers at the Vietnam Day teach-in, May 21–22, 1965, in Berkeley, Arnoni made intense use of testimony:

General de Gaulle is not the only Western leader to have expressed outrage at the American policies in Vietnam, the Dominican Republic, and elsewhere. Even such staunch NATO enthusiasts as D. Halvard Lange, Norway's Foreign Minister, told the recently held ministerial NATO meeting in London that he could not accept the thesis that defends any country's right to contravene in the affairs of another country. Not less outspoken was Per Haekkerup, the Danish Foreign Minister. *The New York Times* summed up that at the NATO meeting ". . . there is a feeling that the U.S. Administration is too inclined to use force unilaterally and to expect the United States' allies to support its use. . . . This attitude has developed among European leaders who in the past have defended the United States hegemony in the Western World against attacks by President de Gaulle." (May 12, 1965) Perhaps even more symptomatic is the fact that the very midwife of the Cold War, and the greatest enthusiast, Paul-Henri Spaak, Belgium's Foreign Minister and one-time NATO Secretary-General, has gotten around to embracing the so-called Rapacki Plan which would denuclearize Central Europe, an East European plan long since vehemently opposed by the United States.[18]

Mr. Arnoni *quotes* only *The New York Times*, but his testimony is much broader by means of reference to and paraphase of other sources. Of course the impact of this section taken from a long speech would be much different in its context.

Testimony may even be from an unidentified source, but student speakers should be especially cautious about such use. But notice what a professor of history does in a speech:

The primary step in dealing with any situation is to gain an awareness of the dimensions of the problem. At the most fundamental level, this involves a focus on self-assessment. Centuries ago, Plato said: "The unexamined life is not worth living." More recently, a feminist friend of mine retorted: "The examined life isn't so hot either." Still, the prominence of self-improvement books on the best seller lists afford evi-

[17] See the Congressional Record, Proceedings and Debates of the Eighty-ninth Congress, First Session, Vol. III, No. 138, Washington, July 29, 1965.

[18] *We Accuse*, Berkeley, Calif., Diablo Press, 1965, pp. 55–56.

dence of consistent concern about self-evaluation (*Passages* and *Your Erroneous Zones* are only two in a long succession of such volumes).[19]

Of course Mr. D'Innocenzo was trying to add a light note. His point was scarcely highly controversial, and, in so far as it was, the point depends on the specific instances that help listeners check their own recent experience to verify the idea.

Selecting and using testimony

Testimony can be used effectively. It is often mixed with other supporting material as was D'Innocenzo's. Look again at Elton Rule's use of example (p. 38). In selecting testimony, you should raise questions like these:

1. Is the testimony precise?
2. Is the person cited known and respected?
3. Is the person cited a good source?
   a. Is he or she in a position to know?
   b. Has his or her opinion on similar problems proved to be sound?
   c. Has he or she a bias?
4. Have I indicated the source quickly and easily?

Speakers frequently use quotations that are quite lengthy. Sometimes the quotations are rather interesting, but often they contain data or opinions that bear on the speaker's point only obliquely if at all. In general, the speaker should prefer several short quotations to one long one. It is perfectly ethical to shorten quotations if one can do so without seriously changing the meaning intended. One may quote a United States Senator on a particular measure and then add the names of several other senators who agree without quoting them directly. Perhaps you noticed that Senator McGee first paraphrased much that President Truman said in his message on Greece before quoting him directly. Paraphrases, of course, should be made clear as such.

One might suggest that if the audience knows and respects the source of a quotation the source is a good one; in some cases the two questions may be synonymous, but not always. We may know and respect a person and recognize that person's disability on a given subject. Often the speaker will be wise to indicate that the person cited is in a position to know about a particular problem and to indicate, perhaps, the person's reliability in the past. It is better, of course, if the testifier's credentials are obvious. If the audience will be inclined to dismiss a quotation because of a bias they attribute to the person cited, the speaker would be wise to find another quotation. It is quite effective to cite a person who testifies *against* what listener's might suppose to be that person's bias, to bring the "reluctant witness." "Even my opponent admits . . ." is a much abused but familiar example.

[19] Michael D'Innocenzo, "The Family under Fire," *Vital Speeches of the Day*, May 1, 1977, pp. 433–34.

In citing a source, be as simple as possible. Sometimes the name of a good source will be unknown to an audience. In such cases it is ordinarily sufficient to indicate the person's position, which is what M. S. Arnoni does several times in the passage we cited from his speech. Notice also that some of those Arnoni uses are introduced by him as "reluctant witnesses."

Ordinarily it is not necessary to indicate the book or magazine containing the quotation. The diposition of some speakers to say "I quote," or "quote" and then "unquote" is distracting and often makes the quotation less rather than more precise. Most speakers with perhaps a conscious effort to pause and probably an unconscious change in pitch can make perfectly clear what is and what is not quoted. There are, of course, exceptional cases in which "I quote his exact words . . ." or similar phrases may add emphasis to the material cited. In all cases, however, "I have a quote here . . ." is too obvious to warrant uttering. Likewise, "A well-known authority . . ." or "reliable sources . . ." should be avoided.

ANALOGIES

Department stores hire comparison shoppers. Reviewers will often compare several recorded versions of the same music. In evaluating essay examinations, college professors will often compare the answers students give to a model answer. Note the frequent use of such expressions as "better than," "not as good as," "similar to," "much like," and "resembles" in ordinary conversation. The impulse to make ideas clear, interesting, and impelling by using comparison is common. It is the principle of comparing that makes analogies useful in supporting ideas.

Analogies are ordinarily classified as literal or figurative. The literal analogy deals with two (or more) phenomena that are essentially alike—one political party as compared to others. The figurative analogy deals with phenomena that are essentially different (thus Plato compared the governor of a city to the steersman of a boat), but which nonetheless contain a critical common element (our destinies are in the hands of our political leaders just as our lives may be in the hands of the steersman).

Literal analogies

One seldom hears analogies in ordinary speeches. This may be because analogies are more difficult to use than other types of supporting materials, or it may be that most speakers simply are not in the habit of seeking out analogies. On the other hand our observation leads us to assert that good speakers frequently use analogy. Consider this long analogy from a radio address by Billy Graham:

A student at an eastern university recently went to Mexico where, in the process of time and discovering true dedication in some Communist workers, he became a Communist. Shortly afterward, he wrote to his fiancee breaking off their engagement.

This letter was given to me by a Presbyterian minister in Montreat, North Carolina, where I live. This is what it says:

"We Communists have a high casualty rate. We're the ones who get shot and hanged and lynched and tarred and feathered and jailed and slandered. . . . We live in virtual poverty. We turn back to the Party every penny we make above what is absolutely necessary to keep us alive.

"We Communists don't have the time or the money for any movies, or concerts, or T-bone steaks, or decent homes and new cars. We've been described as fanatics. We are fanatics. Our lives are dominated by one great overshadowing factor—the struggle for world Communism . . . We subordinate our petty personal selves into a great movement of humanity, and if our personal lives seem hard, or our egos appear to suffer through subordination to the Party, then we are adequately compensated by the thought that each of us in his small way is contributing something new and true and better for mankind.

"There is one thing in which I am in dead earnest and that is the Communist cause. It is my life, my business, my religion, my hobby, my sweetheart, my wife and mistress, my bread and meat. I work at it in the daytime and dream of it at night. Its hold on me grows, not lessens, as time goes on. Therefore I cannot carry on a friendship, a love affair or even a conversation without relating to this force which both drives and guides my life. I evaluate people, books, ideas and action according to how they affect the Communist cause and by their attitude toward it. I've already been in jail because of my ideas and, if necessary, I'm ready to go before a firing squad."

Do you have that much dedication to the Lord Jesus Christ? In Christ, God offers us everything, but He demands no less.[20]

Does Graham's analogy help make his point clear, interesting, and impelling? Notice how the detail of the young Communist's letter serves to indicate specific actions that emphasize sacrifice for a faith.

Figurative analogies

Analogies, like examples, may be minutely detailed or undetailed. Graham's comparison was highly detailed. In contrast, Robert G. Ingersoll uses a simple analogy in his famous speech "The Liberty of Man, Woman, and Child": "Do not treat your children like . . . posts to be set in a row. Treat them like trees that need light and sun and air." We still hear the advice that Ingersoll gave a hundred years ago, but seldom do we hear the grace his imagination produced. The figurative analogy is difficult to use, but it often adds interest to the speech. Perhaps even more important, it may give the listeners a neatly phrased expression of an idea; one they might remember. Perhaps that quality was what Thomas W. Phelps was looking for in making a speech before an ordinary business luncheon. His speech was not ordinary, partly because of his analogies:

[20] "Call to Commitment," Billy Graham Evangelistic Association, Minneapolis, Minn., 1960, pp. 1–3.

What is the difference, you may ask, between a bribe and a commission? It is like the difference between day and night. And just as no one can draw a line between day and night so no one can draw a line between a commission and a bribe, but the difference between them is tolerably distinguishable. Put less philosophically, a commission is a payment to a recognized salesman for effecting a sale. A bribe is a payment to a decision-maker to warp his opinion, corrupt his judgment. If a bribe does not corrupt the decision-maker's judgment it is a waste of money because you would have gotten the order anyway.[21]

Phelps makes a number of arguments all converging on his thesis: dishonesty costs us dearly. Near the end he argues for the concern we should all have for future generations, and says that he cannot argue with a person who says, " 'To hell with posterity. What has posterity ever done for me?' But I can observe with the late Paul Gallico that nature has no concern for birds that eat their own eggs. To my mind a dishonest struggle for wealth puts mankind on a par with the members of a colony of ants fighting for the highest and driest place on a log inevitably drifting toward Niagara Falls."[22] Notice how Phelps uses indirect testimony. Paul Gallico was quite popular when most of Phelps' listeners were young.

Handled well, the figurative analogy can add clarity and interest to an idea, and it can, if the basis for analogy is strong and sharp enough, be impelling.

Selecting and using analogies

The speaker considering analogies should apply to them the same sort of questions that should apply to examples:

1. Is the analogy clearly relevant to the idea?
2. Is the analogy appropriate to the audience?
3. Is the analogy properly detailed?

In addition to those questions concerning the material's relevancy, appropriateness, and detail, in using analogy the speaker should ask these questions:

1. Is the basis of the analogy clear?
2. Are there important dissimilarities in what is compared?

In any question of clarity, one of the best tests is to try the material on as many listeners as possible. Get them to react. The basis of the comparison should be clear with a minimum of explanation. Too often we hear speakers giving painfully inappropriate hints to the audience. In using the ancient story of the Arab who allowed his camel to put his nose in the tent and soon

[21] Can We Afford to Be Honest?" *Vital Speeches of the Day*, Sept. 15, 1976, p. 3.

[22] Ibid., p. 4.

found the camel in and himself out, for example, the speaker ought not feel compelled to speak of "the tent of free enterprise" nor of "the camel of state control." The figurative analogy may be clear, but it becomes ludicrous instead of compelling.

There will be some dissimilarities in anything compared. Generally you should not call attention to them; you should not try to explain them away. You should look for dissimilarities that will render your comparison ineffective and, if you believe you find them, discard the analogy.

Using analogies is difficult, but many fine speakers have used them to advantage.

VISUAL AIDS

The use of a model, a graph, a diagram, or a picture may enable you to clarify an idea that could not easily be made clear through words alone. Wise speakers, ordinarily pressed for time, soon discover that they can often present material much more quickly by using visual aids.

For example, you might want to indicate the rapid rise of the rate of inflation during the decade of the 1970s. You could simply state the percent of the rise each year for ten years, but that would take time and listeners would have great difficulty following all the figures let alone retaining much of an impression after hearing the list. A simple bar graph with the years along the base and the percentages scored off on the vertical axis would be quite easy to make. Perhaps you could add a little visual interest by making each successive bar a deeper shade of red.

One student speaker showing the increase in costs of supporting the military establishment used a simple bar graph. The first bars were pointed, but the shapes became more definite with the bars farther along to the right until the final bar very much resembled a rocket taking off. The drawing was simple, but imaginative and effective.

Preparing graphs or diagrams does not call for a great deal of artistic skill or for expensive materials. With some large sheets of paper (some students have used ordinary wrapping paper and bookstores commonly stock large sketch pads), a marking pencil or pen, and a touch of imagination student speakers can invent or adapt all sorts of visual aids. For example, one student talking about the advantages of the Metropolitan Opera's house in New York City's Lincoln Center executed a drawing of the seating arrangements in the old and new auditoriums (see Figure 1). The sketch was adapted from one he had seen in a magazine. The student's work was scarcely lovely art, but his point that the sight lines had been improved was clearer with the sketch.

Sometimes speakers use simple pictures to help the audience focus more sharply on the ideas. For example, a student talking about the apparent shifts of weather patterns that brought drought to many parts of the country in 1976 and 1977, used an outline of the United States and drew broad arrows with a marking pen. The places on which the speaker focused atten-

THE "MET"

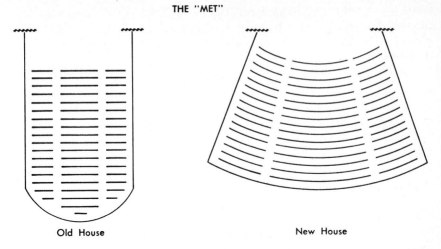

Old House   New House

Figure 1. (Source: sketched from an illustration in *Saturday Review*, Sept. 17, 1966, p. 48. Reproduced by permission.)

tion were already marked, and this foresighted person also had the path of the arrows drawn lightly in ordinary lead pencil so that the marker strokes could be placed rapidly.

Most adults are familiar with line graphs, bar graphs, slices-of-pie, and other methods of indicating statistical information. Line graphs are best for showing trends and can sometimes be used to show comparisons as well. Talking about the apparently waning importance of political party affiliations in the United States, one student speaker produced a simple line graph showing membership in the Republican Party and the Democratic Party. The 1976 elections provided the immediate context for the speaker and a Gallup Poll the information. (See Figure 2). Bar graphs are also useful in showing comparison of one thing to another, when size or amount is the point, and sometimes several lines on a graph can be used to compare one trend to another. Slices-of-pie are excellent for showing the proportions of parts to the whole.

Visual aids may add impact to ideas that may seem at first to be adequately expressed orally. The destructiveness of nuclear explosives may be described in many ways, but enlarged aerial photographs of Hiroshima before and after August 6, 1945, may startle even an audience that has responded quite positively before to other material. The photographs of the Vietnamese killed at My Lai were undoubtedly instrumental in arousing a lethargic public opinion in America. From the student speaker's standpoint, unfortunately, enlarged photographs are expensive. If you were speaking about Hiroshima you might find ways of diagramming from the epicenter of the blast outward in concentric rings the effects of a nuclear explosion. You might overlay the rings on the geographic area of your own community, and you might use such rings to

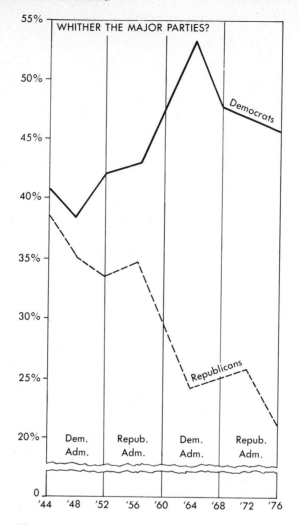

Figure 2.

compare the effects of the old-fashioned Hiroshima type bomb to the destructiveness of up-to-date weapons.

Do not overlook the use of objects. If you were to undertake to explain the steps in binding a book, you might well want the materials available to display during the speech. But you should not limit your imagination to inventing visual aids to help you make simple explanations even though presenting information, especially statistical information, is the dominant use made of such materials. Sometimes visual material will lend persuasive impact.

Although a speaker might be unwise to use such a device these days, some years ago a speaker brought out a stick of dynamite (a dummy, the audience was assured quickly) with a fuse attached and a match. "Would any of you care to light the fuse and put this stick in your pocket?" the speaker asked. "No? Why not? You probably have something in your pocket this very minute that is potentially just as dangerous. The keys to your car." For the audience he made a rather arresting beginning to a speech on safe driving, a rather well-worn subject, but one this speaker found a number of ways to freshen.

Selecting and using visual aids

The speaker who told the audience that a car is as dangerous as dynamite, used both a visual aid and a figurative analogy. Inasmuch as visual aids are usually used to present some other type of supporting material, the speaker ought not overlook questions relevant to whatever other type is involved.

Visual aids are so often poorly used that one is tempted to compose long lists of do's and don'ts. But most of the trouble could be avoided with only a little caution. Too many speakers never practice using their visual aids and therefore overlook some rather obvious problems. In addition to ordinary care, the speaker should raise questions like these:

1. Can the audience see the visual aids?
   a. Are they large enough?
   b. Are they simple enough?
2. Can I handle them?
3. Will they distract my audience?
4. Are they as striking as possible?

Visual aids that cannot be easily seen are worse than useless. They distract and even irritate listeners. You must make them large enough to be seen in whatever situation you are to speak. If you cannot get the photograph enlarged enough to be seen readily do not use it. You should resist the temptation to pass a small object among the members of your audience, remembering that this is about as effective as sending a person among them to whisper an example to each listener in turn while you continue to speak.

Often a visual aid can be seen but cannot be comprehended because it is too complex. Be certain that the details are simplified so that only those essential to your ideas are included. Often it is wise to use several graphs or diagrams instead of trying to put all the information on one.

Frequently a speaker will face an audience with a diagram in mind and a piece of chalk in hand only to find out as the drawing develops that it just does not look like the mental picture at all. In addition the drawing is likely to take much longer than a person expects and the attention of the audience is likely to wander. Unless you are nearly a professional artist, restrict yourself to putting the simplest items on a chalkboard, and those should be well rehearsed so that you can work quickly. Whatever you do should not take your attention from your audience more than momentarily. You must practice changing charts, pointing out details on your graphs, and manipulating whatever objects you will be using.

Too often a speaker will engage in a detailed explanation of a visual aid that is clear to the audience immediately. If the visual aid needs detailed explanation, it probably isn't a good piece of material.

A large, colorful map pinned up at the front of the room at the beginning of a speech and not used immediately will probably command a great deal of the audience's attention while the speaker is concentrating on the ideas. Speakers must remember that visual aids are potentially highly distracting and, if at all possible, should display them only while they actually want to use them. It takes very little foresight to cover a map (or a diagram or a graph) with a blank sheet of paper. Although listeners might wonder what is underneath the paper, they will probably be much less distracted than they would be by the material itself.

SUMMARY

Using supporting materials effectively is a matter of fixing some habits of thinking. Assertions should turn the speaker's mind immediately toward examples, statistics, testimony, analogies, and visual aids. The experienced speaker constantly looks for material to make ideas clear, interesting, and impelling. This is why one so often discovers that good speakers keep files and notebooks to save materials that seem to be useful in supporting ideas in which they are interested. Moreover, speakers continually become interested in an increasing range of ideas because their habits of thought find meaning in the events they meet. A good speaker stocks a full mind and draws from it; a good speaker is rarely satisfied with the material at hand. A good speaker sorts and checks ideas and the materials from which they are drawn and seeks fresh resources for both.

ASSIGNMENTS

For class discussion

Use a short piece of material. The editorial and opinion pages of most daily newspapers are usually a good source of concise prose.

1. Identify the major pieces of supporting material.
2. Ask yourself the appropriate questions as outlined in this chapter about each piece of material. Decide, tentatively, how well-chosen you believe each piece of material is. Then in class, or in small groups, as your instructor prefers,
3. Check to identify agreements and disagreements about classifying and evaluating pieces of material. Can any disagreements be resolved?
4. If the class, or the group, agrees that some pieces of material are not as good as they should be, suggest alternatives. In order to participate, ob-

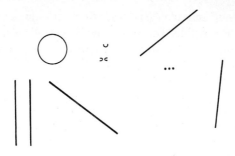

Figure 3.

viously each person must think of alternatives of pieces of material he or she believes to be weak.

Alternative for class discussion

Listen to a speech assigned by the instructor and carry out the discussion as indicated.

An oral exercise

1. The class should be divided into four groups.
2. Each person will make a two- to three-minute extemporaneous talk supporting an assertion.
3. Those in group one will use an example or examples to support their assertions; those in group two will use statistics; those in group three will use testimony; those in group four will use analogies.
4. Simply state your assertion and support it. Limit and phrase the assertion carefully. Search diligently and choose your supporting material critically. *Do not consider this exercise to be a complete speech.* Your beginning and ending will probably seem abrupt.
5. The presentation of the talks should serve as the basis of a thorough class discussion on the selection and use of supporting materials. Let this question be your theme: How can the use of material be improved? Talk about specific efforts made in class.

A one-point speech

1. Each person should prepare a three- to four-minute one-point speech.
2. The thesis must be carefully selected and limited. Make an assertion that you can support directly with supporting material, not one that must be divided into subordinate assertions, which in turn may be supported.
3. Use this pattern: illustrate, state, amplify, and restate.
   Illustrate. Begin with a detailed example, either factual or hypothetical, from which your assertion can be drawn. Do not bother with preliminaries: "I was wondering what to talk about when an idea struck me." "This morning I'd like to talk to you about one of my favorite subjects." Just open with the example.

State. Make your assertion. Try to state the thesis as clearly, concisely, and strikingly as possible. Do it in a single declarative sentence, although you may include several sentences of transition relating the illustration to it.

Amplify. Use other supporting material to make your assertion clear, interesting, and impelling. You may use any supporting material in any order that seems feasible.

Restate. Although you may wish to restate your thesis several times during your speech in relating supporting material to it, make a final restatement that will serve as a simple summation.

4. Discuss the speeches. As students, you should be striving to learn to use supporting material effectively.

4

organizing ideas

Let all things be done decently and in order.
I CORINTHIANS 14:40

Let all your things have their places, let each part of your business have its time.

BENJAMIN FRANKLIN

Each of us is surrounded by phenomena. For some of us listening to a Beethoven symphony is an enjoyable experience; for others it is not. Some of us find modern art meaningful, and some nuclear physics; some of us understand cost accounting and some Shakespeare's sonnets. In experiences with these phenomena we are more or less aware of the sorts of impressions we have, of why we enjoy, why we understand, or why we don't.

Whatever phenomenon we might be interested in—because it pleases us or because it puzzles us—the more meaningful it becomes, the more we recognize that a pattern of parts inheres in it. We recognize that the whole is made up of parts and that the parts stand in a given relationship to one another. To change the relationship of the parts is to alter or to destroy the whole.

We experience other physical beings in various ways. A human being is a structure, or, rather, many interrelated structures. The physiologist can explain the relationships of the physical parts of a person in amazing detail. An artist can represent a person in a drawing, and Picasso may upset us by putting the parts in unusual relationships to one another.

At the end of the last chapter you came upon a senseless jumble of lines labeled Figure 3 (p. 59). You may have glanced at them and wondered what fool had slipped this plate into the presses, but chances are that the lines were not meaningful. Look again. It's a person; what is commonly called a "stick figure." It is scarcely great art, but one can put the elements together to represent a person. If presented with a childish drawing of nearly anything, you can recognize the whatever by the juxtaposition of parts. If you are presented with a drawing of a person with three legs and four arms you may be upset by the impropriety or irritated by the poor joke.

The point is clear. The person who wants to play, to compose, or who just wants to listen to music must become aware, to some degree, of the patterns of pitch and time. He or she soon recognizes that some patterns are traditional ones, that for example, the ordinary rhythmical patterns of Western music are made up of two's or three's. Eastern music, with its complex changes in time patterns may be an upsetting experience for Western ears. One may discover that the second movement of Tschaikovsky's sixth symphony is somehow slightly strange and come to realize that it is written in five beats to the measure. And so persons interested in music recognize that the traditional patterns to which they are most accustomed may be modified with various effects.

The person who wishes to compose speeches will become aware that like most other phenomena, speeches follow more or less orderly patterns or interrelated groups of patterns. The speaker should come to realize that there are traditional patterns that can be used or modified with varying effects.

From the discussion thus far, several generalizations are possible. (1) Speeches should be made up of patterns of ideas and materials. (2) When one is presented with a speech that seems to be unpatterned or improperly patterned, one will probably be puzzled or irritated. (3) There are traditional speech patterns that one can learn. (4) The traditional patterns should be quite useful in helping one construct one's own speech, and because they are traditional and therefore familiar to listeners, should help the audience respond to the speech.

One way you could learn to pattern ideas and materials in a speech would be by listening to and reading a great number of speeches to try to discover useful principles; you could then work with your own ideas and materials to test these principles. In the final analysis, only by this process can you learn in a deeply meaningful way to construct speeches. A book such as this one can only claim to give a few suggestions to make your observation, distillation, and practice somewhat easier and more immediately helpful.

The principles we discuss will be abstract and, therefore, necessarily artificial and somewhat arbitrary. This observation does not mean that the principles will not prove useful nor that they should not be learned and applied. It does mean, however, that not all examples of well-organized speeches will fall neatly and clearly within the patterns described.

Of course students often remark that they do not wish to observe traditions, they wish to break and change them. A fine desire that. But one must know a tradition to be able to break it. One can break a tradition carelessly, but the sense of the desire shifts from the fine one expressed if one is willing to trust to sheer carelessness. Besides, one misses the exhilaration of departing from well-trod paths. Most creative people wish to remould traditions to some extent. And although speech-making is a humble art, it is a readily available creative outlet for many people, as we argued in the first chapter.

THE DEVELOPMENT

Inasmuch as most adults have heard many speeches and read some sort of theory that bears on the composition of discourse, to say that a speech should have a beginning, a middle, and an end—an introduction, a development, and a conclusion—will surprise almost no one. Although it is difficult to say where a speaker will start in his process of organization, he will probably not start, and should not start, at the beginning, that is, by composing the introduction. Because the introduction and conclusion serve definite functions in relation to the development, the development should be at least relatively well composed before the speaker plans how he will begin and end.

The word *development* suggests a natural unfolding or, in some contexts, a careful building of a purposeful design. A good speech should have both of these qualities. Pointing to these qualities is easy enough; actually achieving them in a speech is a difficult but rewarding experience. In this chapter we shall discuss a few ways of looking at basic structure. In the next chapter we shall discuss forming introductions and conclusions.

Patterns of arrangement

Everything in the speech focuses on the central idea. We discussed in Chapter 2 problems of stating purposes and theses. You should be willing to modify your statement of thesis as you compose your speech, because you should become increasingly aware of the content of your speech in relationship to your audience. The sooner, however, you can make a definite, though tentative, statements of purpose and thesis, the better.

"Fraternities should be abolished." Here is an assertion (one used rather commonly for illustrative purposes) that might serve as the thesis of a speech. If I were to make such an assertion in your presence, you might reply, "What makes you think so?" or "Who cares?" I would then be inclined to support my assertion. In doing so, I would probably make other assertions that stand in a subordinate relationship to the thesis:

Fraternities should be abolished.
 I. They distract the student from important activities.
 II. They build false sets of values.

Another person might use a different set of assertions to support the same thesis. Hearing such assertions, you might be inclined to defend fraternities:

We must correct some common misunderstandings about fraternities.
 I. The cinema stereotypes do not represent the average fraternity.
 II. The real aims of fraternities serve legitimate individual needs.

The hypothetical speeches attacking and supporting fraternities have barely been begun. These are only the first indications of what the speeches might become. The point is that the initial development of a speech is composed of a series of assertions. The thesis is divided into subordinate assertions that we shall call *main heads*. The main heads, in turn, may be subdivided. Hypothetically the process of division could be carried on toward infinity. In speeches, however, the pattern of division should be simple; the speaker should learn to come quickly to supporting material that will make an assertion clear, interesting, and impelling. When an assertion is well supported, it in turn supports the assertion that stands above it in the organizational pattern. Too often speeches become a skein of finely divided assertions, few of which are properly supported.

The wise speaker working through ideas and materials will probably have frequent insights into what points might be made and how these points fit together. In short, one should not wait until all the materials are gathered before trying to form patterns of ideas. With scarcely any prompting from textbooks or teachers, students caught up with ideas will jot down sketches that are embryonic outlines.

The constant making of sketches is a good habit to get into and one that tends to save a great deal of time in the long run. Familiarity with a few general patterns of arrangement may help you fix that habit.

Time patterns. The parts of some ideas must necessarily stand in a chronological relationship to one another. First things must come first. If you will find it necessary to explain a process, you will start at the beginning—what must be done first, second, third. If you wish to make a proposal, you may be inclined to indicate what steps will be necessary to initiate the proposal, what steps will be necessary in its operation, and what steps will be necessary to evaluate what is accomplished.

The instructions for almost any mechanical task will probably be arranged in a chronological order. Pick up a booklet in a hardware store or lumber yard (or, more likely in urban areas these days, a home discount center) on installing a light fixture or laying carpeting. Look at the instructions that come with toys that need to be assembled. All of these tasks are modest, but you will soon conclude, if you have not already concluded, that clear explanations are not easy to give and are highly prized by persons who need them. But time patterns are applicable to ideas as well as to mechanical processes. Suppose that you are struggling with the intriguing topic of human conceptions of an almighty being. That topic is open to so many different treatments that it is difficult to start, but you may be interested in history. Such an interest may not answer every question but it might yield some interesting efforts. For example:

Thesis: The Old Testament contains several distinctly different conceptions of God.
  I. The God of the creation and the flood was an angry, powerful, jealous God.
  II. The God of Moses was a personal God—a lawgiver to a tribe.
  III. The God of Job was an inexplicable arguer.
  IV. The God of Micah was a gentle God of love.

Obviously one could make much different interpretations that this example contains, but if one were to support the thesis indicated, or one much like it, one probably would choose a time pattern. One might possibly deal with the concept as it seems suggested in Micah before dealing with Moses, but that order is difficult to imagine.

The use of chronological order is much more apparent for informative purposes than for persuasive, but you should not conclude that time patterns should not be adapted to persuasive purposes. For example, suppose that you are a member of a group and feel that although it is founded around some excellent purposes and has some fine members, the group has lost sight of its goals. You have an opportunity to address the group.

Purpose: to clarify and intensify the feelings of the members toward the group's goals.
  I. Our founders were men and women of vision who established a group with some rather remarkable principles.
  II. At the present time we are carrying forward many of the group's original projects.
  III. In the future we can find exciting new work to do by turning again to the principles of our founders.

Perhaps the second point seems mild. If you decide that it will be more effective to chastise the group directly instead of merely suggesting stagnation, the second point might be:

II. We are failing miserably to live up to the principles of our founders.

The time pattern is quite flexible. It is often worthwhile to think of a subject in terms of *past, present, future;* your effort will not always result in a usable arrangement for a speech, but it may help clarify some relations among ideas and occasionally prove to be a way to share those thoughts with an audience.

Former Secretary of State Henry Kissinger faced a rather difficult task in speaking before the National Press Club in Washington, D.C., January 10, 1977. He was near the end of his tenure and knew that his relationship with the press had been problematic. He could not be maudlin and yet did want to bid for some credit with the press. He was scarcely free of the cloud of bad feeling for the administration of former President Richard Nixon and almost had to take into account his role in the Vietnam war and the negotiations that concluded the fighting there. Moreover, the Press Club setting traditionally calls for humor.

The speech is worth study from several points of view.[1] What is relevant here is to note that Kissinger used a past-present-future pattern to pull together some rather diverse purposes. The *past* was the tradition of American diplomacy. The present, according to Kissinger, is a time of transition, in which the traditions, as precious as they are, no longer suffice. The future is not specified; it is a goal and the speaker concentrates mainly on the role of the press in helping the people and the government create that future.

The order of the speech itself is scarcely remarkable. What is remarkable is the orderliness the pattern gives to the speech in an unobtrusive way.

Topical patterns. If you were to make a speech describing Shakespeare's plays, you might choose a time pattern, talking in turn about the early plays, the middle plays, and the later plays. You would be more likely, however, to talk about the histories, the comedies, and the tragedies. Some subjects have parts—aspects, qualities, types, branches—that tend to be more or less clearly a natural part of them. Some common element seems to recur in different manifestations making what may be called a topical pattern. Think of the speeches you have heard that were extensions of topics such as these: the *benefits* of physical activity (or adequate insurance or reading a newspaper regularly or studying speech); the *qualities* of a good fraternity member (or a cigar or a business letter or a college professor); the *types* of football formations (or tennis players or revolutionaries or patterns of arrangement).

Consider this series of statements culled from a work of Aldous Huxley:[2]

Without an understanding of man's deep-seated urge to self-transcendence, of his very natural reluctance to take the hard, ascending way, and his search for some bogus liberation either below or to one side of his personality, we cannot hope to make sense of our own particular period of history or indeed of history in general, of life as it was lived in the past and as it is lived today. For this reason I propose to discuss some of the more common Grace-substitutes, into which and by means of which men and women have tried to escape from the tormenting consciousness of being merely themselves.

. . . .

[1] A complete text of what has been called Mr. Kissinger's "Valedictory" is available in several sources including *Vital Speeches of the Day*, Feb. 15, 1977, pp. 265–67.

[2] *The Devils of Loudon*, London, Chatto & Windus, 1952, pp. 361, 363, 365.

Alcohol is but one of the many drugs employed by human beings as avenues of escape from the insulted self.

. . . .

Like intoxication, elementary sexuality, indulged in for its own sake and divorced from love, was once a god, worshipped not only as the principle of fecundity, but as a manifestation of the radical Otherness immanent in every human being.

. . . .

The professional moralists who inveigh against drunkenness are strangely silent about the equally disgusting vice of herd-intoxication—of downward self-transcendence into subhumanity by the process of getting together in a mob.

Although we do not find formal outline statements, the first paragraph indicates Huxley's thesis, and the next three statements the main divisions of his discussion. The pattern is topical.

One special manner of applying topical order is to consider it as giving rise to a series of contentions. Take any assertion you would have an audience accept; state it and then ask, "Why?" Your answers to this question will form a series of contentions in support of the thesis. Many television commercials are based on this process at its simplest; a demand is made and enticement is offered: Use this soap! (Why? . . .) Drink this beer! (Why? . . .) Buy this car! (Why? . . .)

In a previous example we imagined that you were about to address a group that you felt had lost sight of its goals. Apply a topical pattern:

Purpose; to clarify and intensify the feelings of the members toward the group's goals.
Explicit thesis: The goals our founders set for our organization should be carefully reconsidered by each of us. (Why?)
  I. (Because) by so doing we shall honor those men and women who by their vigor and imagination formed this group.
 II. (Because) by so doing we shall be better able to serve those purposes to which we have committed ourselves.
III. (Because) by so doing we shall gain personal satisfaction in fresh achievements.

Which pattern will better accomplish the speaker's purpose, the time pattern or the topical? The question is impossible to answer except for a specific speaker and a specific group. The speaker who sees more than one possibility, however, will be in a position to choose which appears to possess the greater potential effectiveness.

A special problem often arises in using a topical pattern: Which main head should be used first, which second, which third? Consider this simple application of the topical pattern:

Thesis: Intercollegiate football should be abolished.
  I. Intercollegiate football is detrimental to the participants.
 II. Intercollegiate football is detrimental to the nonparticipating student body.
III. Intercollegiate football degrades the colleges that sponsor it.

Which of these main heads should be used first, which second, which third? In answering the question the speaker should decide first which is the strongest, that is, the clearest, most interesting, and most impelling point, and which is the least strong. In the present case, the answer would probably be somewhat dependent upon the audience. Is the speaker addressing participants or nonparticipants? Students or a group of professors? Let us suppose that a speaker has decided that in order of strength the points may be ranked 1-2-3. One then has several choices. One may choose *climactic* order, that is, may arrange the points 3-2-1, starting with the least strong and using the strongest last. One may choose *anticlimactic* order, 1-2-3, beginning with the strongest point. Although the evidence available is somewhat contradictory, in general one should prefer anticlimactic order if one's aim is to make the audience remember the points. A recommendation at least as old as Cicero is to begin with the strongest point and use the next strongest last (the old principle of putting the weak argument in the middle)—1-3-2, or with four points, 1-4-3-2. Based on the same inclination to arrange a speech to give a strong beginning and ending, Richard Whately recommended 150 years ago that one use anticlimactic order and then summarize in climactic order: 1-2-3; 3-2-1.

Whatever advice you follow, you should not allow yourself to arrange a topical pattern without a conscious effort to decide in what order the points should come. You should make your decisions with an eye on the audience's possible responses.

In dividing and arranging the parts of a speech, the speaker, especially the inexperienced speaker, should strive for simplicity. A useful guide is to use from two to five main heads. Five is no magic upper limit, but a well-constructed and -supported speech of more than five main points will be a rare occurrence. It may be impossible to support five points effectively in a short speech.

You should ask yourself questions like these, especially if you believe that you have five or more points:

1. Are all my main heads really distinctly coordinate parts of the thesis, or should several of them be combined, or, perhaps one subordinated to another?
2. If I have more than five main points, and I'm sure that they all are distinctly coordinate parts of the thesis, might I be wiser to narrow my thesis, and therefore my span of points, allowing myself more time to develop each point?

Just as the thesis should be divided into main heads and these main heads should be arranged into some sort of pattern, so should the main heads in turn be divided and the subheads arranged. Let's allow one of our samples to grow a little.

We must correct some common misunderstandings about fraternities.

  I. The cinema stereotypes do not represent the average fraternity.
    A. There are three common stereotypes that are frequently presented as being representative of fraternity life.
    B. The sources of these grotesque pictures are rooted in a lack of direct experience with modern fraternities.
  II. The real aims of fraternities serve legitimate individual needs.
    A. Fraternities help serve legitimate scholastic needs.
    B. Fraternities help serve legitimate social needs.

This sample is a combination of topical patterns. You must decide which subhead to use first when you use a topical pattern; and, in arranging subheads, you must be certain that you have real divisions and should hold their number to a minimum. Again two-to-five is a good guide.

Problem-solution patterns. Consider these assertions, all of which are much like many that we have heard again and again: "To meet the energy crisis, we must ration gasoline." "Equal rights for women can be assured only by an amendment to the constitution." "Strategic arms limitations hold the key to continued peace." Each of these statements suggests a problem and a solution. Speeches dealing with them will probably in some way or other utilize statements concerning the nature, extent, and effects of the problem and statements concerning the nature and efficacy of the solution in constructing an organizational pattern.

The simplest and most ordinary use of the problem-solution pattern is a two-step sequence:

  I. The electoral college is a dangerous anachronism.
  II. We should adopt a system for electing the President by a direct vote of the people.

or

  I. Pursuing materialistic values inevitably leads the individual to the sense of a wasted life.
  II. The individual can find complete human satisfaction only through dedication to some cause higher than personal gratification.

Looking at these two examples, you may ask, "Where's the thesis?"

In a problem-solution pattern, the thesis is synonymous with the statement of solution; it should embody the aim of the speech.

The simple two-step use of the problem-solution pattern is capable of being modified in a variety of ways. You may suggest a solution that will raise some objections in the minds of your audience. You must decide what you want to do about these objections. If you believe that they are minor, you may decide simply to stress the virtues of your solution and not mention any possible objections. You may, on the other hand, believe that you cannot safely or legitimately ignore some possible arguments against your proposal; they may be so obvious as almost to demand consideration. In this case, you may decide to meet the objections as you discuss your solution keeping basically the two-step sequence. You may also decide to follow a pattern something like this:

I. Our present methods of controlling pollution on the upper Mississippi are woefully inadequate.
II. We should adopt the methods that have been successful in the Big Horn River valley.
III. The obvious objections of cost and cooperation can be met.

If you wish to utilize the last section of the development for refuting objections, you will probably wish to return to a positive approach to the solution in the conclusion.

You may wish to modify the two-step problem-solution pattern to meet possible objections in a somewhat different sense, that is, there may be another solution or several solutions that would suggest themselves to members of the audience. In such a situation you might feel that you would have to eliminate obvious proposals before making your own recommendation:

I.   We must be able to meet aggression and civil turmoil anywhere in the world if civilization is to survive.
II. Unilateral military action is not feasible.
III. Action by regional alliances is little better.
IV. We must evolve a permanent police force under the control of the United Nations.

Quite obviously, the more complex the modifications of the simple problem-solution pattern become, the more time the speaker must take to support the parts of the speech adequately.

There is one other important modification of the problem-solution pattern that we ought to consider. Thus far the pattern as modified has maintained what could be called a *sequential* form; the problem is developed and then the solution is developed. The pattern can take on what can be called a *parallel* form. One phase of the problem is developed and the solution applied; another phase of the problem is developed and the solution applied; and so on. The result is an alternation of aspects of the problem and aspects of the solution. This "parallel" form is particularly useful when the problem has several rather distinct aspects that can be treated as relatively independent subproblems and when the solution is a rather simple proposal that does not require detailed development to be clear. Consider this example:

I. The electoral college can result in the election of a President who is not preferred by a majority of the voters.

II. Electing the President by a direct vote of the people is our best assurance that
the will of the majority shall prevail.

III. The electoral college system discourages the exercise of the franchise.

IV. Giving the people a direct vote in electing the President would encourage them
to exercise their democratic privilege of voting.

Many of the same difficulties arise in using the problem-solution pattern,
especially when it is modified, as arise in using the time pattern or the topical pattern. To meet many of these difficulties:

1. You should strive for simplicity.
2. You should be certain that your main heads really are coordinate parts of
the whole.
3. You should consider limiting your thesis if it seems that you cannot support all the assertions adequately in the time you have.

If the problem is a fresh one for your audience or if your analysis is
unique, you may wish to concentrate all your efforts on the problem, dis-
carding, at least for the moment, any consideration of the solution. On the
other hand, you may find that you are dealing with a problem that is clearly
recognized as such and concentrate on the solution you would have listeners
accept.

Of course you must divide the main heads of a speech arranged in a problem-solution pattern into subheads. In so doing you must meet the unique
demands of the situation, but there is a traditional group of questions that
may help you discover useful subheads in a problem-solution speech:

Problem: 1. Is the problem serious enough to warrant a change?
2. What are the causes of the problem?
3. If no changes are made, will the problem persist? Or will it,
perhaps, be resolved without making changes?

Solution: 1. Will the solution remove the causes of the problem?
2. Can the solution be put into operation?
3. Will the solution have desirable effects? Do the desirable
outweigh any undesirable effects?

This list is not intended to suggest that these questions constitute a form that
you must follow in constructing the specific points of his speech. It would be
a rare case in which you would want to make explicit use of answers to each
question in order. The listener as well as the speaker may find it useful to
raise these questions in considering problems and solutions.

In this section we have made a few generalizations about patterning the
developments of speeches. Orderly speeches are not simply a matter of mak-

ing models of textbook instructions. Speeches have order in terms of the needs of specific subjects and specific audiences. Learning to make use of traditional patterns will necessitate thought, planning, and practice. You will find a great deal of the material in the second part of this book that you may use to help pattern your speeches, using or modifying traditional forms.

CONCLUSION

If traditional ways of arranging the points of a speech are to be useful, they must be adapted to your subject, to your purpose, and to the situation in which you find yourself and your listeners. In short, every part of the speech must interact with every other part, and we must consider the *parts* to be not simply in the speech but in the world of events and interpreters of events like ourselves.

QUESTIONS AND EXERCISES

In this chapter, we illustrated both *time* and *topical* patterns by trial divisions for a speech concerning a hypothetical organization. Consider again these patterns.

Purpose: to clarify and intensify the feelings of the members toward the goals of the group.

Thesis: The goals of our founders should be carefully reconsidered by each of us.

Time pattern:

I. Our founders were men and women of vision who established a group with some remarkable principles.

II. At the present time we are carrying forward some of the group's original projects.

III. In the future we can find exciting new work to do by turning again to the principles of our founders.

Topical pattern:

[Each point is in answer to the question posed by asking "Why?" of the thesis.]

I. (Because) by so doing we shall honor those men and women who by their vigor and imagination formed this group.

II. (Because) by so doing we shall be better able to serve those purposes to which we have committed ourselves.

III. (Because) by so doing we shall gain personal satisfaction in fresh achievements.

It is not difficult to invent a simple problem-solution pattern to embody the purpose of the hypothetical speech. So let us add another trial pattern.

Problem-Solution pattern:

    I. Our group is threatened by disintegration.

    II. We can save our group by reconsidering the goals of our founders.

Try to answer the questions and then discuss your answers in class:

1. In what sorts of circumstances would each of the above work best?
2. Would it be possible to combine all three of the above into one speech? If so, what sort of combination would be possible?
3. Make other trial time patterns, topical patterns, and problem-solution patterns for the hypothetical purpose and thesis. Did you find time patterns, topical patterns, or problem-solution patterns easiest to invent? Would it be easier to invent trial patterns if you were to specify more specifically the nature of the group? Why?
4. Can you invent another hypothetical purpose and thesis as bases for three or more trial patterns? Try doing so using no more than fifteen minutes time.

5

making introductions, conclusions, and outlines

Every beginning is against nature; the beginning is a leap and nature does not make leaps.

PIERRE THÉVENAZ

All's Well that Ends Well!
SHAKESPEARE

Few things can do so much for a speech as a good introduction and a good conclusion. All of us have heard speeches that began well, that were rather muddled and boring in the middle, and then, miraculously, were concluded with clarity and grace. The total effect was good. Such speeches, of course, are no argument for muddled, boring developments. Much more often, however, we hear speeches that begin and end with remarkable awkwardness and obscurity.

Too often speakers will begin with endless ham-handed references to all their friends present and to the world situation in general. They will quip pleasantly (if we are fortunate) and unfold what they consider to be delightful anecdotes. Somehow or other, we aren't quite sure how, when, or why, such speakers get into their speeches.

If introductions are all too often weak in the speeches we ordinarily hear, the conclusions are worse. "In conclusion let me say to you . . . ." may be the signal for fifteen minutes of dreary effort to bring some sort of order into a development that has been in disarray from the beginning. "Finally I would remind you . . ." from this speaker probably indicates at least another ten minutes. We prefer this person's opposite, the speaker who when we look up after politely having yawned, has suddenly disappeared. Such speakers do not conclude their speeches; they just quit!

The main cause of ineffective introductions and conclusions does not lie in any insurmountable problems posed by these parts of the speech but in the simple lack of attention that speakers give them. Too often a speaker seems to say in effect, "Oh, I'll get started. I have a good speech and can end it." The person who leaves anything to the "spur of the moment" is apt to discover that the moment usually arrives, but the spur often fails to function. If speakers will prepare introductions and conclusions carefully, they can do a good job. Intelligent preparation does not assure success—we all make errors of judgment—but ignorance and indolence will go far in assuring failure. There are two words that speakers who would begin and end speeches effectively should remember—*purpose* and *simplicity*.

INTRODUCTIONS

Remember the point made in the last chapter: Ordinarily introductions and conclusions will be planned *after* the body or development of the main ideas of the speech. Until one has a good idea of just what it is that will be developed, planning an introduction will be difficult, to say the least. Of course one may be struck quite early in the process of preparing the speech by what seem to be good ideas for beginnings or endings and should jot these down in his notes.

Sometimes just "jumping in" works very well. Often speakers will decide to de-emphasize introductory functions and should do so if such a beginning will serve their purposes. But what are those purposes likely to be?

The speaker should realize that there are some legitimate openings that are nonintroductions, in terms of our meaning of the word *introduction*. Some occasions, for example, demand what might be called *preliminary remarks*. When the mayor is introduced to the audience, he will probably acknowledge the speech of introduction and recognize dignitaries, party faithful, the purposes of the organization, and so on. Many speakers face circumstances that call for such remarks. Often skilled speakers will be quite anecdotal in their remarks (that is, they will use detailed examples drawn from personal experience). The beginning speaker, however, seldom speaks on occasions that demand preliminaries beyond perhaps, "Mr. Chairman, ladies and gentlemen."

At other times the circumstances will make an introduction unnecessary. The audience knows who the speaker is; they know what the subject is; they are highly motivated to listen and able to understand. The speaker may begin the development immediately; even, "You know that I'm here this evening to talk about. . . ." is superfluous. But beginning speakers seldom find themselves in such circumstances.

Ordinarily the speaker plans an introduction to fulfill some specific purpose. Three generalizations should guide the speaker:

1. The introduction should arouse the audience's interest.
2. The introduction should dispose the audience to respond favorably toward the speaker.
3. The introduction should give the audience at least a tentative acquaintance with the speaker's thesis and provide an orientation to the speaker's plan of development.

Although the speaker may often safely ignore the second purpose listed, the first and third are essential—*arrest* and *clarify*.

Making a list of the purposes of an introduction should not mislead the speaker into thinking that the introduction will necessarily be composed of three distinct, chronological steps. The speaker might well fulfill these purposes in terms of a specific speech and a specific audience in a sentence or two. On the other hand, it is possible to have a rather elaborate introduction making two or three rather distinct steps. But the speaker should strive for simplicity. It may be that in facing a particularly hostile or apathetic audience the speaker will have to use a rather long introduction, but in general it should be short. The only "rule" possible is to make the introduction as short as possible while fulfilling the purposes demanded by the particular speech situation.

Arousing interest

The introduction should make the audience want to listen to the speech. Although there are some relatively traditional methods for accomplishing this end, you should be constantly alert for methods that seem potentially useful for you. In general, any piece of supporting material may be used to open a speech if, in your opinion, it will arrest the attention of the audience or help clarify your subject. Let us make a variety of beginnings for a hypothetical speech that will deal with the influence of commercial television dominated as it is by three national companies.

A series of relatively undetailed examples

A large number, seemingly a growing number, of incidents recently all seem to point in the same direction. When the hostages were released by the Hanafi Muslims from the Washington, D.C., headquarters of B'nai B'rith, they seemed to be about as angry at the television reporters as at their captors. More and more citizen groups are forming to bring pressure to bear on television. These seem to be encouraged by the example of the success of ACT, Action for Children's Television. Even big business is talking of taking action against what many leaders believe to be unfair treatment; several oil companies took sharp exception to a recent documentary aired on the oil crisis by ABC. Can we discern any pattern to these incidents?

A detailed example

You may have been as fascinated as I was by the well-publicized TV documentary on the energy crisis and the oil companies last week. I watched the dramatic picture of the apparent difficulties the oil companies had in responding to regional demands as they planned to refine more and more imported oil. And we were reminded that eighteen companies control almost all the refining capacities. I was fascinated to see the intricate pattern of tanker fleets that had to be maneuvered like chess pieces. And we were reminded that the decisions concerning where and when the fleets would go are made for the most part by the eighteen huge companies. I listened to the arguments about exploring for more domestic resources and wondered about the sorts of investments the eighteen dominant companies were making. Again and again we were reminded of the small number of companies that control the vital petroleum industry. And many of these companies are involved in coal production, natural gas production, and a network of other energy-related enterprises.

But isn't it ironic that while we concentrated on the combination of a small number of oil companies, we were viewing a program produced by one of the three national companies that dominate television? What of the mental and emotional energies they produce? Should we raise some questions about their behaviors?

An analogy

Suppose that you were to answer your doorbell one nice, bright day and find a well-dressed, middle-aged man standing there. "Good afternoon," he might say, "I want nothing from you. I simply want to come into your living room and sit quietly until you ask me to tell you stories. When you ask, I shall do so. If you tire of my stories, simply ask me to stop. If you'd like to mow the lawn or go shopping on Saturday morning, I'll be glad to tell stories to your children. I'll keep them absorbed and quiet with my tales."

Would you let the man come in to your living room? Would you believe that he wanted nothing from you? Would you leave little kids with him?

Of course my analogy is obvious. And the parallel to the television set that occupies most living rooms is not perfect. But what of the force that controls such a high proportion of the stories that enter our minds, and those of our little sisters and brothers, our sons and daughters?

Testimony

We are used to thinking of television as a vast array of all sorts of things. And indeed it is that. But it is also a combination of a very few, highly centralized groups incorporated to do business. And business they do. Whatever else we think about television, we must think of it as a few companies that are as prone as any of the abuses for which this country has passed antitrust legislation. As Kevin Phillips, lawyer and writer on the media puts it, "Unfortunately, the success of any policy re-evaluation may rest on the extent to which the opinion-molding class of Americans—the bulk of whom, by definition earn their living from communications—can put aside the notion of 'the media' as a moral and intellectual enterprise and think of it as a rich and powerful *industry*." [1]

Let's take a look at Mr. Phillips' proposition.

---

[1] "Busting the Media Trusts," *Harper's*, July 1977, p. 23.

Statistics

We have heard these figures again and again. But still they are difficult to comprehend. Preschool children spend more time watching television than on any other waking activity. By the time the average American reaches eighteen, he or she will have spent 15,000 hours in front of a television set as compared to 11,000 in school.[2] And still the questions persist: What do children see when they watch TV? What effects do viewing have?

These questions are far from easy to answer, and we shall have to focus sharply to gain even a few limited answers this afternoon.

Visual aids can be put to use in an introduction. The student mentioned in Chapter 3 used fake dynamite to arrest the audience. Any statistical information might be dramatized by a graph or chart.

Often you will be able to refer to a recent experience a member of the audience has had, to another speech, or to some aspect of the occasion that you and the audience share, or perhaps to something said by the speaker preceding you in such a way as to help arouse the interest of the listeners. You must be alert, however, to weave such remarks into the fabric of your own speech.

Disposing the audience favorably toward the speaker

In general, the best advice to the beginning speaker on gaining the favor of his audience is simply to plan carefully an introduction that fulfills the other purposes of an introduction. If one can do that, the audience will probably be favorably disposed.

Sometimes the speaker may need to claim a special authority. But such a claim may be best established indirectly in the speech, or perhaps made on the speaker's behalf in a speech of introduction. But occasionally a speaker might make such a claim at the outset of a speech by referring directly to relevant experience. Teachers, for example, commonly refer to the fact that they are teachers when discussing educational issues. The practice is common, and unless one harps on such experience, probably useful.

The speaker should do anything that helps indicate to listeners that they share common ground—common experiences, values, goals, affiliations, but one should not bid too bluntly for favor. Such bids are apt to have the opposite effect.

Clarifying the subject

Some of the examples already used indicate that speakers can scarcely help clarifying the subject to some degree if they choose carefully the material to arouse the audience's interest.

But the question arises, "Just how clear do you want to be at the outset of a speech?" Taking an unpopular position immediately may arouse the audi-

[2] "Improving TV for Children," *Minneapolis Tribune*, July 2, 1977, p. 4A.

ence but may also gain a highly unsympathetic hearing. Of course one will not want to keep one's purpose hidden for the entire speech for then by definition one will quite likely fail. But it may be wise to mention a general topic early ("Fraternities have played highly varied roles on American campuses.") rather than a flat thesis ("Abolish fraternities!"). Sooner or later, however, the thesis will have to be stated flatly or at least strongly suggested.

In general, listeners will be quite satisfied not to know specifically what the thesis of a speech is, provided that they have a strong sense that the speaker has a clear sense of purpose and will reveal the central idea soon. Giving that strong sense of purpose, however, is often difficult. Beginners, especially, should take great care to make their subjects clear.

Often you will want to make an explicit statement of your thesis. If you have worded it carefully, this simple device may be abundantly sufficient. You may choose a question, or a series of questions, that suggests your thesis. (The question, as such, is *not* the thesis, even though it may point quite clearly to the unstated thesis). If questions are striking, they may well serve not only to clarify the undertaking but also to arouse the audience's interest. However, *avoid* the lame, last-minute attempt that unprepared speakers often make to use questions: for example, "Have you ever wondered about water conservation?"

There is the oft-repeated story of the old preacher who explained in a single sentence the whole process of making a speech: "First I tell 'em what I'm going to tell 'em; then I tell 'em what I tell 'em; then I tell 'em what I told 'em." The preacher's first step, apparently, was to presummarize his development. Although a presummary is not always necessary or even advisable, we feel that it is much too seldom used by speakers. The development may be presummarized quite formally: "We should discontinue competition in intercollegiate football because, first, it is harmful to the participants, second, it is harmful to the nonparticipating student body; and third, it degrades our college as an institution of higher education." Or the development can be presummarized more casually: "If we are to assess the merit of our college's participation in intercollegiate football, we should ask what effect it has on the participant, on the student body generally, and on the college itself."

Good introductions take time and imagination to prepare. You must remember, however, that they serve important purposes, which you can ill afford to neglect.

The purposes of an introduction are well exemplified in Russell W. Peterson's speech to the Cleveland City Club. Mr. Peterson is the president of a citizens' action group.

I want to talk to you about world security—about your security and that of your children—about the security of people everywhere. We are in deep trouble and getting in deeper every day. And yet most of our leaders in business and in government continue to make decisions in the same old way. Business leaders worry primarily about this year's operating statement—how can I make a buck today? Government leaders worry primarily about the next election—how can I get re-elected? As a result we are being carried into the future by the momentum of the status quo resisting change in all directions.

There are today four tremendous threats to world security. And all four are the result of a long series of seemingly innocent decisions appropriate to the short-term, special interests of thousands of decision-makers. Each of these threats leads us to the edge of a precipice. What are these threats?[3]

Peterson refers to his subject immediately and directly and asserts its importance. Such an introduction depends on the audience's being at least a little sympathetic; Peterson's audience probably was. He concludes his introduction with a summary of "threats," thus answering immediately the question with which the preceding extract ends. The introduction is moderately good in serving the purpose of arousing the audience and excellent in clarifying the speaker's point of view.

CONCLUSIONS

After a careful development of the four points he summarized in the introduction, Peterson begins a rather long conclusion with a summary of what he has called "serious threats to world security." The main function of the conclusion is to associate individual citizens who wish to act with action groups like the one Peterson heads: "New Directions has been organized to provide citizens with a channel for effective impact on U.S. foreign policy formulation." He uses a series of specific instances about past policies, ones that probably made his audience feel uncomfortable because, although they may have differed with the policies, they probably did nothing. Finally he completes the speech with these words:

Anyone who cares about world security, about our children and future generations has to be concerned about critical world problems—about the poorest of the poor, about hunger, about the exploding world population, about the proliferation of nuclear and other weapons, about the pollution of our oceans and our atmosphere, about running out of energy, about the waste of our resources and about injustice.[4]

Mr. Peterson's speech probably needed a long conclusion; and he made an excellent one. A simple speech, which is clearly developed, may need almost no conclusion, for the purpose of a conclusion is to give the audience a feeling of completion, that things are done, and the speaker may well have done that as he or she utters the last world of the development. Stated a little more elaborately, the conclusion serves two possible functions:

[3] "We Citizens Cannot Sit Back and Relax: World Security as Seen from New Directions," *Vital Speeches of the Day,* June 1, 1977, pp. 490–91.

[4] Ibid., p. 493.

1. The conclusion should restate briefly the substance of the speech.
2. The conclusion should focus the attention of the audience on the response the speaker desires.

These aims may be more or less important depending on the sort of development that has been made. Sometimes more than a simple restatement of the thesis will be superfluous.

Just as presummaries are sometimes useful, final summaries may help the speaker fulfill the purposes of a good conclusion. A summary may be *formal* or *casual*. In his speech, Russell Peterson used both a presummary and a final summary; and both were formal, that is, the points were listed separately and competely stated. He also summarized his points casually twice, that is, the points were ennumerated briefly just using key words in a single statement.

Quite often in concluding, speakers will use a phrase, a sentence, a piece of material that they have used elsewhere in their speeches. It is especially common, and often effective, to use material from the introduction. Consider the conclusion of the speech on highway safety, twice referred to, which began with the speaker displaying dummy dynamite and asking, "Care to light the fuse and put this stick of dynamite in your pocket?" At the end of the speech, the student picked up the object once more.

> This dynamite isn't really dangerous—but your car is. Treat it with as much caution as you'd treat a stick of dynamite.
>
> I have a piece of dynamite fuse taped over the ignition switch of my car. I need a reminder of my responsibility to myself and to others. Maybe you don't need a reminder. But I have twenty-five pieces of fuse which I'll give to you in a minute. Take one and tape it over your ignition—or throw it away. But be careful—don't throw away your life.[5]

This conclusion is one that the speaker's audience is likely to remember.

If the speaker offers some sort of proposal, a solution, he or she might well want to visualize the effects of the proposal if put into operation, or may want to visualize the lamentable state of affairs that will persist if it isn't, or may want to do both, if there is time. In such visualization the speaker can make any number of abstract assertions, but a wise speaker will use supporting material to make the visualization clear, interesting, and impelling.

Like the introduction, the conclusion should be simple. It should be short. As with the introduction, the only sensible "rule" is to make it as short as possible while fulfilling its purposes.

If the conclusion is to give the audience a feeling of completeness, and if it is to "round out" the thought, the speaker, when planning it, might be well advised to look again at the introduction. Good speakers quite often mirror the beginning in the ending.

[5] Adapted from a speech by Orrin Finch, University of Minnesota student, 1959.

Speaking at the Free University of Berlin in 1964, Robert F. Kennedy began by recognizing the occasion and the special relationship of his recently assassinated brother to the Berlin audience:

I greatly appreciate your kindness in asking me to return to the Free University to give this address in honor of President Kennedy. I know he would have been proud to be honored in this way and in this place.

Excellence of education was particularly close to his heart and to be associated with this memorial that reaches to the minds of men would have greatly pleased him. But even more than education, more than any other human quality, President Kennedy admired courage. As Cicero once said, "There is nothing more fair, more beautiful, more to be loved than high courage." He spoke of his visit to Berlin. He admired its vitality and its dedication. But most of all, he admired its courage. And he knew that the Free University was the heartbeat and soul of that courage—that commitment to what is best in man.

Thus Robert Kennedy began his speech. In the conclusion of the speech he reflected many of the same identifications of value and place that he made in the introduction. Consider his last few statements:

Because this University embodies so many of the things President Kennedy cherished, I would like, in closing, to say a personal word about the significance of his death. There were many who felt then that a light had been snuffed out; that the torchbearer for a whole generation was gone; that an era was over before its time; that with him there died idealism and hope and what was clean and best in all of us. To many, it seemed then that the world might lapse again into the empty poses and vain quarrels that disfigured our yesterdays and made of our past a litany of anguish.

But in traveling through my own country, through the far East several months ago and now in Germany, I have come to understand that the hope President Kennedy kindled is not dead but alive. It is not a memory, but a living force. The torch still burns, and because it does, there remains for all of us the chance to light up the to-morrows and to brighten the future. For me, that is the challenge that makes life worthwhile; and I hope it will be the same for all of you.[6]

For most speakers, planning introductions and conclusions is difficult, but that planning can be an excellent opportunity to focus tightly on the thought, feeling, and action that the speaker holds important. These parts of the speech can be especially vital not only in terms of the possible responses of an audience, but also in terms of one's own feeling of worthwhile effort.

OUTLINES

An outline is part of proper speech preparation. Therefore, the question students often ask, "Do I have to make an outline for this speech?" indicates

---

[6] "Address to the Free University of Berlin," in *Voices of Crisis: Vital Speeches on Contemporary Issues*, ed. Floyd W. Matson, New York, Odyssey Press (Publishing), 1967, pp. 96, 103–104.

a deficiency in their understanding of their task as speakers. This deficiency may arise from what they have learned from textbooks about speech outlines. But the moment you put pencil to paper to jot a phrase indicating your tentative thesis and, perhaps, several words to help you remember and consider a possible pattern of main heads, you have begun to outline. What you have made is a rough draft. You should make dozens of such drafts in preparing your speech. Some you will discard; some you will modify. Eventually your outline will grow into a final, completed form.

Too often speakers read or hear advice like that just given and say "A dozen outlines. Sounds like a needless drain on time." So they work hard, gather material, and sit down the night before they are to speak to plan their speeches from beginning to end. In the effort to compose polished speeches, perhaps represented by spic and span outlines, at one sitting students will probably spend more time than they would have had they followed the advice; and the products of their work will probably not measure up to what they are capable of doing. An early rough draft may take only a minute or two to jot down, and in making rough drafts, students will form good habits: *plan, evaluate, modify.*

Outlines in process are not likely to be neat and attractive. As speakers work on outlines they will become less and less neat. Soon speakers discover that they must recopy the modified versions simply so that they can comprehend them and continue to build on them toward the final forms the outlines will take. In making a simple illustration used earlier (Chapter 4, p. 64), one of your authors produced this:

We must correct some common misunderstandings about fraternities.
~~The purpose of fraternities is misunderstood.~~
I. ~~Common misunderstandings.~~ *The cinema stereotypes do not represent the average fraternity.*
II. The real aims of fraternities ~~are far different than many suppose.~~ *serve legitimate individual needs.*

This is, of course, only the beginning of an outline.

What has been said ought not to be taken to mean that complete, neatly written outlines have no value. The complete outline is simply the final step in a long series. It should be neatly done, of course, so that you can see what you have and so that your instructor (or anyone who might help you) will be able to criticize it.

Even when you feel that you have an outline completed, you will be wise to take it apart again. Make a list of the main heads. Are they divided properly? Patterned effectively? Stated clearly? Taken together do they satisfactorily express the thesis? Should the thesis be modified? Look at each main section. Are the subordinate heads well arranged? Are assertions supported? Are all the relationships clear? Have needed transitions been omitted? All of this is necessary because in building a more and more complex structure, the speaker may lose sight of some of the large patterns and reltionships. But some of these questions touch on problems that have not yet been discussed.

Standard symbols

Any system of outlining will be somewhat arbitrary and sometimes seem to be burdensome. You may wish to disregard traditional practices at times, but when you do so, be sure you have good reason, taking care not simply to rationalize carelessness or laziness. Using symbols to indicate parts of the outline will help most speakers achieve an orderly structure. Here is a model to follow:

Introduction
  A. ——————————
  B. ——————————
    1. ————————
    2. ————————
Development
  I. ————————
    A. ——————————
      1. ————————
        a. ———————
          (1) ———————
            (a) ———————
        b. ———————
      2. ————————
    B. ——————
    C. ——————
  II. ——————
and so on
Conclusion
  A. ——————————
  B. ——————————

Several explanations may be necessary. You may not need as many divisions as just indicated. In general, seek simplicity. You will notice that your authors prefer actually to write in "introduction," "development," and "conclusion." We feel that this is a simple but useful reminder. Finally, *you will notice that we have used Roman numerals to indicate only main heads.* This is arbitrary, but there may be some value in having a symbol that says "main head." Some authorities recommend repeating Roman numerals (as we have repeated capital letters, and so on) in each section of the outline; others carry the Roman numerals through from beginning to end.

Take a piece of paper and make two more models similar to that shown. For one, repeat the Roman numerals in each section of the model. For the other, carry the Roman numerals through from beginning to end, which will mean that you will not repeat any of the Roman numerals. Look at all three models, the two you have made and the one above; try to decide which you prefer. Of course your instructor may have a preference and may ask that the entire class follow it in order to make quick comparisons from outline to outline practical.

Stating assertions

Most textbook writers recommend that the beginner compose a complete sentence outline. We feel that it is unnecessary to indicate each minor detail by a complete sentence; often a phrase or a single word will suffice to indicate, for example, a piece of supporting material. There may even be disadvantages to a complete sentence outline, especially for extemporaneous speaking.[7] Too often it becomes a barely disguised manuscript. If one wants to write a manuscript, one should do so and should compose outlines in preparation for writing manuscripts. But a manuscript speech is a manuscript speech whether it is written in paragraphs or in a number of lines with symbols before each.

What you have just read should not be taken to mean that you should not indicate each part of your speech carefully in outlining, nor should it be taken to mean that no complete sentences should be written. *The thesis and each main head must be written as a complete, declarative sentence.* There is no other way of checking these important parts to make certain that they are what one wants them to be. You may write such other complete sentences as may serve to help you compose critical parts of the speech. Many speakers like to write out the first few sentences of the introduction and the last few of the conclusion completely. Often transitions should be written as complete sentences.

We discussed phrasing theses in Chapter 2. Like the thesis, the main heads should be stated as concisely and vividly as possible. If possible, use parallel sentence structure and repeat key words in phrasing main heads to make them stand out boldly in the speech. Consider:

Thesis: D. H. Lawrence's novels are degrading.
 I. The intent of Lawrence's novels is to sensationalize sordid passions.
 II. The effect of Lawrence's novels is to encourage animalistic abandon.

or

Thesis: D. H. Lawrence should be ranked among the world's great novelists.
 I. Lawrence is concerned with timeless problems of human values.
 II. Lawrence treats problems of human values in a frank but uniquely sensitive manner.

You should examine quite carefully any main head stated as a compound sentence. Such sentences usually indicate ideas that should be treated in two (or more) main heads.

[7] Problems of delivering extemporaneous and manuscript speeches will be considered in Chapter 8.

Ordinarily you should state the main heads explicitly at the beginning of the sections of the speech in which they are developed. Sometimes, however, the statement of the main head may be delayed or even left unstated, just as the statement of the thesis may be delayed or left unstated. Often it is effective to introduce some material and to draw the main head from it or to allow the audience to supply the assertion. Inasmuch as the form of outlining requires assertions to be made and development of material to follow in clear subordination, the beginning speaker is often perplexed in trying to indicate a delayed or implicit main head. The answer is to place in brackets, [ ], any assertion that is not actually to be stated at the point at which form requires it to appear in the outline:

I. [Public opinion engineers are usurping our rights of democratic free choice.]
   A. A political campaign in San Francisco.
   B. Experts in conducting campaigns testify concerning their methods.
I. Public opinion engineers are usurping our rights of democratic free choice.

The procedure of using brackets looks more clumsy than it is once one forms the habit. But the vital point to understand is that the actual statement of a main head can be made any time. It may be made first, and then the idea may be developed. Or the idea may be developed with concrete material followed by the statement of the idea. Or the idea may be stated and restated several times while the point is being developed. Or supporting material may be developed concretely and the idea, which could be stated as an explicit assertion, may be suggested silently.

Outlines can only indicate *roughly* the ideas, materials, and sequences of thought. To try to make them do more is a mistake. Outlines can serve you well, but you must be careful not to try to drive them too far. They must help you formulate and present your thought. They cannot be formulas that substitute for thought—either before speaking or during those moments when the speech actually becomes living communication.

Transitions and signposting

Careful attention to transitions is a sign differentiating the experienced from the inexperienced speaker. Transitions may be used between any major divisions in the speech, although usually they are thought of as being the bridge between the developments of two main heads. In a sense they serve as a conclusion to the point just finished and the introduction to the next. In simple, well-ordered speeches transitions may be unnecessary, but the speaker should make certain that this is the case before omitting transitions.

Restatement-forecast is the simplest method of transition: "But a lack of funds is only one of the problems we face; more serious is our lack of commitment to our ideals." "Not only must we hasten to meet this threat, but we must act upon a careful plan. This raises a natural question, 'What can be done quickly?' " As this last example indicates, rhetorical questions serve well as transitions. Often the question will be much like the main head, but it is not itself a main head and should not be mistaken for such. When a question is used as a transition, often the speaker will delay the explicit statement of the main head.

Pieces of supporting material, especially examples and testimony, may serve as transitions. The main problem, especially in short speeches, is to make such transitions quickly.

In the outline, transitions should be indicated by placing the statement or phrase indicating the transition in parentheses:

I. _____

   A. _____

(But there is another problem we must consider . . .)

II. _____

Often a speaker will *signpost* to indicate a new idea, especially to indicate another main head. "In the first place . . ." "Secondly . . ." "My second point is . . ." "Finally we must consider . . ." Although this device may seem awkward, many great speakers have not hesitated to use it. With practice a speaker can signpost smoothly.

Students who have studied this chapter carefully should be ready to build rather carefully ordered speeches. They should not be under the illusion that they will face no difficult problems, that secret doorways have been opened to them. But they should be able to proceed in their private learning process.

EXAMPLES

Study the following outlines composed by college students in preparation for extemporaneous speeches. Very few modifications have been made in them for publication here. They are not perfect outlines; they could be improved as almost all outlines can be improved. But they will indicate the form outlines take and should stimulate you to do at least as well.

Many textbook writers, as we have already noted, would argue that the speaker, especially the beginner, should compose each entry in the outline in complete sentences. Because the following outlines are not composed in complete sentences, some entries will not be completely clear to the reader. But each of these speakers intended the outline for his or her own use and, of course, had to be able to complete the thoughts indicated at subordinate points in the outline merely by words or phrases. In these cases, the young man and the young woman who composed the outlines were able to make excellent use of them.

You will notice that the speakers have maintained a labeling margin on the left-hand side. We recommend this practice for the beginning speaker. Taking stock of what you have done is one good method of laying a foundation for evaluating and improving specific speeches and thereby for becoming a more knowledgeable student of speech.

What sort of notes should you make in the labeling margin? Primarily you should be conscious of your methods of supporting ideas. When you have chosen a piece of material to make an assertion or implication clear, interesting, or acceptable, label the material. You should also be conscious of the organization of your speech. Label main points, transitions, summaries, and other efforts you make to give the sequence of ideas and materials clarity and impact.

Be imaginative in your use of the labeling margin. As a speaker analyzing your own work, you should see the particular procedures you are following and may need a unique word or phrase to describe them.

You will remember that we have chosen arbitrarily to use large Roman numerals *only* in the development section of the outlines. Here you will be able to judge whether limiting the use of that symbol to indicate main points and nothing else seems to make sense to you. Some persons have reported that they are bothered by seeing capital letters in an outline before seeing the large Roman numerals.

An antidote to depersonalized journalism: the case of Norman Mailer[8]

Discussion of purpose

Most Americans are deadened to the incessant flow of "facts and figures" on every hand. Even though we are often "turned-off" by what we see and hear in the media, students like myself may accept the value of "being objective" much too uncritically. My purpose will not be to try to create fans for Norman Mailer but rather to illustrate that events are not simply *out there* somewhere but must be taken in by someone, must be humanized or personalized if finally they are to be meaningful.

INTRODUCTION

Assertion
Detailed examples

A. The news media tend to bombard us with information.
   1. The present space mission.
   2. The troubles of Rolls Royce and Lockheed seem to be our burdens, too, as the facts roll on and on.

A dilemma. Can the audience identify?

B. We feel burdened, but at the same time we want to be informed.
C. A "journalist" like Norman Mailer provides us with a refreshing change.

Quotations

   1. Some of his remarks about Germaine Greer.
   2. Some of Germaine's about Norman!

[8] Adapted from a speech outline prepared by John Trolander, University of Minnesota student, 1971.

Thesis serving also as transition	(Personalized journalism provides a valuable perspective to the news.)
Main point	I. A short sketch of Mailer's career indicates the point-of-view that he brings to journalism.

Sub-point *Examples and quotations from critics*	A. Mailer the novelist
	   1. *The Naked and the Dead*—a "good" novel.
	   2. *Why Are We in Vietnam?*—a "bad" novel.

Sub-point	B. Mailer the politician
	   1. Running for mayor of New York
	   2. Antiwar activity

Main point	II. A self-oriented journalist, he has written about space shots, protests, and political conventions.

Sub-point *Examples involving quotations and my evaluations*	A. He reports about public events while he tells about himself.
	   1. *Fire on the Moon*—and the Mailer ego.
	   2. That his viewpoint is unique indicates that any decent human viewpoint should be unique—witness his self-revealed weaknesses in *Prisoner of Sex*.

Sub-point *Example* *Comparison*	B. Human events, no matter how serious, are comic.
	   1. Organization of the march on the Pentagon in 1967.
	   2. Mailer's drunkenness compared with crowd-intoxication.

Sub-point *Examples of N. M.'s evaluative language*	C. Human events, no matter how comic, are serious.
	   1. The Republicans at Miami in 1968.
	   2. The Democrats at Chicago in 1968.

Transition *Quotations*	(One does not have to like Norman Mailer to recognize the value of making the events that occur around us and *to* us personal. Woman libbers know that.)
	CONCLUSION
Assertion	A. We badly need human dimensions in thinking about "the news."
Restatement of thesis	B. Norman Mailer shows us the complexity and the contradictions of human activities. We need a personal dimension in journalism.

Modern weapons and barbarism[9]

Discussion of
purpose

I expect my listeners to agree with me. My purpose, then, is not to persuade them, but rather to intensify opinions and, especially, feelings already present. An ironic speech praising modern weaponry may help push some over the line toward total repugnance for some of the justifications we use to rationalize our present national and international conduct.

INTRODUCTION

A blatant assertion
Two slightly detailed
examples

A. American society is living proof of the great advance of us moderns beyond our barbaric forebears.
   1. Marvelous electronic mass media.
   2. Complex market management.

Assertion

B. Our technical prowess sets us at the head of world affairs.

Undetailed examples

   1. Trade, tourism; war and welfare.

Transition

(Perhaps the advanced technology of weapons best shows our advances and perhaps even explains in part our ascendancy.)

DEVELOPMENT

Main point

I. Arms have played an important role from the earliest periods of American history.

Example
Details

A. Consider the solution of the "Indian problem."
   1. The musket: slow but efficient.
   2. Better than bow and arrow, but one still had to see and think about "the enemy."

Contrast

B. The example contrasts our crude beginnings with savage tactics of the Indians.

Details

   1. Indians didn't try to kill but often counted "coups."
   2. Settlers used advanced skills to eliminate future threats.

Assertion

C. Challenges caused our forebears to refine techniques.

Example

   1. Indians lack of cooperation in face-to-face combat created a need for long-range weapons—thus the rifled barrel.

[9] Adapted from a speech outline prepared by Milo Schefers, University of Minnesota student, 1970.

More detailed examples	2. Need to eliminate numbers quickly gave birth to rapid advances.
	a. The Treeby chain gun in 1858.
Quotation and figures	b. *London Standard*, 1859, reported the firing of 30 rounds in precisely one minute and twenty seconds.
Somewhat detailed example	c. The Colt revolver soon eclipsed this record.
Assertion	D. The outbreak of the Civil War intensified the search for efficient rapid-firing weapons.
Example	1. Richard Jordan Gatling of Chicago developed a gun that fired 350 rounds a minute.
	2. Gatling's modern weapon helped civilize the American plains.
Transition and an example and contrast	(Modern human endeavor was symbolized by the developing of a fully automatic weapon by Hiram S. Maxim in 1884, but by contemporary standards, nineteenth-century weapons, as wonderful as they were, are still semibarbaric.)
Main point	II. Today we have numerous weapons that would have been science fiction a century ago.
Comparison	A. Unlike the relatively crude but advanced methods of the warfare against the American Indians we have many "better ideas."
Detailed examples contrasted	1. Smallpox infested blankets were crude methods of biological warfare.
	2. Truly advanced pathogenic organisms allow sophisticated delivery and much more certain effects.
Assertion	B. We have eliminated barbaric face-to-face combat.
	1. Recall August of 1945. A milestone.
Specific instances	a. August 6, 78,000 people were killed at Hiroshima by a bomb dropped from only
Facts and figures	one plane.
	b. Three days later, 74,000 were killed at Nagasaki by the device that eliminated the need to come into personal contact with the enemy.
Assertion	2. It is possible with sheer threat of "the bomb" to maintain control.
Assertion	a. Advanced countries have bombs that can destroy the world hundreds of times over.

Questionable
assertion

    b. Less civilized countries respect our tremendous power.

Assertion

C. When face-to-face combat is necessary techniques are used that make it more efficient.

Detailed example

    1. Popularity of the hand grenade established in World War I.

    2. Training of men has advanced also.

Slightly detailed
examples

      a. Consider a modern "Green Beret."

      b. Even guerrillas are becoming modernized.

Transition

(Even more advanced weapons stagger one's financial imagination.)

Main point

III. The money spent for different types of weapons is a clear indication of our great advances.

Example statistics

A. The sentinel antiballistic missile system: $40 billion—a dollar of taxes per second won't cover the. cost.

Example figures

B. Nuclear attack submarines especially designed to seek out and attack other submarines: introductory cost, only $12 billion.

Summary assertion

C. Countering the advanced weapons of others make us even more advanced, as the cost figures show.

Transition

(The progress of war technology has been without doubt staggering in terms of human ingenuity, energy, and cost. Such accomplishments could only be gained by truly advanced societies.)

CONCLUSION

¡ A. Our nation has become civilized to the point that technology can plan and counterplan every human motive. Remember, that I used weaponry only as one example of our abilities.

B. We can be proud of our rapid advancements beyond our forefathers in the rate of extending civilization.

Thesis implicitly but
strongly suggested

B . [We should be ashamed of much that we call "progress" and reassess the values of "civilization."]

ASSIGNMENTS

Group exercise

1. Divide the class into groups of about four students each.
2. Preliminary meeting. Each group should
  a. choose a subject for a speech.

b. discuss the purpose of the speech for the class-audience.

c. phrase a tentative thesis.

3. Each group member should work out an outline using the tentative thesis.

4. In group meetings, compare and discuss the outlines. Try to work out a "best" outline.

5. Optional: let each group discuss organizing a speech on its particular thesis, telling what they did and why.

Speaking assignment

1. Choose a speech from *Vital Speeches*.

2. Describe the organization of the speech.

3. Criticize the organization using this question as a guide: "What could be done to improve the organization?"

6

adjusting ideas to audiences

> Speaking generally, we may say that the rhetorical function is the function of adjusting ideas to people and people to ideas.
>
> DONALD C. BRYANT

The speaker's commitment to ideas and materials is a theme that we have constantly reiterated in this book. It is a theme that will be developed more deeply in Chapters 10 through 14 when we set forth a problem-centered system of analysis.

The inclination of people to commit themselves to ideals, institutions, and programs is a major force in bringing progressive improvements into human life and in conserving past gains from the threat of corruption. But unless we are inclined toward totalitarianism, we must recognize that such commitment is not enough. We must believe not only in a particular analysis of a problem and a plan or a program but also in the right and ability of others to assent or dissent intelligently.

Good speakers, in short, must temper their own convictions in the crucible of communication. As our metaphor suggests, good speakers do not relinquish their commitments. Too often adjusting to audiences is taken to mean compromising in the negative sense that word often carries, or to be even more pejorative, to "sell out" or to prostitute one's thought and effort.

Few feel admiration for the person whose opinions change with every breeze, but neither do we praise the person who may think critically on shared public problems but who cannot or will not bring that thought in some way into the public forum. On the other extreme, we sometimes label "courageous" the person who, in effect, says, "Here are my ideas; I will not modify them to suit anyone!" Occasionally it *is* courageous to forego the immediate prospect of appealing to a majority in order to serve more long-range convictions. Too often, however, what we know as "the courage of one's convictions" is simply the result of a person's being too lazy or too stubborn to take the responsibility of making ideas as effective as they could be for an audience.

Ordinarily a sincere effort to make one's ideas effective, to adjust "ideas to people and people to ideas" in Donald C. Bryant's phrase,[1] takes more ability and courage than does striking the take-it-or-leave-it posture. One's thought may be tempered, as steel is tempered, in heat. Seldom, however, will the proper temperature be reached merely by the flash of hot proclamation. Much more often it is the friction of fine minds working to find an alloy that will suit the situation that brings the strongest fusion.

Quite commonly, we read advice to be open-minded. Strangely, this advice is often seemingly addressed solely to listeners: "Listen carefully to what others say! Set aside your own biases! Actively seek information that may be useful to your needs and even that may extend those needs in ways you do not immediately understand!"

Those are excellent pieces of advice. In Chapter 9 we shall be concerned with giving similar advice to listeners. But if listeners should be open to speakers, should not speakers be open to listeners? The barrier to understanding here, in addition to the fact that the question itself may be a little unusual and hence seem odd, is that we tend to consider our thought process as somehow separated from the speaking process. That is one difficulty with the word "and" in the title of this book, although we have sought at every step to show (1) that thinking should carry one into speaking, and (2) that the process of speaking should direct and continue into thought. Certainly there are time sequences in the planning and delivery of a speech. But the good speaker is one who can make the parts of the process interpenetrate one another.

It is probably a sign of poor thought when a speaker thinks "Here's what has to be said; now how can I say this to them?" The facts of the matter, if they are worth talking about at all, have human relevance, and the speaker should be thinking about the facts from the outset in terms of people.

At this point a perceptive student may remark, "Yes, these arguments are obvious enough. They have, as a matter of fact, been present in the book from the beginning." The student is quite right and might predict further

---

[1] "Rhetoric: Its Functions and Its Scope," *The Quarterly Journal of Speech*, XXXIX 4 (Dec. 1953), p. 413.

that the task of adjusting ideas to audiences will be a major theme of most of the following chapters. The title we chose for this chapter would be descriptive of most speech textbooks, including this one. What we say in this chapter will be most useful if the student sees in it an opportunity to review Chapters 2, 3, and especially 4, and recalls it in studying the problem-centered system of analysis set forth in Chapters 10 through 14.

What is vital in studying all this material is to recognize the reciprocal relationship of speaker and audience. Each depends on the other, at least momentarily, for whatever meaning their joint efforts may make.

IDENTIFICATION—THE FUNDAMENTAL PROCESS

"To persuade a man is largely a matter of *identifying* the opinion or course you wish him to adopt with one or more of his established beliefs or customary courses of conduct,"[2] James A. Winans observed [italics, Winans']. Even the speech in which one sets as his basic task putting forth some body of information must relate somehow to the needs of auditors if it is to be attended to seriously; we may extend therefore Winans' remark to apply generally to the rhetorical function of adjusting ideas to an audience. (The student may wish to review our discussion of *purpose* in Chapter 2.)

Often in introductions the effort of speakers to identify their interests with those of the audience is especially apparent. When places, occasions, and participants give speakers opportunities to refer to experiences, goals, or associations they hold in common with their listeners, many take advantage of the circumstances. For example, in speaking to a Black audience of civil rights activists, Malcolm X recognized that most of the leaders with whom his listeners identified were Christian ministers, so he lists them, declares his own religious affiliations, and then says,

Although I'm still a Muslim, I'm not here tonight to discuss my religion. I'm not here to try and change your religion. I'm not here to argue or discuss anything we differ about, because it's time for us to submerge our differences and realize that it is best for us to first see that we have the same problem, a common problem—a problem that will make you catch hell whether you're a Baptist, or a Methodist, or a Muslim, or a nationalist.[3]

Whereas the identifying of interests in introductions may give us the quickest, most obvious examples, one should not expect to find the function fulfilled there and the matter put aside. Fundamental identifications should undergird the entire speech and will often appear only in subtle signs throughout. The basic nature of identification is neatly caught in the central metaphor of this statement of Kenneth Burke's:

[2] *Speech-Making*, New York, Appleton-Century-Crofts, 1938, p. 370.

[3] *Malcolm X Speaks*, ed. George Breitman, New York, Grove Press, Inc., 1965, p. 24.

True, the rhetorician may have to change an audience's opinion in one respect; but he can succeed only insofar as he yields to that audience's opinions in other respects. Some of their opinions are needed to support the fulcrum by which he would move other opinions. (Preferably he shares the fixed opinions himself since, "all other things being equal," the identifying of himself with his audience will be more effective if it is genuine.)[4]

Extending Burke's parenthetical remark, we must observe that a speaker who has reason to address an audience at all should be able to find some rather substantial grounds on which to identify interests.

On what sorts of grounds may one identify with an audience? This question is natural enough. The answer will entail making a choice of a set of terms to guide the speaker's thought in preparing a speech. As we have said constantly in setting forth our nomenclature, other terms could be chosen, and whatever terms are chosen, they constitute merely points of departure for specific analysis.

Before discussing possible bases of identification, however, we shall suggest that the process of adjusting ideas to audiences, although it is a general process that may manifest itself in an infinite number of ways in speeches, may be given special focus if the speaker will concentrate on three elements of speech composition that we have already discussed.

Identifying in the statement of purpose

As we said in Chapter 2, the careful speaker constructs a guide by composing a statement of the purpose that the speech is intended to accomplish. Although some traditional "ends" of public speaking may help focus the effort, each purpose statement should be a unique one setting forth the specific response or group of interrelated responses sought from the audience.

The student who begins his statement of purpose with "I expect my audience to agree that a basic purpose of higher education is to enable us to learn to exercise free choice intelligently. In light of this belief, it is inconsistent for us to accept an administrative policy that limits strictly the political affiliations of speakers invited by student organizations to address them. Furthermore . . ." is probably seeing the purpose in the light of adjusting ideas and listeners. "It is the existence of some inconsistency within the microstructure of most auditors' opinions . . . that makes possible opinion change on controversial questions," Theodore Clevenger, Jr. has argued.[5] Whether or not the speaker highlights possible inconsistencies, and whether or not he is dealing with issues that are obviously controversial, he will be saying in some way or another, in effect, "These ideas are consistent with beliefs or behaviors that you already find important."

Because planning a statement of purpose should be a very early step in the

[4] *A Rhetoric of Motives*, New York, Prentice-Hall, Inc., 1950, p. 56.

[5] *Audience Analysis*, Indianapolis, Inc., The Bobbs-Merrill Co., Inc., 1966, p. 114.

preparation of a speech, and one that the speaker often reconsiders as preparation continues, indicating in it the identifications that will be attempted helps the speaker to keep focused on productive lines of thought development.

Identifying in the key assertions

In discussing organization, Chapter 4, we focused on arranging patterns of the statements of ideas directly supporting the thesis. These we called *main points*. The thesis, main points, and formal transitions are the key assertions to which the speaker may turn with profit in seeking to reflect fundamental identifications in the speech.

Abraham Lincoln's "First Inaugural Address" is a clear example of an effort to identify common interests in these key structural elements. Consider this major transition: "That there are persons in one section or another who seek to destroy the Union at all events and are glad of any pretext to do it I will neither affirm nor deny; but if there be such, I need address no word to them. To those, however, who really love the Union may I not speak?"[6] The main points that follow this transition indicate clearly the grounds on which the speaker hopes to identify his interests with those held by his auditors, e.g., "All profess to be content in the Union if all constitutional rights can be maintained."[7]

When he delivered his proposal for a comprehensive energy policy, President Jimmy Carter was careful to refer constantly to what he considered common interests, needs, and experiences. At one point in the speech he lists what he calls "ten principles" to guide policy. Consider a few of these:

The first principle is that we can have an effective and comprehensive energy policy only if the Government takes responsibility for it and if the people understand the seriousness of the challenge and are willing to make sacrifices.

The second principle is that healthy economic growth must continue. Only by saving energy can we maintain our standard of living and keep our people at work. An effective conservation program will create hundreds of thousands of new jobs.

The third principle is that we must protect the environment. Our energy problems have the same cause as our environmental problems—wasteful use of resources. Conservation helps us solve both at once.

The fourth principle is that we must reduce our vulnerability to potentially devastating embargoes. We can protect ourselves from uncertain supplies by reducing our demand for oil, making the most of our abundant resources such as coal, and developing a strategic petroleum reserve.[8]

---

[6] This speech is available in many anthologies. We are quoting from *Speeches for Illustration and Example*, ed. Goodwin F. Berquist, Jr., Chicago, Ill., Scott, Foresman and Company, 1965, p. 136.

[7] Ibid., p. 137.

[8] "President's Proposed Energy Policy," *Vital Speeches of the Day*, May 1, 1977, p. 419.

These are assertions, but they are assertions that recognize certain interests (e.g., in jobs) and experiences (with the difficulties a very brief oil embargo created) and the speaker seeks to identify with listeners by these means.

Identifying in supporting materials

Quite often the identifications the speaker hopes to make with auditors are reflected in the supporting materials. In choosing and forming supporting materials, the experienced speaker will keep in mind the need to adjust ideas to listeners.

As a senator from Massachusetts, John F. Kennedy addressed a Harvard University commencement on "The Intellectual and the Politician." It was mainly for those who thought that there was an antipathy between these roles that Kennedy spoke: "Authors, scholars and intellectuals can praise every aspect of American society but the political. My desk is flooded with books, articles and pamphlets criticizing Congress. But, rarely if ever, have I seen any intellectual bestow praise on either the political profession or any political body for its accomplishments, its ability or its integrity—much less for its intelligence."[9] One can predict quite early that Kennedy will argue that in some way intelligence and politics are not mutually exclusive, but the genius of the identifications rests in the amazing quantity of specific supporting material, especially the examples, which reflect the speaker's thought. Consider just part of the development of one point:

First, I would ask both groups to recall that the American politician of today and the American intellectual of today are descended from a common ancestry. Our nation's first great politicians were also among the nation's first great writers and scholars. The founders of the American Constitution were also founders of American scholarship. The works of Jefferson, Madison, Hamilton, Franklin, Paine and John Adams—to name but a few—influenced the literature of the world as well as its geography. Books were their tools, not their enemies. Locke, Milton, Sydney, Montesquieu, Coke and Bolingbroke were among those widely read in political circles and frequently quoted in political pamphlets. Our political leaders traded in the free commerce of ideas with lasting results here and abroad.

In these golden years, our political leaders moved from one field to another with amazing versatility and vitality. Jefferson and Franklin still throw long shadows over many fields of learning. A contemporary described Jefferson, "A gentleman of thirty-two, who could calculate an eclipse, survey an estate, tie an artery, plan an edifice, try a cause, break a horse, dance a minuet, and play the violin."[10]

THE BASES OF IDENTIFICATION

Keeping in mind constantly the need to adjust ideas and materials to the audience and focusing especially on the *statement of purpose, key assertions,*

[9] See *Contemporary American Speeches*, ed. Wil Linkugel, R. R. Allen, and Richard Johannessen, Belmont, Calif.: Wadsworth Publishing Co., 1965, p. 281.

[10] Ibid., p. 282.

and *supporting materials* in making substantial identifications of interest, the speaker may seek some guidelines in considering the nature of the audience to whom the adjustment is made.

Probably no part of one's formal education and experience will be irrelevant to the task of gaining insight into the nature of people and society. All speakers use the accumulation of their pasts in trying to understand their audiences. The division suggested here will serve as one rudimentary approach to the problem.

Most speakers will find it useful to consider the abilities and knowledge, the physio-psychological needs, and the commitments of their listeners. We shall discuss each of these factors in turn.

The abilities and knowledge of the audience

The class-audience that the beginning speaker faces is in many ways a difficult one. The speaker must realize that for the listeners, a particular speech is not a special event. They are apt to be easily distracted from listening by the events of the day that have preceded and will follow it. On the other hand, the student speaker has the advantage of speaking to a peer group with similar abilities and knowledge.

In general, the speaker should ask two basic questions, each of which must be applied specifically to the subject of the speech: (1) "What is the educational level of my audience?" and (2) "What experiences of my audience relate specifically to my ideas and materials?" These questions will help the speaker determine whether the audience has special knowledge concerning the subject or whether it is markedly deficient in needed background, and whether the listeners will probably readily understand complex ideas or be easily perplexed by anything out of the ordinary. These inquiries will be especially useful to the speaker in planning the statement of purpose.

James B. Conant's statements concerning his response to an invitation to speak indicate the importance of considering the abilities and knowledge of an audience:

When I was honored by the invitation to be the Bampton lecturer for 1952, President Eisenhower, then of Columbia, expressed on behalf of the committee the hope that I would undertake to provide "some understanding of the significance of recent developments in the physical sciences." On my inquiring as to the nature of the audience, I was assured professional philosophers and scientists would be conspicuous by their absence. My exposition, if not aimed at the proverbial man-on-the-street, was to be directed at the equally proverbial college graduate—the hypothetical individual whom college presidents welcome each commencement to the fellowship of educated men. Being thus assured that I was not expected either to give an appraisal of the impact of physics on metaphysics or a technical account of the inner workings of the atom, I gratefully accepted the privilege of being a guest lecturer at Columbia University.

After some further remarks on his subject matter, Conant shows clearly that his speech is founded on an appraisal of the sort of persons his listeners might be:

I wish to include in my survey the impact of modern science on the philosophic presuppositions of the average enlightened citizen of a modern democracy—on his ambitions, his hopes, his fears, his outlook on the world. So in a sense I shall relate physics to philosophy, but only by handling both subjects in a general fashion and viewing each from the point of view of a deeply troubled modern man.[11]

Conant's lectures are "popular" in the best sense of the word. They should be challenging to a well-educated audience. In judging the ability of an audience it is much better to overestimate than to underestimate. Nothing is as likely to irritate an audience as to be "talked down to." Whereas listeners may be perplexed or bored by intricate explanations for which they do not possess sufficient background, they may be irritated by elaborate explanations of what is immediately understandable.

The needs of the audience

The men and women who compose any audience will have basic needs. These needs grow out of their physiological nature but are considerably modified by the particular social context in which they live, as, indeed, the social context has in turn been molded by the needs of men and women. In large part, the study of speaking is the study of the needs of the persons addressed. The speaker should constantly seek different viewpoints from which to gain insight into the needs of people. Knowledge, gained from the study of many subjects—anthropology, sociology, and psychology in particular—should help in drafting some styles of thought that will be useful in determining how best to adapt ideas and materials to the specific audience.

The particular analysis we shall follow here is based on the work of Abraham H. Maslow.[12] Maslow classified human needs into five categories:

5. The need for self-actualization.
4. Esteem needs.
3. Belongingness and love needs.
2. Safety needs.
1. Physiological needs.

These human needs form a kind of ladder; it is necessary to climb the lower rungs in order to reach the higher rungs. The base of the ladder is composed of those needs that are necessary for life to exist at all. Unless the

[11] *Modern Science and Modern Man*, New York, Columbia University Press, 1955, pp. 3 and 5.

[12] *Motivation and Personality*, New York, Harper and Brothers (now Harper & Row, Publishers, Inc.), 1954.

physiological needs are met we cannot reach the higher rungs of the ladder any more than a person who is being smothered can appreciate the most magnificent performance of Beethoven's Ninth Symphony. The physiological needs are those associated with hunger, thirst, elimination, balance of body temperature, and the like. We are seldom more than momentarily deprived of physiological satisfactions in our affluent society. At the same time, some of our habits relating to these satisfactions may be interrupted and thereby cause tensions that will affect our behavior. We are used to certain foods on a certain schedule, for example, and if this schedule is interrupted, we may be affected. The speaker should sometimes consider potential tensions arising from physiological needs.

The next rung on the ladder is formed by the safety needs that emerge when the physiological needs are met. Security is apt to be a concern for any listener. We are driven by a sense of needing to provide security for ourselves, our families, and various groups—state, nation, political party, economic group, and so on. Simple self-preservation is likely to play a heavy role in the consideration of questions from traffic safety to safety from nuclear fallout. In general, we have learned (perhaps not always or even usually consciously) that the activities and institutions we have established provide safety or at least make us feel safe. Therefore, changes of any sort are likely to be threats.[13] The speaker should consider safety, especially as it is represented in established economic, social, political, religious, and educational institutions, when choosing and stating ideas for speeches.

The third rung is occupied by the need for love and belongingness. Belonging in and of itself is satisfying; therefore individuals will want to preserve those groups to which they belong and will want to establish, probably, groups in which they can satisfy their need for love and belongingness. Our increasingly complex, mobile society is making satisfaction of needs on this level more and more difficult. The family, for example, has been considerably weakened as a source of satisfaction for love and belongingness needs. One might speculate that the definite increase in church membership and attendance is due at least in part to an effort by great numbers to make identifications with groups that have traditionally helped satisfy belongingness needs.

The fourth rung of the ladder is the need for esteem. All men and women whom we call normal want a high evaluation of themselves—by themselves and by others. They are apt to undertake whatever modes of behavior they feel will help win this esteem and to avoid those that they feel will interfere with it. It is possible, of course, for demands for self-esteem to conflict with those for the esteem of others. But at the present moment, men and women in our society can be counted on to pursue external symbols to display as means of gaining esteem. The use of this tendency in advertising is too well

---

[13] Eric Hoffer builds an entire book on this theme. His *The Ordeal of Change*, New York, Harper and Brothers (now Harper & Row, Publishers, Inc.), 1963, is instructive for the speaker.

known almost to bear mention. The alert reader will not be able to go through a day without finding a score of advertisements in newspapers and magazines or radio and television that offer some sort of promise of acquiring symbols the display of which will win the esteem of others.

Many of the words that indicate virtues we associated with our society have grown out of our particular sets towards the satisfaction of love and belongingness needs and esteem needs. We honor freedom, competition, curiosity, loyalty, and fair play. And these virtues are intimately associated with acceptable need satisfaction.

The highest rung on the ladder is occupied by the difficult concept of the need for self-actualization. It is a recognition of unique potentiality in every human. "What man *can* be, he *must* be."[14] Although speakers will have more difficulty seeing the application of this level of needs, they ought to recognize the inchoate yearning for "something higher" in most people, and the especially strong feelings of dissatisfaction in those who are observably well satisfied in all other needs. It is a uniquely human need that has emerged in our society with increasing strength.

A close study of the speeches of Martin Luther King, Jr. will reveal how much he depends on identifying his analysis of problems and his programs with the love and belongingness and the esteem needs of his audiences. In one speech, for example, he says typically: "But the Negro has a new sense of dignity, a new self respect, and new determination. He has re-evaluated his own intrinsic worth. Now this new sense of dignity on the part of the Negro grows out of the same longing for freedom and human dignity on the part of the oppressed people all over the world. . . ."[15]

Almost any speech dealing with the current international tensions will illustrate how speakers build on safety needs. Regard for these needs is connected by speakers to wide varieties of proposed actions. This tendency is by no means a wholly recent phenomenon. In his famous "quarantine" speech delivered in 1937, President Franklin D. Roosevelt, speaking to people who had been repeatedly exposed to the idea that the Atlantic was an effective barrier to involvement in European conflicts, laid the basis for a developing pre-World War II foreign policy on the need for security: "War is a contagion, whether it be declared or undeclared. It can engulf states and peoples remote from the original scene of hostilities. We are determined to keep out of war, yet we cannot insure ourselves against the disastrous effects of war and the dangers of involvement. We are adopting such measures as will minimize our risk of involvement, but we cannot have complete protection in a world of disorder in which confidence and security have broken down."[16]

[14] Maslow, p. 91.

[15] "Love, Law, and Civil Disobedience," *Contemporary American Speeches*, p. 53.

[16] "The 'Quarantine' Speech," in Donald C. Bryant and Karl R. Wallace, *Fundamentals of Public Speaking*, New York, Appleton-Century-Crofts, 1960, p. 543.

Neither the beginning speaker nor anyone else should expect to be able to state immediately and precisely what needs are operating within listeners. What one should gain from general understanding of human needs, however, is awareness of the potential of one's ideas for speeches that will be meaningful to particular audiences and ways of selecting and handling speech materials.

The commitments of the audience

Just as the speaker will have his commitments to ideas, people, institutions, programs, and so on, so will his listeners. Sometimes looking for these commitments will give the speaker a clearer view of the nature of the audience than will anything else.

People tend to make commitments that they believe will have utility in satisfying their personal needs. Therefore, the lines of thought that we have suggested are scarcely independent. Whereas humans share the same basic needs, their commitments may differ widely and may be more immediately involved in responding to the ideas and materials of a speaker.

A speaker often makes the mistake of seeing an audience only in terms of its agreement or disagreement with a commitment that speaker holds dear. There may, however, be other commitments that might be utilized to change audience alignments.

Adlai Stevenson worked adroitly to show a group of listeners that they were probably committed to two viewpoints that were less consistent with one another than one of their fundamental views would be with another that he recommended. The editors of an anthology, which includes the speech, "The City—A Cause for Statesmanship," write that "in his address he met with consummate skill the audience's desire that its own policies and objectives be rendered urgent and impressive through fresh, exhilarating restatement."[17] They are certainly correct. But Stevenson did more.

The group before which Stevenson spoke, ACTION (American Council to Improve Our Neighborhoods), was composed of eminent business persons. His listeners were explicitly committed to programs of urban reconstruction, but on the other hand, they were probably also affiliated with political groups that mistrusted the participation of a strong, centralized, federal government in municipal affairs.

Throughout his speech, Stevenson identified himself with the goals of urban reconstruction to which the group was committed. Moreover, he warmly affirmed the proper role of profit-making private enterprise in such programs. But he pictured this role as interwoven with the participation of governmental agencies:

The problems of the American city will be met when, and not until, we recognize that they are already and inexorably committed to the *joint* [emphasis Stevenson's]

17 *The Speaker's Resource Book*, ed. Carroll Arnold, Douglas Ehninger and John Gerber, Scott Foresman & Co., 1966, p. 219.

trusteeship of private enterprise and public responsibility; that they demand a shoulder-to-shoulder, two-fisted attack; that their solution depends entirely upon an alliance of private and public agencies—with each respecting its own limitations and the capacities of the other, and with each acting in support of the other.[18]

Later in the speech he was even more pointed, saying, "In the face of these great opportunities, I hope we are ready to stop the demagogic political debate which assumes that government and private enterprise are inherently antagonistic." This demand, politely put but a demand nonetheless, was well prepared for by a detailed consideration of the problem that identifies the speaker with goals and means to which the audience was probably strongly committed.

The values of the audience

The word *value* indicates the patterns that develop as we make decisions. These patterns are individual in that each person makes decisions as a person and develops personal values. But no person builds values in isolation because most decisions are made in a social context. The decisions of others affect each of us; they affect us because often they directly impinge upon us; they affect us also because we sometimes consciously or unconsciously model our decisions on the examples of others.

We may think of our values, then, as "social values." As such, values give us rather direct sources of identification with others. Identifications that can manifest themselves both in speeches and in the thought that precedes and follows speaking should be sought in value terms.

Any listing of values must be arbitrary and abstract. No listing will be a perfect reflection of reality. Any listing must simply be considered at best as a possibly useful starting point for thought. One such starting point may be a list of traditional values used by the Daniel Yankelovich researchers in studying the so-called generation gap as a basis for a Columbia Broadcasting System television documentary.[19]

1. Hard work will always pay off.
2. People should save as much as they can regularly and not have to lean on family and friends the minute they run into financial problems.
3. Depending on how much strength and character people have, they can pretty well control what happens to them.
4. Belonging to some organized religion is important in a person's life.
5. Competition encourages excellence.
6. The right to private property is sacred.
7. Society needs some legally based authority to prevent chaos.
8. Compromise is essential for progress.

[18] Ibid., pp. 220–21.

[19] "Generations Apart," A Study of the Generation Gap Conducted for CBS News by Daniel Yankelovich, Inc. 1969, Columbia Broadcasting System.

We do not suggest that each person *should* agree with these statements of values, but the Yankelovich survey indicated that most people *did* agree with them. Of course each person should think about these as points of departure in dealing specifically with ideas and materials for the special groups who will comprise the audiences. In many cases the individual will decide to speak contrary to the apparent indications of some general value. If one is to do so usefully, one should recognize the contradictions being posed. One should also recognize that speaking contrary to one value probably arises from the speaker's believing that there are some more specific, or deeper, or at least different values to which others should commit themselves. In short, it is the inconsistencies in the situation—between the speaker and others, between others and reality, between one aspect of reality and another—that may enable the speaker to identify interests with listeners while at the same time opposing some aspects of other interests.

Generalizations about broad values are safe only so long as one thinks in terms of very large groups. It is widely believed, for example, that youth are less "traditional" than their parents—and so they are—but the differences within each group are probably as great as those between the groups.

The most striking aspect of the Yankelovich survey for CBS was that the agreement on traditional values was consistently high for both parents and youth. The lowest percentage of youth expressed belief in the value of organized religion, and on this value the difference between youth and parents was the greatest (youth, 64 per cent; parents, 89 per cent). The next lowest expressed belief by the youth surveyed was in the value of "hard work"; and 74 per cent of the youth agreed that hard work *always* pays off. The average of the differences between the youth and their parents on all eight of the statements of traditional values was 6 per cent.

Moreover, college youth and college parents tended to agree. On the basis of this survey, at least, one can argue strongly for a generation gap only if educational level is ignored.

In Chapter 14 we shall return to the concept of *value*. Here we have tried to indicate large groups as starting places. Later we shall discuss the possible functions of analyzing and speaking about problems in such a way as to develop values. It is the sharing of common problems and seeking solutions to problems recognized as common that bind men and women into communities. And speech is one of the means that makes such sharing possible.

SUMMARY

A summary of ideas concerning "adjusting ideas to people and people to ideas" is possible only in a very limited sense. Our effort has been to indicate the multiplicity of possibilities rather than a closed set or formula for success.

Perhaps a good summary might be found in a concrete example of adjusting. One of the best known short speeches in our culture is St. Paul's recorded in Acts 17:16–34. In Athens, Paul was at once a "propagandist for foreign deities" and a man well educated in the Hellenistic centers of learning. He was able to identify himself with experiences immediately shared with his listeners. Notice his drawing on the familiar concept of craftsmanship to explain God as a maker. Notice how the speech tends to suggest the potentials for progressively higher fulfillment of human needs.

Most striking, perhaps, is the relative lack of success, for the text suggests that no throng followed Paul that day. Success, however, is a highly relative concept. The few followers named and the potentiality created for the future could be labeled highly successful outcomes. By mentioning the potentiality for the future, we mean to call attention to the fact that one does not simply believe, but one believes in something on some basis. It is laying the bases for sharing beliefs that is the speaker's vital task.

Now while Paul was waiting for them at Athens [for Silas and Timothy] he was exasperated to see how the city was full of idols. So he argued in the synagogue with the Jews and gentile worshippers, and also in the city square every day with casual passers-by. And some of the Epicurean and Stoic philosophers joined issue with him. Some said, "What can this charlatan be trying to say?" others, "He would appear to be a propagandist for foreign deities"—this because he was preaching about Jesus and Resurrection. So they took him before the Court of Areopagus and said, "May we know what this new doctrine is that you propound? You are introducing ideas that sound strange to us, and we should like to know what they mean." (Now the Athenians in general and the foreigners there had no time for anything but talking or hearing about the latest novelty.)

Then Paul stood up before the Court of Areopagus and said: "Men of Athens, I see that in everything that concerns religion you are uncommonly scrupulous. For as I was going round looking at the objects of your worship, I noticed among other things an altar bearing the inscription 'To an Unknown God.' What you worship and do not know—this is what I now proclaim.

"The God who created the world and everything in it, and who is Lord of heaven and earth, does not live in shrines made by men. It is not because he lacks anything that he accepts service at men's hands, for he is himself the universal giver of life and breath and all else. He created every race of men of one stock, to inhabit the whole earth's surface. He fixed the epochs of their history and the limits of their territory. They were to seek God, and, it might be, touch and find him; though indeed he is not far from each one of us, for in him we live and move, in him we exist; as some of your own poets have said, 'We are also his offspring.' As God's offspring, then, we ought not to suppose that the deity is like an image in gold or silver or stone, shaped by human craftsmanship and design. As for the times of ignorance, God has overlooked them; but now he commands mankind, all men everywhere, to repent, because he has fixed the day on which he will have the world judged, and justly judged, by a man of his choosing; of this he has given assurance to all by raising him from the dead."

When they heard about the raising of the dead, some scoffed; and others said, "We will hear you on this subject some other time." And so Paul left the assembly. However, some men joined him and became believers, including Dionysius, a member of the Court of Areopagus; also a woman named Demaris and others besides.[20]

As we suggested at the outset, the basic concern of this chapter will scarcely be exhausted herein. We believe that the principles discussed will bear review as you prepare for your own speeches. Only as you try to state, support, and organize your own ideas will the problems of adjusting ideas to audiences and your ability to meet them become sharpened.

You will find the principles of this chapter reinforced and clarified as you study in Chapters 10 through 14 of this textbook. The problem-centered system of analysis is one that constantly encourages speakers to become more deeply and intelligently committed to their own ideas and to see those ideas in relationship to patterns of thought that intelligent listeners are likely to manifest.

ASSIGNMENTS

For class discussion

1. Prepare for a class discussion by collecting advertisements from popular magazines that you believe indicate clearly efforts to gain response based on some need discussed in this chapter. Probably several students will chose the same advertisement but will interpret it as involving different needs. What accounts for the difference in interpretation? What is the significance of the differences?

2. Prepare for a class discussion by collecting several letters to the editor of your local newspaper. What commitments to groups or programs are reflected by the letter writers? Do the writers simply stand for their commitments or against the commitments of others? Do the writers attempt to use some common commitment as the basis of gaining assent to an idea that may be fresh or unaccepted for potential readers?

3. In his book *Toward a Psychology of Being*,[21] Abraham H. Maslow argues that every person is torn between two sets of forces—those associated with security and those associated with growth. He presents this schema:

Enhance the dangers   *Enhance the attractions*
Safety ▶——▶ PERSON ◀——◀ Growth
Minimize the attractions   *Minimize the dangers*

"Safety has both anxieties and delights; growth has both anxieties and delights. We grow forward when the delights of growth and anxieties of safety are greater than the anxieties of growth and the delights of safety."

---

[20] From *The New English Bible*. © The Delegates of the Oxford University Press and the Syndics of the Cambridge University Press, 1961, 1970. Reprinted by permission.

[21] New York, D. Van Nostrand Company, 1962; see pp. 42–45.

Do you agree with Maslow? Can you illustrate either your agreement or disagreement? What possible *anxieties* can be associated with safety? Will growth always be associated with danger? Are there any applications of Maslow's schema to the central concern of this chapter?

A writing assignment

1. Choose a speech for analysis from *Vital Speeches* or from an anthology containing contemporary speeches.
2. Describe the speaker's purpose and the audience from which response is solicited.
3. Using the principles discussed in this chapter as a guide, analyze the manner in which the speaker tries to identify with the interests of the audience.
4. Try to discover opportunities for adjusting to the audience that the speaker did not choose. Would these have been wise or unwise choices?

7

developing confidence[1]

Confidence does more to make conversation than wit.
                                        LA ROCHEFOUCAULD

Hypnotized persons, when told that they are very strong, are able to perform feats that they previously thought were impossible–feats showing that they had nearly twice the strength they believed they had. Almost all can do better if they have confidence, whatever they are doing. Lovers who lack confidence will likely not receive nor give much love; but give them confidence instead of fears, see that each gives the other encouragement, and love may catch fire. "You can because you *think* you can" runs the adage. Your best theme may be the one you dashed off quickly when you knew you could; you played your best game when you felt confident. You can ski better, fight better, sing better, cook better, and certainly you can talk better if you are confident. Belief in one's self is often a partial cause of success; such belief heightens and increases natural ability; belief in one's self is a neces-

[1] This chapter originated with an article of the same title by Otis M. Walter, published in *Today's Speech*, II (Sept. 1954), pp. 2–7, and has been expanded in each edition; in this edition, a computer retrieval system searched over 17,000 articles as a check against the ideas in this chapter.

sary ingredient of the champion as well as of one who would merely like to do his or her best, champion or not.

Speakers need confidence, however, not only when they are speaking, but at every step of the process of preparing the speech. Of course we must not be paralyzed by the audience, but we also need to feel confidence that we know how to find good supporting material, that we can discover significant ideas to develop, and that by systematic work, we can evolve a speech worth hearing and that the audience will want to hear. At every point in the process of preparing and giving a speech, confidence can increase our natural and learned abilities.

At the same time, the speaker must not be overconfident. Confidence is not a substitute for skill. However overconfident the novice may be as he buys stock just before the market crashes, his confidence does not prevent him from going broke. If a teacher is unprepared for students and lacks good materials for the subject, a mindless confidence does not prevent disaster. Nor will overconfidence offset poor work from a student. Overconfidence can only make the speaker look ridiculous and can stimulate the audience to reject the speech. But if the prepared teacher and the prepared student can develop also the power of confidence, they may rise to heights quite unexpected. Perhaps Wordsworth expressed the kind of confidence needed when he said "True confidence abides in him alone who in the silent moment of his inward thought can still suspect, yet still revere himself."

The development of the kind of confidence that enables one to use skills best does not come from easily stated nostrums; there are no cheap recipes for confidence, although there are good ones. We can gain some understanding of confidence and its enemies, and thereby gain some knowledge of how to develop this powerful boost to our abilities.

STAGE FRIGHT AS ANXIETY

Serious lack of confidence among speakers is often called stage fright, although "stage fright" is not limited to the stage, but is a common response experienced in a variety of "threatening" situations; this response is given the name *anxiety reaction*. Anxiety in front of audiences is not new: although Cicero was the greatest orator of Rome, his contemporaries reported that he shook visibly before an audience; even so experienced an opera star as Madame Shuman-Heink, the greatest star of the late-nineteenth- and earlier-twentieth-century, reported that she wished that the stage would open up so she could fall through it. Although anxiety was common, only until recently have we learned how to reduce it. Even by the beginning of the twentieth century, students of the subject could do little more than produce a long list of the symptoms of stage fright. Although such a list was accurate, it was worse than useless, because far from suggesting treatments, the formidable list could induce additional symptoms in those already alarmed. Recommended treatments such as "Relax," "Breathe deeply," and "Think positively," were superficial and dubious at best, and at worst, harmful. Before the 1930s, few speech books discussed stage fright; because of our superficial knowledge of it, the best books on public speaking avoided the subject.

Today our knowledge of stage fright is still incomplete; by no means do we know enough to offer a guaranteed cure. Nevertheless, we understand much about the physiology and psychology of stage fright and about its causes and treatment; today we can help those for whom stage fright is a serious problem. The subject is especially interesting, moreover, because *the causes of stage fright and its treatment are remarkably like the causes of maladjustment and its treatment. Inasmuch as the nature and treatment of stage fright are much like the nature and treatment of human maladjustment, insights into one leads to insights into the other.* The treatment of either leads to the kind of confidence that enables a man to do his best. To begin, we must first have a brief understanding of the physiology of stage fright.

The physiology of anxiety and stage fright

Some lucky speakers are stimulated by an audience; audiences excite their imagination. And yet the unfortunate speaker who is terrified by an audience and the lucky one who is stimulated by them undergo indistinguishably similar physiological responses. As far as we can determine today, the physiology of excitement and that of fear are the same. Nothing about this physiological response leads to discomfort; the discomfort is a psychological matter. The physiological response itself only readies one for action, for it performs the following function:

1. More blood sugar, which furnishes energy, is available.
2. Insulin, which increases the permeability of the membrane surrounding the cells to the blood sugar, is secreted, with the result that more food can get inside the cells.
3. Thyroxin, a catalyst that speeds the burning of sugar inside the cells, is added to the blood stream.
4. Blood pressure increases.
5. Respiration increases.
6. The conductivity of nerves increases slightly.
7. More oxygen is available so that more fuel is burned.
8. The poisons from metabolism are removed more speedily so that toxicity and fatigue are reduced.

Metaphorically, these changes simply add fuel to the furnace, increase the draft so that the fires can burn faster, and carry away the smoke from combustion at a more rapid rate. The energy from the reaction may be misdirected and may end in tensions and shaking, but the physiological reaction itself is not debilitating.

Experienced speakers, while undergoing this reaction, report that they think more rapidly in front of an audience than in the less stimulating comfort of their armchair. One study of stage fright among experienced speakers reports that 77 per cent of them had some stage fright before they began each speech; most of these speakers believed that a little stage fright helped one make a better speech.[2] The explanation may be that the stage fright of the experienced speaker is generally limited to *initial* fears that diminish as soon as the speaker begins talking; when speakers do not have this initial re-action, they lack the energy furnished by the reaction, and, consequently, they give a less effective speech. Not surprisingly, therefore, the presence of an audience may stimulate memory.[3] The physiological aspects of stage fright, therefore, *do not* commit one to discomfort, but they *do* ensure abun-dant energy and reserve power. Insofar as we can tell, the physiological changes in stage fright are beneficial. Nevertheless, the speaker must pre-vent the conditions, often associated with these physiological changes, that produce anxiety, nervousness, and the resulting incapacity to think well. To understand how one may keep the effects of the physiological reaction and yet avoid anxiety, we must examine the psychology of stage fright.

The psychology of anxiety and stage fright

As we said before, stage fright and anxiety are, despite their differing names, the same thing. Let us look at the evidence for this sameness. We can see that stage fright and anxiety are the same, because the physiological reaction in each appears to be the same: Each is characterized by increased heart-beat, increased tension, and increased metabolism. Moreover, the psycholo-gical reactions in stage fright and anxiety seem similar: Both are character-ized by dread and in both, the dread is not justified by the situation that produced it. The beginning speaker, for example, faces a classroom of stu-dents who are also beginners, who are friendly, who are pulling for him, and who may suffer with him. But the beginning speaker with stage fright often fails to perceive the situation for what it is, namely a friendly situation in which mistakes are not only tolerated but expected. Rather than so perceiv-ing the situation, he sees it as does the anxious person—as a fearful situation, full of threats and dangers.

Because stage fright is anxiety, it we can determine how to reduce anxiety, we can likewise know how to reduce stage fright. Let us examine the psy-chological causes of anxiety. *Anxiety occurs in people—and even, experi-mentally, in animals—whenever they are placed in an unresolved conflict sit-uation.* The medieval donkey who starved to death between two stacks of hay because each stack was equally attractive, equally succulent, equally large and equally distant may serve as a paradigm of the unresolved conflict situation. Such a conflict situation is the key to emotional responses that are

[2] Elma Dean Orr Wrenchey, *A Study of Stage Fright in a Selected Group of Experienced Speakers*, Unpublished M.A. Thesis, University of Denver, 1948, p. 37.

[3] N. G. Hanawalt and K. F. Butler, "The Effects of an Audience on Remembering," *Journal of Social Psychology*, XXIX (May 1944), pp. 259–272.

disorganizing and tortuous; when one is in constant conflict, he is likely in a constant state of discomfort and disorganization.

A few examples will help us understand the nature of conflict. The mother who tells her boy to go out and play, but not to get dirty, may place the child in a minor conflict situation: If the child plays with the roughness required to gain and keep the respect of his peers, he will get dirty; if he gets dirty, he will be punished. The boy probably will resolve the conflict in some way, such as by playing just hard enough so that he isn't quite dirty enough to be punished. The less normal child may alternate between, at one moment, staying clean, and at the next moment playing hard. His energies will be divided, and he likely will meet neither the requirements of his peers nor of his mother. A young man who wishes to get married but who does not make enough money to support a wife may be in a perpetual conflict situation. If he does not marry the girl he loves, he risks losing her; if he does marry her, he cannot support her. This perpetually unresolved conflict situation batters his nervous system, and he may begin to respond in an undesirable way to situations not even remotely related to his conflict: his employer may notice that he is less efficient at his job, and his girl friend may notice both a decrease in his capacity for warmth and an increase in his irritability. He is undergoing a reaction like that in stage fright, and exhibits tension, unhappiness, dread, and fear.

The speech situation is of the same sort; it is often a conflict situation: the speaker with stage fright is trying to speak well; yet he wishes he were not on the platform. He must continue the speech; yet he would like to run away or disappear. He is trying to earn a good grade; yet he is fearful that he will make a spectacle of himself. He must speak; but he doesn't want to. He is in conflict, and responds with the temporary anxiety that we call stage fright.

THE LARGER SIGNIFICANCE OF CONFLICT

Reduction of anxiety not only reduces stage fright, but the reduction of anxiety is a key to a productive existence; what you learn about reducing conflict in stage fright may help you learn how to reduce conflict in other parts of your life.

That the resolution of conflict leads to greater productivity and greater happiness is no new discovery. Over thirty years ago, Symonds recognized that the resolution of conflicts led to a better life, while failure to resolve them led to a less satisfying life:

The happy man is one in whom conflicts are at a minimum of depth, frequency and intensity. His life is one that has a straightforward pattern. He can face outward, and meet with zeal and adequacy the situations that each day presents. The successful resolution of the conflicts, both major and minor, which beset one in daily living is the road to maturity. Integration depends upon the successful resolution of the conflicts inevitably met at all stages of development. A person's emotional stability is closely related to his conflicts. The stable person . . . is the person who has found a way through his conflicts. On the other hand, the person whose conflicts are intense gives way earlier to emotion and we recognize him as an emotionally unstable individual. . . .[4]

To face a conflict situation and see each aspect of it clearly is difficult. We wish to be polite to our parents, but their demands provoke us to anger; yet we do not fully understand why. Much of our behavior is devised to hide our conflicts, or to use a somewhat ineffective way that we have learned—a way that more often or not helps blot them out but does not help us solve them in the best possible way. We may develop excessive shyness, for shyness can keep us from confronting people who engender fear in us. Others turn to alcohol or narcotics to anesthetize themselves; still others blot out awareness of the world, as does the catatonic patient, who dares not respond to the world and who sits motionless wherever he is placed, oblivious to the world and unmoved by it. "Most tragedy," says Gardner Murphy, the well-known psychologist, . . . is a matter of a personality divided against itself. . . .[5]

Yet the integration of conflicts—even conflicts that appear diametric opposites—as in desiring to speak and yet being afraid to do so—is necessary for continued health and effectiveness. To avoid the misery of unresolved conflicts that can tear powerfully, they may be skilfully and ingeniously integrated. In a famous passage Abraham Maslow, formerly President of the American Psychological Association, suggests that the integration of conflicts is the key to exceptionally good psychological health, a state of health only a small minority of people possess:

What has been considered . . . to be polarities of opposites or dichotomies were so *only in unhealthy people*. In healthy people these dichotomies were resolved, the polarities disappeared, and many oppositions . . . coalesced with each other to form unities.

For example, the age-old opposition between heart and head, reason and instinct, or cognition and conation was seen to disappear in healthy people. . . . In these people, desires are in excellent accord with reason. St. Augustine's "Love God and do as you will" can easily be translated "Be healthy and then you may trust your impulses."

The dichotomy between selfishness and unselfishness disappears altogther in healthy people because in principle every act is *both* selfish and unselfish. Our subjects are simultaneously very spiritual and very pagan and sensual. Duty cannot be contrasted with pleasure nor work with play when duty *is* pleasure, when work *is* play, and the person doing his duty and being virtuous is simultaneously seeking his pleasure and being happy. If the most socially identified people are themselves also the most individualistic people, of what use is it to retain the polarity? If the most mature is the most childlike? If the most ethical and moral people are also the lustiest and most animal?[6]

[4] Percival Symonds, *The Dynamics of Human Adjustment*, New York, Appleton-Century-Crofts, 1946, p. 360.

[5] *Personality*, New York, Harper and Brothers (Now Harper & Row, Publishers, Inc.), 1947, p. 296.

[6] A. H. Maslow, *Motivation and Personality*, New York, Harper & Row, Publishers, Inc., 1954, p. 233.

The healthy persons are not divided: What they want to do, what they are doing, and what they think they should do are the same. Because they are "united" persons, whether on the speaker's platform, in class, playing with their peers or having dinner with their parents, they plunge wholeheartedly into their activities, enjoy them more, and produce more than a person who is at war with himself. The resolution of anxiety—caused by conflict—can create not only a better speaker, but a better person.[7]

Limitations to integration

But is there not danger—to one's self, and to others—in being "too well" integrated? May not total integration produce a monomaniac—a man divided, following a single unhealthy drive? The Hitlers, the Napoleons, the Joseph Stalins of the world seem at least on superficial evidence, to be "integrated." Yet these men probably were not: Each of them was known to have deep depressions that halted activities; each made seriously mistaken judgments, trusting men who were untrustworthy, and suspecting those who were trustworthy; each displayed symptoms of serious maladjustment, and at least one died insane. Their integration was not a general pattern of their existence, but a temporary state that permitted activity of such unusual and vigorous nature that it functioned to conceal their depressions and anxieties both from themselves and from others. The monomaniac does not display the kind of integration Maslow describes, in which the selfish and the altruistic blend together, in which the reasonable and emotional are one. We need not fear this latter sort of integration, for far from producing a diversity of interests, and who, unlike the monomaniac, are closely in touch with reality.

In some ways, however, a civilized person is one who *will* experience conflict—the soldier who must kill when killing may be required, the judge whom the law requires to sentence the hapless product of a bad environment, the teacher who must fail the student, all probably should experience conflict and sense the tragedy of what they do. But their conflict, unlike that of the neurotic, remains tied *only* to the situation that warrants conflict, and does not permeate their lives apart from that situation. Of course the well-integrated person has doubts, where doubts are warranted; he knows it is a mark of maturity to be unsure where no one *can* be sure. Probably some psychologists have overdone the idea that one must live a life without doubts and without uncertainty. After all, the hero in *Hamlet* for all his conflict and uncertainty, is still the play's most civilized character, and among the most civilized in all dramatic literature.

The intelligent speakers, therefore, will have doubts. But they will have

---

[7] See Rollo May, *Power and Innocence: A Search for the Forces of Violence*, New York, W. W. Norton & Company, 1972, for further confirmation of the disastrous results of powerful unresolved conflicts in creating addicts, insanity, violence, and shyness, especially Parts I, and II. Yet the resolution of conflict can produce desirable people who seem to have more influence and who get more satisfaction from living. See Part III.

most of their doubts about whether or not they are giving the audience the right answer or for that matter whether or not they are asking the right question. His doubts are *subject-matter* centered, rather than *self-centered*. Has he read the best sources on the subject? Has he located the strongest supporting material? Is the theme of his speech important enough? Is his information accurate? Is his speech as clear as possible? These doubts an intelligent speaker will have over and over again.

But healthy speakers will not have doubts when they deliver their speech—at least not doubts that are *ego-centered*. Their energies, at the time of speaking, will be unified to communicate with as much vigor and power as wisdom allows—and they will not be divided because of unwarranted timidity or fear. Their energies are expended in communicating, and not in restraining themselves or in developing nervous tension. Their dobuts in preparation, moreover, are reconciled as time goes on, and drive them to prepare the speech so thoroughly that self-centered doubts will not arise during the delivery of the speech. Let us see some of the ways unjustified conflict may be treated to permit this kind of confidence.

The influence of personality on stage fright

Some types of personalities can reduce conflict and, hence, overcome stage fright more easily than others. The development of confidence is easiest for those who lack shyness, who feel self-sufficient, who are somewhat uninhibited, who have relatively weak feelings of guilt, who have a sense of their own worth and who are socially active; stage fright is strongest in those who lack these qualities and who have a generalized sense of maladjustment.[8] Even severe stage fright, however, can be reduced, so that if you are among those who experience it, take heart. More than one superior speaker began his career terrified by audiences.

Those who have a sense of severe maladjustment and who have strong

[8] See Stanley Ainsworth, *A Study of Fear, Nervousness and Anxiety in the Public Speaking Situation*, unpublished Ph.D. dissertation, Northwestern University, 1949, abstracted in *Speech Monographs*, XVI (Aug. 1950), p. 323. See also, William Hamilton, "A Review of Experimental Studies of Stage Fright," *Pennsylvania Speech Annual*, XVII (Sept. 1960), pp. 44–45. Regrettably, studies of stage fright have not greatly increased in recent years. Just as they are styles in clothing and architecture, so are there in the sciences, and with some exceptions which we shall note, there have been very few helpful studies produced during the decade of the seventies. Studying stage fright is out of fashion, even though it is important.

In place of stage fright, some people are studying concepts such as reticence and communication apprehension. These concepts, although related to stage fright, are not quite the same. Nevertheless, if the reader is interested in these related concepts, see the following: Gerald M. Phillips, "Reticence: Pathology of the Normal Speaker," *Speech Monographs*, 35 (1968), pp. 39–49. Gerald Phillips and Nancy J. Metzger, "The Reticent Syndrome: Some Theoretical Considerations about Etiology and Treatment," *Speech Monographs*, 40 (1973), pp. 220–230. J. C. McCrosky, "Measures of Communication-bound Anxiety," *Speech Monographs*, 37 (1970), pp. 269–277.

stage fright, however, should give their maladjustment serious attention and, perhaps, seek expert guidance. Severe conflict can reduce one's ability in solving problems and, as the conflict grows, one's ability to deal with conflict intelligently may decline. Some of Pavlov's famous dogs illustrate the debilitating effect of intense conflict: A dog can be taught to discriminate between a circle and an ellipse; the conditioned discrimination occurs if the dog is given food when the circle is flashed on a screen in front of the dog, but not given food when an ellipse is flashed on. After the dog had been conditioned so that he salivated whenever the circle was present, but not when the ellipse was present, the experimenter tested the dog's ability to discriminate between the circle and ellipse by making the ellipse more and more like a circle.

The axes of a circle are, of course, ten to ten; and those of an ellipse can be such that one diameter is seven while another is ten. When the axes of the circle were eight to ten, the dog could still discriminate easily and avoided the ellipse—which if he had chosen it, would have resulted in his receiving an electric shock. Now picture the hungry dog: He must have food; he has learned that he can safely get food whenever the circle is shown, but that if he tries to get food when the ellipse is shown, he gets a shock. Suppose, however, one axis of the ellipse is increased from seven to ten to eight to ten. The dog can still tell the two apart and knows when to and when not to try to get food. But when the axes of the ellipse are expanded so that the ellipse is almost circle-like from nine to ten, the dog can no longer tell the ellipse from the circle. Now he is in a geniune experimental conflict situation: He must have food, but he must avoid the electric shock. What is he to do now there is no reliable sign to tell him when he could safely secure food and when he might receive a painful shock? The dog, of course, now not only lacks the ability to discriminate the circle-like ellipse with axes of nine to ten, but is in such a state of conflict that he can't even perform the previously learned discrimination when the axes were seven to ten. Moreover, the conflict is so severe that the dog *breaks down:* He salivates indiscriminately for circles, ellipses, and even for the experimenter. He whines, barks, and tears at the harness, and henceforth proves useless as an experimental animal. (One is tempted to comment on how useful is the human being who puts the animal in such state.) But we must not miss the point: Conflicts can reduce our ability to behave intelligently, to tolerate other conflicts; and intense conflicts can cause inability to solve almost any problem intelligently. The person who has too many conflicts in his life may be plagued by stage fright because he, somewhat like the experimental dog, has lost, momentarily, the ability to resolve conflict in other situations. With an increase in his ability to handle conflict in life, his ability to reduce stage fright will also increase. Therefore, those who are seriously upset by stage fright should consider seeking expert guidance to help them reconstruct their general state of adjustment; as this reconstruction is achieved, their stage fright will probably decrease.

THE TREATMENT OF STAGE FRIGHT

Because stage fright is caused by conflict, its solution lies in the reduction of conflict. *Conflicts are reduced by increasing desires that make one want to speak and by nullifying, preventing, or weakening desires that pull in other directions.* The medieval donkey need not have starved to death between the two stacks of hay had he reduced the desire for one of the stacks and increased the desire for the other. He might have remembered that he was a "left-footed" donkey and taken the stack of hay to the left, and thereby reduced the conflict sufficiently to permit his survival. The speaker is not given so simple a choice; on the other hand, so many possibilities for reinforcing the desire to speak and reducing the fear of speaking exist that he has a strong chance of reducing conflict in the speech situation. Let us look next at the ways in which he can unify himself so that when he *must* speak, he will *want* to.

Resolving conflict: some reassurances

Once speakers know of them, some reassurances can help a speaker. Speakers can take heart from the knowledge that if they have stage fright, the audience will not realize that fact. Observations have shown that audiences—including experienced speech instructors—notoriously *underrate* the degree of stage fright a speaker has.[9] When a speaker realizes that his stage fright will not be noticed, some of the speaker's apprehension may vanish.

A second bit of reassurance may come from the realization that stage fright decreases with age. Adolescents in the tenth grade experience less stage fright than those in grades below them, and by the time one reaches twenty, stage fright will have dropped even more. Inasmuch as time seems to decrease stage fright, you may trust that time will also help you to feel more confident.[10]

Thirdly, and far more importantly, experience in speaking reduces stage fright enormously. "All the investigations . . . showed that on the high school as well as on the college and adult level, practice was a significant factor in influencing gains in confidence.[11] Most students gain confidence as they proceed through a course in public speaking. So certain to reduce stage fright is practice that it is recommended by textbooks more than any other single remedy,[12] and is recommended as a treatment by instructors them-

---

[9] See Theodore Clevenger, Jr., "A Synthesis of Experimental Research on Stage Fright," *Quarterly Journal of Speech*, XLV (Apr. 1959), p. 137.

[10] Ibid., pp. 141–42.

[11] Hamilton, *op. cit.*, pp. 46–47.

[12] Edward R. Robinson, "What Can the Speech Teacher Do About Students' Stagefright?" *The Speech Teacher*, VII (Jan. 1959) pp. 10–11.

selves more than any other treatment.[13] The more frequently one speaks, the less will stage fright be a problem. Stage fright especially lessens in the classroom where the attitudes of the instructor and of the classmates are unthreatening, and when the student is taught so well that the beginning speaker receives genuine insights and techniques useful in preparing and delivering speeches. Students who speak frequently can expect a reduction in their fears.

Finally, students may take heart from realizing that nearly all beginners feel some stage fright. Inasmuch as one's classmates have the same disadvantage, one need not feel upset.

These four reassurances, therefore, may help reduce stage fright: How much stage fright one has cannot be recognized by the audience; as one grows older, the degree of stage fright will lessen; experience in speaking will greatly reduce fears; your classmates have the same difficulty that you have. These reassurances will help reduce the fear of speaking, but there is much more the speaker can do to reduce fears and to increase the desire to speak. These other means of reducing stage fright are more recent discoveries and are based on an understanding of the causes of stage fright and how to eliminate or reduce such causes.

Resolving conflict: combating unfortunate previous experiences

Some students may have had an alarming experience with speaking in which they may have felt publicly embarrassed. The fifth-grader, who, on Parents' Night, was asked to recite a poem, but who, when he stood in front of his classmates, parents and teacher, couldn't remember the first line, may have become so frightened that he is afraid to get up in front of another audience. The young actor who accidentally stumbled against the canvas scenery during the class play and pushed his arm through the canvas "wall" may feel alarmed at the thought of being before people again. Such experiences are usually passed off lightly, but once in a while, the experience may cause undue stage fright. The student who has had such an experience should take the following steps to reduce or nullify the effect of the experience:

1. Recall the experience fully. The process of recalling may be temporarily painful, but to "forget" the experience may cause harm. Such "forgetting," which psychologists call *repression*, may be harmful and may continue to cause trouble. A standard treatment for phobias—unjustified fears—is to trace the origin of the phobia to the incident that caused it. This incident usually is painful to the person, and difficult to recall, because the experience makes him feel guilty. The guilty feelings, however, are unjustified, and as soon as the incident is fully recalled, the unjustified guilt feelings disappear, *as does the fear itself.* To reduce any feel-

[13] Lawrence Edward Cole, Jr., *A Critical Evaluation of Methods of Controlling Stage Fright*, Unpublished M.A. Thesis, Emerson College, 1964.

ings of anxiety caused by such an incident, recall the incident completely.

2. Discuss the experience with the instructor. The instructor will probably want to know about any students who have been "traumatized" in front of an audience. Moreover, the act of talking over the experience with a sympathetic listener is, itself, therapeutic. Discussion of the episode with others not only reduces the repression further, but often helps one gain perspective about the situation so that one can realize its unimportance.

3. Above all, work as hard as possible to prepare fine speeches. One good speech given by a traumatized student may reassure him more than kind words from the class or from the instructor. As the student continues to give good speeches, his successes will nullify the old experience and begin to build strong feelings of confidence that will do more than merely heal the old scar.[14]

The methods of reducing conflict suggested so far have been limited to a discussion of ways to *reduce the fear of speaking*. There are, however, ways to *increase the desire to speak*. These ways may be more important, for they tend to develop that kind of confidence that contributes to success, and that makes the speaker, when he *should* speak, *want to* speak.

Resolving conflict: choice of subject

A speaker can reinforce his desire to speak by choosing a subject that makes him want to speak. If he knows his subject is interesting, important, or unusual, that subject will reinforce his desire to speak. However, if the speaker has chosen a banal, trite, superficial, or otherwise insignificant, subject, he will feel less impelled to speak; instead, he may be reluctant, fearing that the audience will recognize the shallowness of his ideas. Having reinforced his desire *not to speak* by choosing a poor subject, he will be more prone to suffer conflict.

Resolving conflict:
preparation of the materials of the speech

Careful preparation can powerfully reinforce the desire to speak; lack of preparation will increase the fear of speaking and only add to the conflict situation. A speaker who has prepared the speech materials carefully, that is, one who knows the subject well and who knows that it is well chosen, who has vivid and valid supporting materials that are sure to intrigue the audience, who has an introduction that is "sure fire" and a good conclusion,

---

[14] The steps herein described are probably sufficient to reduce the fears of most students who have been traumatized by some previous speech situation. Those whose fears are not reduced— and these will be very few in number, my guess being fewer than one per cent—may be helped by the desensitization technique described by Joseph Wolpe. See Joseph Wolpe and Arnold A. Lazarus, *Behavior Therapy Techniques: A Guide to the Treatment of Neuroses* (Oxford: Pergamon Press, Ltd., 1966). Using the technique on tramautized speakers has been described by William L. Barnett, "Adoption of a Behavior Therapy Technique for Combatting Stagefright," *Pennsylvania Speech Communication Annual*, XXXII (June 1976).

knows that there is little to fear. The prepared speaker will want to speak and can plunge into the speech wholeheartedly with a minimum of conflict and little or no anxiety. But the speaker who suspects that the ideas and supporting materials are dull and unclear, and who knows less about the subject than one should, cannot help but be worried, and perhaps such a speaker should be. Unlike the speaker who is prepared, the unprepared speaker cannot anticipate success, but will, likely, anticipate failure. Such anticipation decreases the desire to speak. Although the speaker must speak, he or she won't want to, and conflict and anxiety not only add to discomfort, but may reduce even further the already limited possibilities for success.

Even the beginning speaker, if prepared, can feel competent when giving the speech; likely the speech will be at least somewhat successful and this success will breed further confidence. Eventually the speaker who prepared carefully for each speech begins to find an audience stimulating rather than frightening.

Reducing conflict: the moments before speaking

An inexperienced speaker may "work up" an unnecessarily strong case of stage fright by overreacting to his or her weaknesses and by falsely imagining the coming presentation as an embarrassing spectacle of blithering idiocy. A low opinion of one's self increases the desire not to speak, and in other ways as well adds to the conflict and anxiety of the speaking situation. Almost any speech will have some weaknesses, but the moments just before giving the speech are not the moments to rehash the ideas of the speech nor to dwell on one's ineptness. Rather, think about something else.

It is not easy to "think about something else." One suggestion, however, may help. If you force yourself to concentrate intensely on whatever is being said just before you speak, you will probably be able to keep your mind off alarming thoughts. The more intensely you concentrate on the speeches that precede yours, the less you can think about your own plight. Moreover, you may find, in one or more of these speeches, some idea or fact which you can refer to, capitalize on, or refute in your own speech. (Classroom audiences listen closely when a student speaker refers to another student's speech.) Before you speak, avoid thoughts about yourself and about your speech by listening carefully to whoever is speaking; try to find a way of referring to this speech when you give yours, and you will not only be more calm for having avoided unnecessary—and, usually unjustified—fears, but will have simplified the conflict situation by removing at least one of the causes of anxiety.

Resolving conflict:
commitment to the significance of one's ideas

That you may reduce the fear of speaking and increase the desire to speak by thinking about matters that have nothing to do with the subject of your speech may already have occurred to you. You may reinforce the desire to speak by any of the following notions, all of which are *extrinsic* to what you say: You may wish to give the speech simply to get it over with. You may increase the desire to speak by wanting to finish the speech so as to complete one more requirement of the course. Some, it is hoped, will want to finish the speech to gain more experience and expertise, or because they realize that not to give the speech at all would be embarrassing. Although such reasons are extrinsic to the speech itself, they may make a contribution to stimulating the desire to speak. If these extrinsic reasons help, use them.

One can develop confidence better, however, by reinforcing the desire to speak for reasons that spring from the ideas of the speech—for *intrinsic* reasons. *One should speak because one is committed to one's ideas, because one is alive with a crucial idea, because one feels he knows something that is important to the audience, because he understands or has clarified a significant problem, because he has found the right answers, or even the right questions. Probably the best way to develop confidence is to be driven to speak because one catches the significance of one's ideas.* One who suffers stage fright is, literally, self-conscious, self-aware. "True neuroses are best defined," Gordon Allport says, "as stubborn self-centeredness."[15] The speaker, on the other hand, who speaks because of committment to an idea is not *self*-centered, but *idea*-centered. When one is so committed to an idea that one has caught its fire, one will want to speak, and can do so wholeheartedly, with every desire to speak, without conflict, and hence, without anxiety.

Too many beginning speakers to not grasp the significance of their ideas, and seldom is one ever "on fire" with an idea; their delivery reflects this lack by its timorousness, its lifelessness, and its ineffectiveness. *The speaker must show that he knows that he has something important to say. Good delivery reflects the significance of one's ideas, and this sense of significance is the most important element in delivery. Without the sense that what one says is important, instruction in delivery is of little avail, and with this sense, most speakers have little need for further instruction.* Moreover, the intensity that springs from speaking with a sense of the importance of one's ideas is one of the roads to *individuality* in delivery. The speaker who reflects the spirit and importance of his or her ideas will not be an imitation of the instructor or of anyone else; rather, such a speaker will be so immersed in the ideas that his or her selfhood emerges uniquely and fully.

But how does one grasp the intrinsic significance of one's ideas? This grasp stems from depth of knowledge about one's ideas. In particular, the person who in a mature way recognizes this significance is one who has certain kinds of knowledge about the ideas, suggested by answers to the following kinds of questions:

[15] *Personality and Social Encounter*, Boston, Beacon Press, 1960, p. 173.

1. In what way are these ideas important today?
2. How do these ideas relate to the material needs of my audience? To their psychological needs? To their philosophic or spiritual needs?
3. In what ways might my ideas influence the attitudes and behavior of the audience?
4. Are there times in the past when these ideas have performed an especially useful service?
5. If these ideas are accepted, how might they change the course of events?

When one is vividly aware of answers to these questions about the subject, one will *want* to speak; moreover, one will have a deeper understanding of the subject, as well as of its importance, and will begin to develop the kind of attitude toward the ideas, toward one's self and toward the audience that is in itself persuasive. The reflection of these ideas in delivery will encourage the natural development of directness, variety, vitality, intensity, and poise that dedication to ideas bring. Thus, one will, through developing a deeper understanding of the significance of one's idea, have also developed many of the skills of delivery.

The speaker who cannot answer at least some of these questions in such a way as to provide ideas that increase the desire to speak may have either a superficial understanding of the subject or may have chosen a poor subject. But if one has chosen a worthy subject, one must not fail to grasp its importance. To miss the power that can be derived from the significant idea is to miss one of the speaker's sources of strength. The power of a great idea is the source of strength that gave confidence—and much more—to men such as Socrates, Lincoln, Churchill, Martin Luther King, Jr. and others. Great ideas have inspired people and nations to wholehearted effort during times of danger. Those *possessed by a great ideal seldom fear.* Many have endured hunger, pain, persecution, and even torture or the threat of death with less terror than the neophyte giving his first speech. If the perception of a great truth can do so much to alleviate real tortures, it is not too much to expect that a speaker who begins to grasp the significance of an idea, will reduce the weak-in-the-knees feeling on the occasion of a short speech in a beginning class.

There are some limits, however, that one should place upon commitment, inspiration, and the drive to accomplish. The person who seems to raise his aspirations too high may fall victim, by the very strength of the desire, to stage fright. Neurotics are often those whose aspirations are too great for their capacities. The student who expects to save the world by one speech is out of touch with both his own limitations and those of the classroom situation. But what constitutes too much commitment and what is too little is never easy to determine. The student is probably the best judge. Nevertheless, one should keep in mind that most beginning students reflect the kind of delivery that is characterized too little by the fire of commitment, and that the student's spark would be increased by a deeper understanding of the significance of ideas.

Because overcoming stage fright requires one to be *idea*-centered instead of *self*-centered, the real challenge to the student is a call to stretch one's mind. It is a challenge to recognize, appreciate, understand, and commit oneself to ideas. The challenge calls one to discover ideas of worth and to turn one's mind toward the significant. It calls one to bury self-centered ideas and to fix attention outside one's self. When one answers the challenge to stretch one's mind around a great idea, one not only gains confidence, lays the foundation for good delivery, and further develops one's own individuality, but one becomes a speaker deserving of the attention of the audience. Such a person is not only a more effective human being but likewise a more worthwhile one.

Resolving conflict: habit formation[16]

Emotionally charged situations—those in which the rewards for success or the penalties for failure are great—do not always produce anxiety or breakdown *unless the situations are too complicated to be met skillfully*. Remember, for example, the first time you drove an automobile. Because you could have had an accident, the event was not only emotionally charged, but it was also too complicated for you. You had to manipulate the steering wheel, push down or let up on the accelerator and brake (and perhaps operate the gear shift and clutch pedal), and do these things not only in coordination with each other, but also in correspondence with what you saw through the windshield. You probably had anxiety—stage fright—and if a real emergency had occurred, you might have experienced breakdown, e.g., stepped on the accelerator when you intended to stop the car, or thrown up your hands in horror. One experiences anxiety and breakdown in an emotionally charged situation that is too complicated for one to respond to ably.

Complexity produces a special form of conflict situation. The responses a beginning driver can make are, perhaps, infinite, and the novice doesn't quite know which response to make at a given time. One can speed up, remain at constant speed, lift one's foot from the accelerator and slow down, touch the brake lightly or firmly, and make innumerable adjustments with the steering wheel (and perhaps with the clutch and gear shift or gear selector). These possibilities provide one with a multi-conflict situation; at the right time, each of these things must be done. The poor novice lacks the skill either to do these things well or to recognize when the right time is. The driver is, therefore, in a multi-conflict situation, and is likely to behave as

---

[16] The writer is indebted to the late Professor Clarence T. Simon for his article "Complexity and Breakdown in Speech Situations," *Journal of Speech Disorders*, X (Sept. 1941), pp. 199–203, and especially for the writer's interest in the psychological means of preventing stage fright, which received its first and greatest stimulus in Professor Simon's classes over a quarter of a century ago.

many do in conflict: sometimes he will over-respond, sometimes under-respond, sometimes not respond at all, and often respond the wrong way—and he is anxious most of the time.

But notice what happens eventually. At first, these complexities required all of one's attention, but one soon learned to make appropriate responses so that one could speed up or slow down with ease, turn corners without even slight difficulty, back up, park the car, and at the same time listen to the radio or carry on a conversation. The learner made *habits* of the skills of driving and therefore could respond easily and appropriately in a variety of situations. *Habits converted the previously complex situation into a simple one.*

Habits convert complex situations into simple ones because *habits are relatively independent of one's attention.* Note how habits are performed without much awareness: Putting on shoes is habitual; can you remember which shoe you put on first this morning? Or remember tying the shoes? Unless something unusual happened, unless one shoe was missing or you found a knotted shoe lace, the act was independent enough of your attention so that memory of it will be dim or, perhaps, nonexistent. Because habits do not require your full attention, they simplify complex situations for you. *The development of skills that are habitual may reduce the discomfort of anxiety-producing situations.*

Habits help reduce anxiety. The good football player responds on the field (in front of perhaps a hundred thousand spectators) without disintegration because he has habituated techniques of passing, dodging, and running; because these techniques are habits, he is free to expend his attention and his energy searching for the pass-receiver or finding the hole through which he can plunge with all his strength. The complicated techniques of playing are made simple because they are independent of his attention, permitting him to play with courage and to put his full strength behind his skills. In the same way, the surgeon remains calm and in possession of his or her skills because of knowing what to expect, and through practice what to do as the incision is made. But place the surgeon, for a moment, in the huddle, or give the football star a scalpel at the side of a patient, and neither star nor surgeon would display coolness or deftness. *Confidence is born of competence.* When one faces an emotionally charged situation for which one does *not* have habituated skills, one will lack the calm assurance of the star or the swift and quiet skill of the expert. To take another example, basic training in the armed forces, in some of its more worthwhile aspects, is an attempt to habituate certain skills of fighting. The soldier, properly trained, will know how to react when faced by the enemy, and instead of disintegrating, will use habitual fighting know-how. Because habits of fighting will be semiautomatic, the soldier, instead of breaking down, fights. The seasoned Marine probably has an abundance of raw courage, but *also* has habituated, through training, superior skills of combat; what would disintegrate other strong people will not do so to him. When good airplane pilots are faced with an emergency they have a repertory of skills that they use semiautomatically, and remain effective in a situation that would terrorize us. Teach us the same skills, and we might behave as well as they. Because habits can simplify a complex situation, they can help reduce anxiety and prevent breakdown. *Confidence and courage are built, in part, out of knowing what to do.*

The same principles apply to the speech situation. It, too, is a complicated situation. The beginning speaker must walk to the platform with ease and dignity, wonders how to stand when getting there, worries about what to do with one's hands, would like to loosen one's collar, can't seem to use his or her voice normally, occasionally forgets items he or she intended to include, and cannot think well, or respond fully to communicating thoughts. The speaker has not yet formed habits that will free attention form the more petty skills of delivery.

One reduces complexity in an audience situation in the same way that one does in driving, surgery, or fighting, for wherever complexity causes anxiety, by habituating the required skills that reduce complexity. We now can see one reason that students who take a speech course experience a reduction in stage fright. In the process of giving several speeches they form habit patterns of the skills of delivery. (Some reductions in stage fright come from a different source—the student who speaks frequently before an audience not only forms habit patterns that reduce the complexity of speaking, but he also learns *what to expect* from an audience. Knowing what to expect often can help reduce anxiety; when the student finds the audience does not respond with catcalls or rotten eggs, but is mildly sympathetic, his anxiety lessens.) Experience not only builds habits that simplify the speech situation, but also gives one a healthy set of expectations that also help reduce anxiety.

The student should not rely only on the slow progress of the term to form habits that will build his confidence. He can speed the process of forming habits by practicing his speeches. Practice, however, does not make prfect; practice only makes more permanent. The wrong kind of practice may intensify the complexity. Therefore, the student should practice so as to incorporate the best skills of speaking in the easiest way. The following sugestions will help form habits of good speaking.

1. After the speech has been carefully outlined to include the best main points, subheads, supporting material and the like, memorize the outline. Memorize the outline so well that you *overlearn* it, for things that we overlearn are not forgotten, even under stress. (You have overlearned your name and address, and are not likely to forget them even before an audience.) A good test of sufficient degree of overlearning is to see if, without reference to your outline, you can repeat it from the last line to the first. When you can recall it line by line from the bottom to the top, you know it so well that no audience will cause you to forget. Moreover, because your outline is well stamped in, you will feel more confident.

2. Practice the speech from this memorized image of the outline, until you can give the speech reasonably well. When a speech is delivered from the

memorized image of an outline—without notes or a manuscript—it is called *extemporaneous* delivery (see Chapter 7). This sort of delivery is best for the beginner because it will help one learn to think before an audience. The speaker must think to recall the outline, and then must think to put it into words so that the thoughts are fuller than the sketchy outline. If, instead of delivering the speech extemporaneously, one memorizes the speech, one is not forced to think. Nor is one forced to think if the speaker practices reading from a manuscript. Extemporaneous speaking therefore, is preferable because it helps develop the ability to think while speaking.

3. Practice the speech as if presenting it to your class, imagining that you are standing before it and looking at it. Such practice best habituates the skills you will use when you give the final presentation. If you practice sitting down, for example, you will reinforce habits that you can't use on the platform; such reinforcement may increase the complexity of your final performance, because the *wrong* rather than the *right* habits, are stamped in. Practice, therefore, as nearly as possible, in the same circumstances as those in which you will give the speech.

4. Practice the speech reflecting the significance of your ideas. (See pp. 124.) It is especially important that the beginning speaker recall the significance of the subject before starting to practice the speech and keep that significance in mind throughout the speech. Especially, the speaker should try to reflect the significance of each sentence and each idea, checking himself or herself occasionally and asking, "Did I say that so as to reflect its importance?" As James Albert Winans put it, "what the speaker needs . . . is such preparation that his ideas will command his attention and awaken him to energetic thinking and earnestness." [17] If one practices being idea-centered, one will be more likely to give the speech in such a way as to preserve the idea-centered attitudes of the practice session and be less self-centered in front of the audience.

With abundant extemporaneous practice, you will find that, inadvertently, you will memorize parts of the speech. But you will also, inadvertently, make habits of some of the skills of delivery. With practice you can habituate good posture, responsive use of voice and body, and a strong spirit of communication. If you can stamp in these skills *before* you deliver the speech, the speech situation will be all the more simple. Because you know your speech and know that you can deliver it well, you are quite certain to face the speech situation with less anxiety. You will be freer to think, to respond to your thoughts, and to speak in such a way that the audience catches and feels the same thoughts.

[17] *Public Speaking*, New York, The Century Co., 1917, p. 51.

AN OVERVIEW OF CONFIDENCE

Confidence springs not from a bag of tricks, but from two more difficult but more certain remedies: *competence* and *commitment.* Either one is probably enough, but confidence—courage—can be developed by (1) knowing what to do and by (2) dedication. Let us examine competence first. The surgeon who knows surgery well opens the abdomen of the anesthetized patient without fear, trembling, or fainting. Such surgeons learned what to do; they know their skills, and what to expect. They are confident because they are competent. Or take the football player who, before 80,000 people sees the pass coming, and even before he catches it is looking for a place to take the ball. He, too, knows what to do. But reverse the two: Put the surgeon on the football field with the football spinning toward him, and the football player in the operating room with a scalpel in his hand. The surgeon may be frightened on the football field, and more than one novice in the operating room has been known to faint at the first sight of blood. Neither is competent. Neither has confidence. Courage is often built by knowing what to do, whether in fighting, preparing a dinner for company, talking with the boss, or giving a speech. Stage fright may be inevitable if you do not know what to do, for courage is often built only from competence. Competence in speaking comes from knowing and being able to use as many skills of preparing and delivering a speech as possible. To develop these skills is one of the objectives of taking a course in speech.

Developing commitment is the other basic road to confidence, and one that presents a different set of problems. To what should one be committed? Each of us must probably find the answer for ourselves. But here, too, there are guides. Many academic subjects can be viewed as potential sources of commitment. The study of history can illumine the worthy and unworthy commitments of the past; literature often has at its heart the nature of a person's commitment, and where that commitment led. Philosophy might be viewed as the study of commitments. So, too, might religion, science, the arts, and social sciences. Developing commitment is a longer process, involving a search or ideas, movements, problems, and values. The study of speech, especially as it is presented in this book, will be of some help. Nevertheless, the students must search their hearts, and look for help from whatever sustaining forces they can find. Perhaps the search through literature, history, philosophy, religion, science, or art will help one discover those things that merit dedication. Perhaps in one or more of the problems of the present age or the high values of the past you will find that which is worthy of commitment. At any rate, the kind of confidence that stems from competence and commitment is the kind that not only enhances success, but also makes one worth hearing and worthy to influence the lives of those who listen to the speaker. And when one is committed to a cause worthy of belief, that belief brings courage, as the lives of martyrs suggest.

The major task in developing confidence is to develop competence and (or) commitment. There is no instant way to develop these attributes, but one can begin any time, and in some ways the college speech class can be among the better places to begin.

ASSIGNMENTS

1. Give examples of people you have known or read about who were confident because of their competence. Discuss the experiences they had that developed their competence. To what extent were there limits to their competence?
2. Give examples of people you have known or read about whose confidence seemed to result from their commitment. By what means did each of them achieve the commitment that gave them confidence?
3. Give examples of people you have known or read about who lacked confidence. What factors seem to account for their lack of confidence? If you could advise them, what would you tell them in order to increase their confidence?
4. Write an autobiography in which you perform the following:
   a. Explain those factors in your life that have increased your own confidence.
   b. Explain those factors in your life that have decreased your confidence.
   c. Set out a program for your life proposing means by which you may develop confidence by developing competence.
   d. Set out a program for your life proposing means by which you may first locate those matters in which you believe you can or already have located ideas, causes, and beliefs that are worthy of your commitment. Then set out a program for yourself by which you can become more committed to these matters.

8

delivering ideas

Speak fitly, or be silent wisely.
Scottish proverb

"It's not what you say but how you say it!" This too-common remark is one of the most insidious catch-phrases ever invented. The serious student of speech should despise it, for it suggests that what is said is not important, that ideas that are frivolous and ill-supported can be "said well," and, worst of all, that the person who does say something well is to be suspected of being skillful but empty-headed.

In reacting strongly in opposition to those who consider delivery to be all there is to speechmaking, we should not assume that delivery is without importance. A speech is not a speech until delivered to an audience. We have all listened to speakers who seemed to lack either the interest in what they were saying or the energy necessary to present their ideas vigorously. We have found our attention wandering and looked about us to see others in the audience meeting the apparently bored speaker with equal boredom. Often we have made an effort to listen and understand what the speaker was saying and found that intrinsically it was sometimes quite interesting and even vital. Yet the speaker's manner was such that the listeners found it easy to let their attentions drift. Such speakers are the opposites of the legendary peddlers of patent medicines: Instead of making something worthless sound valuable, they make something valuable sound worthless.

On the other hand, we have heard speakers who live in auras of enthusiasm. Their eyes fix us; they point, they pound, they smile, they frown. But back of it all we sense an emptiness and are repelled by what seems to us to be grotesque parody of what public speaking should be. These people really believe that "it's not what you say but how you say it."

We should not pretend that either of these sorts of speakers is always easily detected. Lackluster speakers are usually successful in concealing the value of what they have to say, and there are those who through knack and practice are experts at making vacuousness sound attractive. We assume that the student wishes to avoid being the former sort of speaker and has no interest in becoming the latter sort.

GOOD DELIVERY

What is good delivery? Although it is difficult to give a description that will satisfy every student, some standards may be set even if absolute standards are impossible to set. The judgment, "That was well delivered," is at least partly a matter of taste. Individuals vary, often markedly, in what they like. Groups tend to vary also. In one set of circumstances at one time and before one group, what will seem quite proper and appropriate will seem inappropriate to another group at another time. Recognizing these differences and without trying to account for them, some generalizations about delivery are basic to good public speaking.

From the point of view of the listeners, delivery is good when it focuses attention on the speaker's ideas and enables them to grasp the speaker's meaning. From the point of view of the speaker, delivery is good when it permits communication of the intended message. In general, good delivery is simple, lively, and emphatic.

The speaker should continually ask two questions:

1. Do I have the audience's attention?
2. Do my listeners grasp my meaning?

Although no speaker will probably ever be able to give an unqualified "yes" to each of these questions at every moment, the questions will direct the speaker's attention where it should be—*on meaning.*

Meaning is a broad word. Meaning in oral communication is dependent upon more than the sum of the dictionary definitions of the words uttered. The oral cues to meaning are many and often subtle, but any listener recognizes some obvious ones. A rising inflection indicates a question although the same words with a final falling inflection would indicate a declarative sentence. Thus we readily distinguish, "I am?" from "I am." We recognize that different meanings arise when different words in a sentence are emphasized. "*I* am going shopping," carries a different meaning from "I *am* going shopping." Or consider these statements: "I believe that I shall go home." and, "I believe that I shall go [long pause] home." These are different statements; although they are in no context, they carry different meanings.

The oral communication of a message, furthermore, gives the audience some cues about the person communicating the message. The attitudes the speaker suggests are an important part of the meaning. What about, for example, the attitude of the speaker toward the subject matter? Toward the audience? Is the speaker matter-of-fact or impassioned? Pleased or angry? Antagonistic or conciliatory? The person's manner of speaking helps convey meaning in this broader sense. The speaker who wishes to conciliate the audience but sounds antagonistic will probably fail. The speaker who believes that the message is vital to the welfare of the listeners should not chat as if making polite conversation at an afternoon tea. In short, the audience should feel that the delivery is appropriate—appropriate to the speaker, to the ideas, and to the situation.

ATTAINING GOOD DELIVERY

Paradoxically, the best way to attain good delivery is *not* to attend to it, that is, not to attend to it directly. Speakers should give their attention to their messages and to the audiences for which the messages are intended. The best foundation for well-delivered speeches that beginners can lay are well prepared speeches—speeches that contain ideas to which they feel committed, speeches with purposes that they want to accomplish.

Although oral cues are important in indicating meaning just as changes in inflection, in rate, and in loudness indicate to a listener changes in meaning, nevertheless the importance of these cues does not mean that the speaker should try to plan such changes consciously. To plan every inflection, pause, change in loudness, or gesture is probably impossible; to plan many will consume time heavily. For most speakers planning any of these details of delivery will probably result in observable artificialities that will distract the audience and interfere with the communication of the intended meaning. One of the authors remembers listening to what he considered to be an excellent speech by a college student in a contest. At a critical point near the end the speaker stepped stiffly backward and placed his hand over his heart. At that moment worthwhile ideas became ludicrous. The speaker was embarrassed, and so were many of his listeners. Except for that false note, his speech was well delivered. His mind had seemed to be on the ideas of the speech in which he was vitally interested and about which he wished his listeners to feel just as strongly, but at the climax he withdrew his attention from the thought of his speech and made a studied gesture.

The point is not to avoid pointing, or shouting, or whispering, or speaking more loudly or less rapidly. The speaker referred to had gestured time and again during his speech. He had made many changes in his vocal pattern, some subtle, some quite marked, but these had seemed to arise spontaneously from the ideas. The problem is to get and retain *spontaneous* delivery.

Watch people in conversation. Most of them without conscious attention to voice and body respond quite vigorously when they speak. They gesture; their facial expression changes; they modify intensity, rate, and inflection. Think of speaking as a conversation, a rather advantageous conversation in which you may think and talk with little interruption from your polite listeners.

Even though the speaker will have to be somewhat more intense, more vigorous simply to be heard when talking to an audience rather than a few, conversation makes a good model. To gain the natural responses of conversation, Richard Whately gave this sound advice well over a hundred years ago: "The practical rule then to be adopted . . . is, not only to pay no studied attention to the voice, but studiously to *withdraw* the thoughts from it, and to dwell as intently as possible on the Sense; trusting to nature to suggest spontaneously the proper emphasis and tones."[1] What is needed is, in James Winans' memorable phrase, "the full realization of the content of your words as you utter them. . . ."[2]

Much of the speaker's success in concentrating on ideas, not on manner, and thereby improving delivery, will depend upon rehearsal, a topic we shall discuss presently. Some difficulty may arise for the beginner simply from feeling awkward speaking before an audience. In Chapter 7 we discussed reducing tensions, and quite obviously, the problems are closely related. Beginning speakers should expect to feel awkward when talking to an audience just as they would in undertaking any other new activity, whether it is skiing, bicycling, golfing, or swimming. Your first kiss was probably rather clumsily executed, but you learned.

INDIVIDUAL PROBLEMS IN DELIVERY

Each speaker will meet many problems in developing an effective delivery. One must come to recognize them, large and small, and seek to overcome them. There is little sense in trying to predict precisely what these problems will be or to try to meet them in advance; the best advice is to concentrate on ideas and to follow some positive directions that will help fix good habits of delivery. A friendly listener, preferably one whose experience in speaking is quite broad, can help each learner identify and meet individual problems as they arise. In the speech classroom, the instructor will probably take this advisory responsibility.

What do we mean when we talk about individual problems in delivery?

[1] *Elements of Rhetoric*, London, B. Fellowes, 1836, Pt. IV, ch. II, Sec. 3.
[2] *Speech Making*, New York, Appleton-Century-Crofts, 1938, p. 25.

Take one general example—the problem of distracting mannerisms. Every speaker, even the very experienced, is in a state of tension in speaking. This is natural and it is, in normal degree, desirable. This tension may manifest itself in many ways, some of which will tend to make the delivery of the speech more effective, some of which will help release tension in ways that are not likely to draw the audience's conscious attention, but some manifestations of tension are intrusive and distract the audience. A speaker may pick up a pencil, move it from hand to hand, put it down, pick it up, shake it, and put it down again. This sort of activity is likely to distract the audience's attention from the ideas that the speaker wants to communicate.

The problem of distracting mannerisms may seem petty, and in a sense it is. The friendly critic ought not be too quick to call them to the attention of the speaker. A mannerism may be a good releaser of tension, and be at most minimally distracting. Often as the speaker becomes used to the public speaking situation, much of the tension will flow into useful bodily and vocal activity. On the other hand, if the mannerism persists and seems likely to interfere with communication, the speaker should be told about it and urged to make an effort to eradicate the tendency. Sometimes negative practice will help, that is, in rehearsal to rattle loose change, or pace, or scratch, or do with conscious exaggeration whatever is interfering with communication. The main point is, however, that individual problems should be met as they arise with the help of a friendly, knowledgeable observer.

FORMING SOME POSITIVE HABITS

Beginning speakers raise all sorts of questions about how they should conduct themselves before an audience. They ask, for example, "What should I do with my hands?" The answer, of course, is "Do what you feel like doing (unless a friendly observer has urged you to concentrate on removing some distracting mannerism), but don't think about it. Concentrate on your ideas and let your hands do what they will. Chances are that you will find yourself gesturing to reinforce your meanings." In general, this is good advice, but some positive habits that the beginner can cultivate will reduce tension, probably, and will encourage concentration on communicating ideas to the audience.

As simple as it might seem, the beginner would do well to concentrate a little practice on posture. Sit in a chair near the back of a room. Stand up, walk quickly and firmly to the front, turn around purposefully and face an imaginary audience. Do this until you start to become accustomed to "rising to speak." Stand erect before your imaginary audience, your weight distributed about equally upon each foot. Starting with your left foot, move a few steps to your left. Starting with your right foot, move a few steps to your right. When you move, move firmly. When you stand, stand erect. You will soon start to feel comfortable, and, although you are doing only what is natural for you to do, most natural activity feels awkward at first. Give yourself a chance to become used to facing an audience. Practicing facing an imaginary audience will help you develop these helpful rudimentary habits.

Just as ordinarily in conversation you look at those to whom you are talking, do so also in speaking to larger groups. There are two reasons for this advice: Listeners, consciously or unconsciously, expect you to look at them and become uneasy or distracted if you do not; moreover, you will probably find it easier to keep your mind on communicating your ideas if you will fix your eyes on your audience. This suggestion does not mean that you must never glance away to check your notes or simply to rest for a moment, but it does mean that you should not bury yourself in your notes or fix your attention more than momentarily anywhere except upon your audience. You probably cannot see everyone at once, but you can look at one portion of your audience, and then another, and another, giving each part about equal attention. Do not shift your gaze constantly, but do distribute your attention to all parts of your audience. Forget any tricks you might have heard about how to appear as though you are looking at your audience. These tricks are of dubious merit. See your listeners, watch them react; although now and again a listener may disconcert you, usually the audience will serve as a stimulus to a positive, effective manner.

Finally, you should realize that delivering a speech is a physical activity. You must work—your vocal mechanism works; your body works. You should consciously exert yourself. Be vigorous. You need not rant and shout. Far from it. A normally quiet person can be energetic; in order not to seem vapid, the quiet person must be energetic. It may be well to over-react to ideas in practicing, to be too energetic. Overdo gesturing in practice. Few speakers are too energetic before an audience so there is little cause to worry about carrying too much activity with you from your practice sessions.

The speaker needs to develop a sense of communication. This means feeling that one is conversing directly with listeners who, although they remain silent for the most part, are actively engaged in the communication process. If the listeners are to be actively engaged, the speaker must be actively engaged. A speaker who rises and faces an audience purposefully, who stands erect, gives attention to the audience, and speaks energetically will find the power to develop a strong sense of communication.

MODES OF DELIVERY

Speakers may speak impromptu or extemporaneously; they may write manuscripts and then either memorize or read them. Each of these modes of delivery presents special challenges.

An impromptu speech is one for which the speaker has made no specific preparation. Ordinarily, the impromptu speaker is moved by specific circumstances to deal with ideas and materials with which he or she is familiar.

Courtroom lawyers, for example, may engage in a good deal of impromptu speaking simply because they must meet ideas as ideas arise. They will, however, be dealing with cases for which they have made a thorough general preparation and will speak in familiar surroundings. Furthermore, insofar as possible they will prepare specifically. Congressional debaters will speak impromptu at times, but, like lawyers, they will draw from ideas, materials, and procedures that are familiar. They may, indeed, have discussed the issues involved again and again even though they may not have prepared the particular debate speeches. You have done and will probably do some impromptu speaking. In general, preparing specific speeches will give you the sort of experience that will be useful when circumstances demanding impromptu speech arise.

In speech classes, probably, most if not all of the speaking you do will be extemporaneous. Extemporaneous speeches are prepared in advance. The speaker plans the purpose, thesis, a pattern of main heads, and subordinate heads. The speaker chooses supporting material to make ideas clear, interesting, and impelling but does not set the language of the speech specifically. Generally in speaking extemporaneously, one speaks as in conversation, the words coming as one concentrates on expressing an idea.

If the speaker writes a manuscript, it can either be read or presented from memory. Although some authorities argue otherwise, we can see little merit in memorizing speeches. The time spent in memorizing could be more profitably spent in composing and rehearsing the speech. Reading a manuscript is difficult, but some occasions demand a speech that is carefully phrased in detail. The best advice is to learn to speak well extemporaneously before undertaking to compose and deliver manuscript speeches. With a thorough grounding in extemporaneous speaking, you will be better equipped to deliver speeches in a direct, communicative manner.

Before discussing the rehearsal of extemporaneous and manuscript speeches, there is one other remark about manuscript speeches that should be made. Too many beginners are tempted to write out speeches in full immediately thinking that having ideas written verbatim will help them. Almost universally, however, writing out a speech hinders its development; the written draft tends to become a final draft immediately. In composing a manuscript speech, the speaker should proceed as if the speech were to be presented extemporaneously. One should plan large units, outline, and revise. It is even a good practice to rehearse the speech extemporaneously to check on the appropriateness of one's plan and to reinforce the feeling of talking one's ideas through conversationally. Only after this preparation should a speaker develop the specific phrasing of the manuscript.

Unfortunately many speakers treat the manuscript as a short cut. The manuscript speech has the advantage of allowing the speaker to choose words carefully. This advantage is wasted, however, unless the ideas and their support are carefully crystallized first.

REHEARSING

Speakers cannot be told too often that the speech must be practiced. This advice means that one must prepare far enough in advance to allow adequate rehearsal time. Only through rehearsal can you gain the familiarity with ideas and materials that enables you to present ideas in a clear, interesting, and impelling manner.

You may take advantage of all sorts of odd moments in preparing and rehearsing speeches. Riding a bus, or walking across campus, or waiting for a meal in a busy restaurant, you may turn over in your mind ideas for a speech you are preparing, or you can even engage in silent rehearsal of a speech that has been thoroughly planned. But even though such efforts may be quite useful, they should not be considered as substitutes for careful preparation with paper and pencil resulting in a series of outlines leading to the final plan, nor should silent rehearsal be thought to obviate any need for oral rehearsal.

Repeated oral rehearsal is necessary. A ten-minute speech could be practiced a half dozen times in an hour's time. You are unlikely to spend an hour of preparation more profitably. Actually, however, it is unwise to practice several times consecutively. It is better to practice and revise; then practice again. Or if you feel that little revision is necessary, to wait a short while before practicing again. If at all possible, spread your rehearsals over several days.

Oral rehearsal is difficult. At first it will seem utterly ridiculous to stand talking in an empty room. As a matter of fact, it is easier and better for most speakers to recruit a few friends to listen. Unfortunately friends are not always available, so you must get used to imagining an audience in an empty room.

There is another reason why oral rehearsal is difficult. Except in those rare instances when every turn of fortune is good, speeches, the first few times they are delivered, are likely to be much less than adequate. It can be a rather trying experience to make a good speech, even before an imaginary audience. Quite obviously, however, it makes more sense to try the speech out orally, to revise it, and to bring it under control before facing a real audience.

As we have suggested, a primary reason for practicing orally is to lay a basis for revision. Most speakers do not begin practicing soon enough. They feel that rehearsal is to be undertaken only after the speech is finished. By this attitude they lose a potent instrument of composition. A good deal of the composition of an extemporaneous speech can be oral. Mark Twain is supposed to have commented that he sometimes practiced stories (detailed examples) as many as a hundred times "before I got them the way I wanted them." Whereas most speakers will not go to this extreme, Mark Twain's example is worth emulating. By practicing orally you will be able to discover what parts of your speech need more support, need rearrangement, or perhaps can be omitted. Having a friend listen to rehearsals, especially one who is willing to react in detail to the speech, will help in deciding upon revisions. You ought to question anyone you get to listen to you practice in order to find out what is clear and what is not, what is interesting, and what is impelling to that particular listener. But with or without the help of a friendly critic, you must practice and revise repeatedly.

Another function of oral practice is to help fix the speech in your mind. You should not try to memorize the speech, but as the ideas are developed and refined and practiced repeatedly, you will find yourself choosing without effort words that you have used before. Ordinarily it is better to practice the speech from beginning to end without stopping to repeat or to correct.

In practicing, you should use your outline. Many speakers find that the complete outline they have planned, as necessary as it is, is not a good outline to speak from. The detail distracts them. You should try preparing a vastly simplified outline after you have prepared thoroughly and rehearsed a few times. Cut down words. Use a few key terms to indicate ideas; the key word outline will resemble an early draft, but it will represent careful and complete preparation. On the other hand, some speakers work well from rather complete outlines. You should find out what works best for you; whatever sort of outline you use to speak from should help you be a direct, energetic speaker.

Some speech instructors request that for short classroom speeches students use no notes at all, except perhaps a few cards for complex statistical material or direct quotations. In this case, careful rehearsal is essential. A clear, simple outline, perhaps one that has been reduced from the full outline to a key word outline for initial rehearsals, will help you hold the sequence of your ideas and your materials in mind.

In practicing orally, try to simulate as closely as you can the surroundings in which you will finally speak. If you will have a speaker's stand, practice with one even though it may have to be a makeshift. Try to find a room approximately the size of the one you will speak in. If you can, go to the room itself and practice.

For the overwhelming majority, direct, energetic manuscript reading is much more difficult than good extemporaneous delivery. Part of the problem lies in the fact that too many speakers feel that once the manuscript is written, the job is done. Not only do they often fail to prepare a good manuscript, as we have already mentioned, but they fail to practice what they have prepared.

In general, the procedure for practicing a manuscript is like that for practicing an extemporaneous speech. But the speaker will have more difficulty in concentrating on ideas because the impulse will be to read words. The first step in solving the problem lies in having a good manuscript, one that is well organized. The speaker should study the outline repeating the pattern of assertions without the detail of support. It is often helpful to practice the speech as if it were extemporaneous, using different material even to develop the ideas. In this way the speaker becomes familiar with the ideas and fastens on the ideas while reading the words.

The speaker must practice reading the manuscript repeatedly no less often than one would rehearse an extemporaneous speech. Without trying to memorize the manuscript, one will become freer and freer from the written document through practice. The speaker's goal should be to be able to look at the audience while reading. A well-delivered manuscript speech can be nearly as direct as a good extemporaneous speech.

The speaker should prepare a clean manuscript. If you have penciled in many changes, you should recopy the pages on which they occur. Recopying takes time, but a legible manuscript is necessary if it is to be read well. Some speakers like to mark cues on the manuscript—perhaps underlining an emphatic word or writing a note, "slow down," and so on. Quite frankly this procedure is not advisable. It may indicate simply that the speaker is not familiar with the pattern of ideas or with the manuscript. If you feel impelled to indicate such cues, however, keep them simple and hold them to a minimum.

CONCLUSION

Actually delivery is not a separate topic. It is a part of the speech. Rehearsing for a speech is not so much a time set aside as part of the preparation, the very composition, of a speech. The speaker who develops a sense of communicating to an audience will probably carry this sense over into the choice of material and the patterning of ideas. The speaker who chooses material and patterns ideas carefully will probably lay the basis for good delivery and will be impelled to deliver the speech in a direct, energetic manner. The result should be a speech that is clear, interesting, and impelling.

ASSIGNMENTS

1. Prepare a speech of self-introduction, three minutes in length, in which you write your name on the board, and give the class three main ideas about yourself that you would like them to remember about you. Jot these three points down on a piece of paper. Phrase them and rephrase them until they are parallel: That is, until they are of the same grammatical structure and of approximately equal importance. To illustrate: The following points are not parallel:
   a. I enjoy sailing and own a small sail boat.
   b. I'm president of the campus chess club.
   c. Speaking to audiences scares me.
   But the following are parallel:
   a. I enjoy sailing.
   b. I enjoy chess.
   c. I hope I enjoy speech.

After you have devised three points that are parallel, think of ways to support them. You might support the points by, in the case of point a, saying that you own a sail boat, telling about some of the experiences you have had in it, and perhaps concluding the point by describing the thrill of sailing. Jot down the ideas you will use to support each point. Memorize the outline; it will take you less than four minutes. Give the speech from your memorized outline without the use of notes. It is unlikely that the instructor will grade the speeches, and because you will be talking about the subject you know best, namely yourself, you will not experience great stage fright. If you do get worried, remember that all your classmates are in the same position.

2. Prepare a speech presenting a significant problem to the class. No solution is necessary; simply be sure the class understands that what you speak about is an important problem. Prepare a careful outline of the speech and memorize the outline. Practice the speech attempting first not to have (in Winans' words) a "full realization of the content of your words as you utter them." Then go through the speech, sentence by sentence, trying to feel the meaning and import of the words, phrases, and sentences as you speak them. Constantly listen to yourself, asking "Do I reflect a vivid realization of the idea at the moment I speak of it?" "Am I running this material through my head *before* I run it over my vocal chords?"

9

listening analytically

We have two ears and only one tongue in order that we may hear more and speak less.

DIOGENES LAERTIUS

The attitudes and skills that the speaker studies and applies can be turned to good use by the listener. As a listener you have asked yourself such questions as these: "Just what is this person driving at?" "Is this the point?" "Is that example relevant?" "I wonder if this notion will be proposed as the solution?" You have raised such questions for two reasons: (1) to learn more about speaking, and (2) to help determine the merits of the ideas that the speaker has recommended to you. If you already listen analytically, why bother with a chapter on the subject?

Undoubtedly you have learned some attitudes and skills that you can turn to excellent use as a listener. You probably had some good habits of listening before you ever opened this book. But on the other hand, all of us probably assume much too readily that listening is no problem for us. Paradoxically, we know all too well how easy it is to fail to listen analytically, or to listen at all for that matter. We have sat too often in an audience and suddenly realized that our minds have wandered off. We have been given directions, often important directions, and discovered to our dismay that although we thought we knew what we were to do and how we were to do it, we did not know. How many times has each of us taken an action on someone else's advice and said later, "I wish I'd listened more carefully." We are not much different from the average person.

Too often we blame the speaker for our lapses. "What a boring sermon," we say as we drowse in our pews. "If that professor could only make an idea clear . . ." as we find ourselves unable to reproduce the ideas in writing an essay in an examination. Sometimes when we listen carefully, we find ourselves the possessors of an inferior product or find a belief hollow. There can be no doubt that there are uninteresting, unclear, and unethical speakers in the world, but too often our judgments are simply excuses for our own inadequacies. And even when such judgments are accurate, they should be the spur to better, not less analytic listening. Whereas the brilliant speaker who is interesting, clear, and ethical may be able to carry even poor listeners along, the poor speaker must have fine listeners.

WANT TO LISTEN

"I can listen well when I want to." This statement tends to represent our attitude toward listening. In one way it's a good attitude; in another way it is not.

To say, "I can listen well when I want to," is to imply, "but I may not want to." Herein lies the problem. We live in a society that has learned to shift the responsibilities from listeners to speakers. We say, "Make me want to listen. I dare you." If we are distracted, it's not our fault but the speaker's. As speakers, we should recognize this common attitude and try to meet it. But we cannot expect the impossible from ourselves nor from others and, try as we might, we shall not always be perfectly clear and interesting. To use an analogy that's at least as old as Plutarch, one may throw a ball, but another must catch it. Even with the best of pitchers, a catcher will have to move off his haunches once in a while. Poor listeners tend to dwell on the responsibilities and the disabilities of speakers. The only person who has a right to say, "That was a boring sermon," is the person who has listened as closely as possible to it. And the only person who has a right to say, "That point was really garbled," is the person who has made the utmost effort to ferret out the idea.

On the other hand, the person who says, "I can listen well when I want to," may make the statement a resolution to listen well. Motivation, wanting to listen well, is the starting point. It is possible to give many detailed reasons to anyone who asks, "Why should I want to listen?" Among many reasons are three general ones.

1. *Personal integrity.* We inevitably make judgments concerning the value of speeches and speakers. Even an almost unconscious turning of the mind from the speaker to other matters is a kind of judgment. Sometimes we com-

municate these judgments to others, perhaps at length verbally after the speech, or during the speech by merely raising our eyebrows. Sometimes we keep the judgments private. In either case, to be honest we must listen carefully. An irate student once brought a term paper to a professor. The paper had just been returned to him by another professor. It was neatly typed, well written, and had an "A" marked boldly upon it. Why was the student angry? Buried in a long paragraph in the middle of the paper was a sentence much like this, "I'll bet you didn't read this, you. . . ." Although the student did not mind getting "A's," he did resent deeply the apparent lack of effort on the professor's part to evaluate the paper meaningfully. Not long ago a home owner asked in exasperation after the assessor had just left, "How could he assess our property? He didn't get out of the living room." We recognize that the professor and the assessor had no right to make evaluations in these cases, but how many evaluations of speeches, of ideas, of materials, of motives, do we make that are essentially dishonest ones?

2. *Personal profit.* As a student of speech, you are no ordinary listener. You can learn about speaking in no better way than by listening carefully to speakers. It is not enough to say that a speech is effective or that it is not. You must try to analyze just what prompts this judgment. The student of speech, then, will be an especially busy listener and must be an especially alert listener. We have discussed, for example, the necessity of good organization, but nothing will drive the lessons home more quickly than to hear some poorly organized speeches. The student may learn to handle supporting material adroitly by listening to speakers who do so. The possible lessons are too numerous to mention, and the possible benefit too great to overemphasize.

Even if we were not trying to learn more about speaking, we should, as intelligent persons, resolve to listen carefully to speakers. What are the ideas in the speech? On what materials do these ideas rest? Herein lie high potential profits. We should resolve to find as much as possible in any speech out of sheer acquisitiveness. We are inclined much too quickly to say, "There's nothing here for me." If we were wise, we would turn our attention away from a speaker only when we could use our time profitably for some other activity. If for no reason than to make the best out of a bad situation, we should listen carefully; and quite often we shall find that the situation is not so bad after all.

3. *Simple courtesy.* Even if we could turn profitably to something else, we probably should not do so. As speakers we should be interested in creating the kinds of listening situations in which decent communications can prosper. As human beings we should be interested in creating a social situation in which all of us can respond intelligently to one another. If a speaker takes the time to prepare a speech for an audience, that audience owes him the courtesy of listening carefully. What if the speaker does not take the responsibility of preparing carefully? No doubt we hear too many speakers who do not make honest efforts to prepare, but on the other hand, as listeners we

should assume that speakers have taken the time. If there is blame that can be attached to a failure in communication, we should take care that as listeners we do not deserve that blame.

The person who resolves to listen carefully will take the first step toward being a good listener. Although this resolution by itself is not enough, without consciously deciding that one should listen and wants to listen, no one is likely to become a good listener.

DECLARE A TRUCE WITH BIAS AND EMOTION

One of the authors happened to be in the home of a friend at presidential election time a few years ago. The television set was on. As the announcer informed us in ringing tones that we were about to hear a speech by one of the candidates, the set owner turned vigorously to another channel, snapping, "We don't want to listen to that guy. He won't do anything but tell a lot of lies anyway." We would be safe in saying that even if this person had not tuned out the candidate he would not have listened, not listened well at any rate, to the speech.

We tend to concentrate on those things we like and to turn away from those things we dislike. Our existing attitudes—toward ideas, toward people, toward groups—shape what we hear, until, at times, we hear only the weird phantoms of what is said if we hear at all. Consider this hypothetical example:

The firm's accountant goes to the general manager and says: "I have just heard from the Bureau of Internal Revenue, and . . ." The general manager suddenly breathes harder as he thinks, "That blasted bureau! Can't they leave me alone? Every year the government milks my profits to a point where . . ." Red in the face, he whirls and stares out the window. The label "Bureau of Internal Revenue" cuts loose emotions that stop the general manager's listening.

In the meantime the accountant may go on to say "here is a chance to save $3,000 this year" if the general manager will take a few simple steps. The fuming general manager may hear this—if the accountant presses hard enough—but the chances are he will fail to comprehend it.[1]

We could cast this hypothetical case in a hundred different forms; and, if we try, we can probably remember ourselves in the role of a listener who let emotional responses get in the way of understanding what was said.

Our problems are not new ones. Among other pieces of advice that he gave his own contemporaries in regard to listening, Plutarch declared, "He therefore who comes to hear must for the time come to a kind of truce and accommodation with vainglory. . . ."[2] Although there are a few who may be

[1] Ralph G. Nichols and Leonard A. Stevens, "Listening to People, *Harvard Business Review* (Sept.–Oct. 1957), pp. 88–89.

[2] Plutarch, "On Hearing," sect. 6.

so impressed with their own powers as a speaker that they cannot listen carefully to others, this feeling is probably not going to be a principal problem with most of us. Still Plutarch's advice is apt; we do need to come to a truce. Whenever we sense the tug of our own strong feelings on a subject, we must be cautious. We must not, of course, forget our own beliefs. Far from it. We must remember them; but in remembering them, we must recognize our inclination to tune out, to distort, to forget conveniently those ideas and materials that do not fit our prevailing attitudes.

When we listen to ideas to which we are opposed, our inclination is to start to compose rebuttals. In so doing, we turn our attention from the speaker to another task and so are not to hear much of what he has to say. We have all had the experience of attending a lecture to hear afterwards someone ask a question, probably one framed to embarrass or expose the speaker, which indicated that the listener had tuned out at some point to work on his own composition because the speaker had quite clearly (we thought) answered the question in the speech. If you are actually debating and must refute what is said, you will be faced with an extremely difficult task of combined listening and composition. You should be well prepared in advance, but even so you will need to make sure that you hear and understand the entire argument if you are to respond to it intelligently.

Learn to set aside your judgments temporarily. "Hear me out," a speaker may answer a questioner who interrupts him, and that is a fair request. We must wait for the speaker to complete each idea, and we must wait to see the relationship of one idea to the next. Only if we are willing to wait and listen can we decide on the basis of what is said whether the material is clear or the requests are reasonable. It may be well for us to bring our own beliefs and the basis of these beliefs forward, to compare what we have heard with what we already believe, but if we let our beliefs step in too soon we may be doing ourselves and the speaker a disservice. Final comparisons and decisions will take time; we do not have the time during another's speech for careful, final decision making.

It will not be easy to declare a truce with each speaker, but if you make a conscious effort to do so, to keep your attitudes from interfering with your comprehension of what is said, you will begin to build a habit of listening that will serve you well. If you respond fully to speakers, you will be fairer to your own beliefs in the long run.

LISTEN ANALYTICALLY

What we have discussed thus far is, in a sense, preliminary to listening. Listeners are active. We do not sit back like blotters ready to absorb anything that comes along. We have minds, and our minds work, and herein, strangely enough, lies the problem.

Although as listeners we do not have time to make detailed comparisons, evaluations, decisions, and refutations, we do have time to do more than listen to each word the speaker utters. The average person will speak from 125 to 150 words per minute, but the average person can think at a much more rapid rate. Most persons reading this book can read at least 300 words per minute. Who has not impatiently taken a magazine away from a friend who was reading some tidbit aloud in order to get through the material at a much faster rate? The average listener, then, has spare time. The question is, how will we use that time?

Too often we use our spare time for nonlistening activity. While the speaker is poking along at 125 words per minute, we compose a grocery list. We return to the speaker satisfied that we have missed nothing and soon dart away to ponder some tangential thought the speaker has raised in our minds. "When was it that I heard Milton Rokeach lecture? Oh, yes . . . It was . . ." By the time we return we may well have missed some critical detail. The good listener learns how to turn the spare time to use as a listener; a few suggestions for the use of "spare time" follow.

Search for ideas

As students of speech, you know that speaking is a purposive activity, that the speaker has a pattern of ideas to communicate to listeners. As a listener you should search for the speaker's ideas. This search must be a conscious and diligent one. We cannot expect every speaker to be efficient enough to make us recognize every idea with little or no effort on our part. Try to find the thesis. Try to determine the main points upon which the thesis rests and the ideas subordinate to the main points. In so doing, remember three key words: *anticipate, verify,* and *review.*

Try to predict from the outset what the speaker's thesis will be, and what each succeeding point will be. Attempting to predict what the speaker will say is one way to use your spare listening time constructively. Some speakers may unwittingly mislead you, so you should make your decisions tentative. You know, as a speaker, that ideas are not always stated explicitly; you must, therefore, search for unstated ideas.

Try to verify your predictions about the ideas underlying the speech. Search for statements and materials that would lead you to reject or modify your interpretations. Do not be easily satisfied that you know what the speech is all about. If a speaker is good, even an idea explicitly stated and recognized will be made increasingly clear and meaningful to you as the speech develops.

Take notes

You will try to make a pattern of the ideas as the speech unfolds. In so doing you will be tempted to make notes. This impulse is a good one. You have a record of what you have heard and making notes often helps you sharpen your understanding. But making notes can be hazardous. It is easy to become too involved in the note-making process and thereby to lose the thread of the speaker's thought. Keep your notes brief, and do not start making them immediately. Think and rethink an idea and then jot it down. Do not try to set it down in elaborate detail. The most useful notes, the notes that will indicate most accurately what was said, will be just a few reminders from which you can rework ideas carefully at your leisure later if you feel that the ideas are important ones to record. You'll probably understand better what is said and remember longer if you make few notes as you anticipate, verify your anticipations, and review the speaker's ideas.

Reviewing is important. Use your excess listening time to recapitulate for the speaker, even as the speaker should occasionally review for you. A review will help you anticipate new ideas and make a pattern of the whole. You will be better able to discover how ideas fit together or fail to fit together. A final review should summarize your search for the ideas of a speech.

Find the basis of ideas

As a student of speech, you should recognize examples, statistics, analogies, and testimony. When you recognize pieces of supporting material you should be looking for the relationship between them and the ideas that they are purported to support. Finding an example may help you recognize an idea or understand it more clearly; it will also help you determine whether or not the idea is founded upon substantial material. This is not to say that you can immediately judge the quality of ideas. You should be willing to delay that judgment, but you should also note the material upon which the ideas rest and make some tentative estimates to which you may return.

Lay the groundwork for analyzing the quality of ideas

Your aim in searching for the speaker's ideas and the materials upon which these ideas are based should be to establish a basis upon which to analyze the worth of those ideas. As we have indicated consistently, this final analysis will be the result of painstaking listening during the speech and careful thought after the speech is over. A final analysis will ordinarily not be reached through a quick flash in which all truth is made clear. Accept or reject ideas tentatively, but be sure you understand those ideas. Continually analyze and check the ideas from a speech as you understand them. As far as the speech itself is concerned, you will often be made uneasy by an unsupported assertion or the relation of one assertion to another or to the supporting material the speaker uses. When you find symptoms of something amiss in thought, you should seek out the causes. You may not decide finally that the speaker's ideas or materials are deficient. If you do decide that the speaker's beliefs do not merit acceptance, be sure that you are not being blinded by your own biases and emotions. Remember, you are interested in judging not simply the speaker's ideas, but your own as well.

In judging the acceptability of claims made, the material that we have already discussed, especially in Chapter 3, should be of use to you as will the material in Chapters 10 through 14 of this book. Listeners as well as speakers analyze social problems, causes, solutions, and values. You should study the material in these later chapters; they will provide an introduction to the sort of analytic activity you must carry on in order to listen intelligently to others.

Use feedback to check perceptions

Although we have been discussing speeches as uninterrupted units of discourse not allowing much freedom for speaker and audience to interact, skillful use of feedback to a speaker can facilitate listeners' checking their perceptions of a speaker's message. Since a good speaker will be scanning the audience, trying to use their responses as a guide to continuing thought development, the facial expressions that indicate confusion or uncertainty in normal conversation may be used to suggest that the speaker restate or rephrase an idea. When confronted with such cues, some speakers will even pause in their development of ideas to ask listeners to identify the point or points of confusion.

When a speaker solicits verbal feedback during a speech or, more frequently, during a question period after the speech, listeners can check their perceptions best by paraphrasing what they have heard and asking the speaker if that paraphrase accurately expresses the speaker's intended message. Unless you have simply not heard the words spoken, asking for repetition of a statement does little to clarify the message; a restatement gives the speaker clearer indication of how you have perceived the idea and that, in turn, allows the speaker opportunity to adapt to the level of understanding that has been reached. When speaker and listener work together in this manner, they both can be more confident that the audience's response, whether positive or negative, will be based on mutual understanding rather than misperception.

Be alert for the signs of poor listening

No matter how well-intentioned we may be as we begin to listen, we shall be prone to lapse into inefficiency in this activity just as we may in any other. We should, therefore, be alert for the signs of our poor listening. We have mentioned the principal signs already, but we shall review them briefly.

Beware of negative evaluations of the speaker, especially of the small matters of delivery. If you find yourself beginning to dwell on these, you are probably not searching for ideas. It would be a shame, for example, to have heard Einstein speak and to have come away only with the impression that he had a pronounced foreign accent. Negative evaluations are often the beginning of a rationalization for not listening. If, in the classroom situation, you wish to make a friendly suggestion to the speaker concerning some distracting mannerism, note it briefly and turn your attention to ideas and the material upon which those ideas are based. There will be plenty of time later to list and consider in detail negative evaluations of the speaker as a person after you have exhausted the potential worth of the ideas that you have heard.

If you find yourself composing rebuttals to what the speaker is saying, resist this impulse temporarily. Be sure you have heard and understood the message first. Often the tendency to make rebuttals is a sign that our attitudes are interfering with our listening. We should resolve to hold our truce until we have heard the speaker out.

Check your note taking. If you find yourself trying to copy in detail what is being said, you should remember that you are taking on a task that will probably prove impossible. Make only a few notes to help you remember. Expand and organize these notes later. Concentrate on ideas; anticipate, verify, and review them. With such concentration and a few jottings, you will understand and remember more of what the speaker has to say.

LISTEN TO CLASSROOM LECTURES

We have been discussing listening to speeches in general. Whereas most of what we have said will apply to the special case of listening to classroom lectures, you may need to make some special adjustments to your particular circumstances, adjustments you would not necessarily make if you were listening to a political campaign speech or to a speech after a dinner. Most especially, you must adjust your note-taking habits. Inasmuch as classroom lectures are undoubtedly the listening situation most frequently encountered by users of this book, we should consider their special circumstances briefly.

A college lecture has been defined, not always inaccurately, as a device for getting notes from the notebook of the professor to the notebook of the student without going through the head of either. We discussed the listener's motivation earlier; remember two assertions in relation to your motivation: (1) Intend to remember. You cannot listen passively to a lecturer and expect to retain much; you must listen actively intending to understand and to remember. (2) Do not always expect to understand the importance of what you hear immediately. Often one must submit frequently to a great deal of preliminary data before one can start to see connections between ideas and the value of the material presented.

Although students will vary in the amount and sorts of notes they take, we can generalize somewhat about taking lecture notes. Our generalizations will differ somewhat from those we made before concerning note taking. It is, of course, possible to try to take too many lecture notes just as it is quite possible to try to take too many notes in other situations. The graduate student who writes down everything the professor says, including "Good morning," takes too many; but the average college freshman takes too few. Sketchy notes may fail to record many of the lecturer's subordinate ideas, the limitations the speaker puts on some general statements, and the support given for these ideas. The poor student's notes are thus oversimplified to the point that even if all that is recorded becomes committed to memory, the student cannot hope to perform well in an examination, much less have a thorough knowledge of the subject studied. *One should take as many notes as one can while still comprehending the relation of what is being said to what has been said.* One should, therefore, try to record the speaker's main themes, subordinate ideas, and support of them as accurately as possible.

Again we should warn the student that it may not be possible to make a perfect record while listening. One should be willing to invest a few minutes after the lecture to reorganize one's notes, perhaps filling out in more detail some of the items; one may even have to rework and recopy everything jotted down during the lecture.

Reworking lecture notes will not only create a more orderly record, but it will help your memory considerably. Most forgetting occurs immediately after learning. Thus after hearing a lecture, we forget more during the first five minutes than we forget in any subsequent five minutes. We can slow the curve of forgetting and further stamp in the lecturer's ideas and materials by spending even as little as five minutes reviewing immediately following the lecture. When one reviews lecture notes immediately following a lecture, one remembers six months later twice as much as would be recalled had this time not been spent in review.

Good listening is especially valuable in a speech class. A class discussion after speeches, which concentrates on the speaker's ideas and upon the basis of those ideas, will probably reveal how difficult it is to communicate accurately one person's thoughts to others. As a speaker, such discussion should stimulate you to plan your purpose and thesis carefully, to pattern ideas simply, and to find a variety of concrete supporting materials to help make your ideas clear, interesting, and impelling. Such discussion can give you an insight into your listeners and into the general problems of communicating to an audience.

These guidelines will help you form good listening habits. Forming these habits is not a matter of applying a set of absolutely dependable rules; such rules do not exist. Skillful listening can only be built slowly and consciously by each individual.

LISTENING ASSIGNMENTS

For class speeches

1. After each speech, write quickly on a piece of paper the speaker's thesis and his main ideas. You might make brief notes during the speech, but do not try to make final, full statements of the ideas until the speaker has finished.
2. Give the notes to the speakers. Each speaker should summarize the statements, noting agreements and disagreements.
3. At the next class period, the speaker should report to the class the apparent successes and failures in achieving understanding between speaker and audience.

4. Discuss possible reasons for significant disagreements and lack of understanding among the listeners. Do not assume that all difficulties lie within
the speeches.

A report on a speech heard outside class

1. Choose a speech for the class to hear. If possible, find a speech that is
likely to be controversial, one toward which the members of the class are
likely to respond differently in terms of their beliefs.
2. Each person should write a report of what the speaker has said, stating
the speaker's thesis, summarizing the major ideas, and indicating briefly
the supporting material on which each idea is based.
3. Each person may write several paragraphs responding to the worth of the
speech in general and any of the ideas in particular that stimulate comment.
4. In class discussion, compare what the listeners heard. Concentrate, especially at first, on item two. Are there significant differences in the reports?
Can these differences be accounted for by differences in the beliefs held
by the listeners?

10 thinking and speaking about problems

He who does not understand history is doomed to repeat it.
SANTAYANA

Great speeches have only one characteristic in common: *Each great speech is concerned with a great problem.* The kinds of problems may vary, the manner of the speaker may vary, but a brief glance at some great speeches shows that they never vary from their concern with a great problem. The first great speech of which we have record was the announcement by Moses of the Ten Commandments; this speech was generated by moral problems that were destroying the Children of Israel. The most famous speech in ancient Greece was Pericles' Funeral Oration, a speech that may have been ghost-written for him by a famous woman, Aspasia, and was the first speech known to ask and answer the question "What is the nature and significance of a free society?" The speaking of Socrates was of a different sort; Socrates gave no speeches, but rather asked questions. The questions were of such decisive brilliance that they performed two great functions. First, Socrates' questions revealed the unintelligent ethical base of Athenian life with such brilliance that some Athenians knew that they must either change their way of life or destroy Socrates. These people regrettably took the easy way: Socrates' death marks the end of the Golden Age of Greece. Nevertheless, even after his death, the speaking of Socrates performed its second function, namely, generating dozens of schools of philosophy. There is no philosophy originating in the Western world that does not claim Socrates as its founder; he may well be the greatest Founding Father of all time. Different problems generated the speaking of Pericles and Demosthenes: their speeches were fired by the necessity of understanding and preserving the first free society. The speaking of Jesus also arose from problems; one need not be a convinced Christian to recognize that the Sermon on the Mount is one of the great speeches, and that it was generated by the problems of the artificial ritualism into which religion had fallen, and by the desperate need of religion, and of man himself, for a transformation.

In modern times as well, great speeches come about only when they are generated by a great problem. From the speaking of Moses to that of Abraham Lincoln and on to that of Franklin Roosevelt and John F. Kennedy, only problems of significance have generated speaking of genuine excellence.

And so will it always be. There is no possibility of writing a great speech, or even a significant one, unless in some way, the speech is a response to a significant problem. Nor can a great speech be understood apart from its concern with the problem that sparked it.

Great speeches are generated only by great problems and this reason is sufficient for devoting the rest of this book to the study of problems. Nevertheless, additional and compelling reasons justify a strong concern with problems in a book about speaking.

But what of us more ordinary mortals who will, likely, never give, nor have the opportunity to give, a great speech? We, too, must learn to understand problems, for problems usually represent the reasons we speak. We speak if our rights are being trampled on, if our opportunities are not fulfilled; and if we learn to speak well about problems we will be in a stronger position to help lead to the solution of the problems we face, and in a stronger position to help our people, our nation, and our culture solve problems. All of us who take the care to become informed can learn to speak well about problems we face. Let us look carefully at the nature of problems, for therein lies our chance for understanding them and solving them.

THE VALUE OF PROBLEMS

The ideal world, we might think, would be a place without any problems; indeed, Valhalla, Nirvana, and Heaven seem to be places where problems cannot exist. But on earth, the situation is different, because *when human beings respond to certain kinds of problems with great intelligence, and at the same time, with great vigor, we often rise to a higher level.* Some examples show the way problems help us develop: When we responded intelligently and vigorously to the problem of disease, we ended the great plagues, learned to restore the sick, and found ways to maintain good health until advanced age. When, at long last, we reacted intelligently and vigorously to the problem of poverty, we created scientific agriculture and invented means of producing great abundance. So successful has the industrial-scientific revolution been that it suggests that, at last, we can create enough goods to free the world from want, provided that the products from the industrial-scientific revolution are distributed to the people and provided that this same revolution does not, while producing goods, pollute the air, the land, and the water. At any rate, for the first time in history, in some countries, surpluses are a "problem." The same growth from intelligent and vigorous responses to problems develops not only great civilizations, but great nations as well: England solved the problem of being a small island that could not be self-sufficient by developing the most far-flung Empire in history. Holland, even though a tiny country, has at times led the world in art, philosophy, and in per capita wealth; even today she responds so intelligently and vigorously to the problem of land scarcity that if we managed all arable lands on earth as efficiently and productively as those in Holland are managed, our planet could support a population of ten times those now alive. America responded to the challenge of an almost perpetual labor shortage—which we still occasionally experience—not only by the tragic and cruel importation of slaves but also by becoming the most industrialized country on earth. If industrialism is not an unmixed blessing, at least it has been, since wage and hour controls, a more humane solution to a labor shortage than slavery, or than serfdom, or than cottage industry, all of which took a heavy toll of human time and human life. Thus do intelligent reactions to problems raise one to a higher level.

Not only does this principle of growth apply to civilizations and nations, but also to cities: Pittsburgh was infamous for being the world's smokiest city; after its smoke prevention program went into effect, it was, for a while, probably the cleanest of the Northern metropolises. The principle applies to individuals: perhaps it is not an accident that the greatest orator of antiquity, Demosthenes, was a stutterer, or that the greatest composer in history, Beethoven, became deaf, or that Milton, who could see so many things so clearly, was blind, or that the most active United States President up to his time was paralyzed. When we react intelligently and vigorously to certain kinds of problems, we reduce human misery, create new sources of strength, and find fresh possibilities for humane fulfillment. Problems, then, are like Mephistopheles in Goethe's *Faust:* They may "try" to do evil work, but in the end, they increase—instead of stultify—growth, provided, of course, that they are reacted to with both great intelligence and great vigor.

Why do problems—certain kinds, anyway—seem to bring out the best in human beings? At least five major reasons suggest that much of our speaking—as well as much of our education—should direct itself to means of locating and solving the great problems that beset us.

Thought

First, as John Dewey discovered, a problem is necessary to start thought. We do not think about our feet until the shoe pinches, nor about our health until we get sick, nor, perhaps, about achieving a genuine education until we realize we are dangerously ignorant. No man, said Dewey, even begins to think until he first notes a perplexity, a need, or as he put it, a "felt difficulty."[1] Because thought does not begin without a problem, a corollary is that when we are absorbed in petty problems, our thoughts are correspondingly petty. The suburbanite who believes his greatest problem is crab grass is not likely to reach great heights, except in lawn growing. The challenge of a significant problem may stimulate the best thinking and, with it, the best speaking.

Civilization

Second, problems bring out one's best—provided, again, that one responds intelligently and vigorously—because certain problems are the generating force behind all civilizations. Arnold Toynbee showed that each civilization arose not because the living was easy and human beings had time to think, but because the living was extremely difficult and *to survive, people were jolted into the necessity of thought.* To use his own words, civilizations arose as a result of a "challenge followed by a hitherto unprecedented effort."[2] Those societies that have remained primitive, Henri Bergson pointed out, are probably those in which the living was too easy and which never were required to stretch their minds by solving demanding problems.[3] Problems not only provide the necessary jolt to get a civilization going, but they seem to be the generating force behind the continued growth of civilizations. Whether or not a civilization continues to grow depends on the ability of a culture to respond to further problems—not merely problems of creating wealth, although wealth is needed, but also to problems in philosophy, in government, in the arts, or in economics, science, law, and religion. The failure of a culture to recognize such problems can cause the stultification and eventually the death of that culture. A response to problems is necessary not only to generate a civilization, but also to ensure its continued growth.

---

[1] *How We Think*, Boston (now Lexington) Mass., D. C. Heath & Company, 1910, p. 9. Perhaps the discovery that thought proceeds from problems—rather than from syllogisms—may turn out to be Dewey's greatest contribution to philosophy.

[2] Students interested in the study of civilizations will be stimulated by reading A *Study of History*, abr. by D. C. Sommervell, New York, Oxford University Press, Inc., 1946. The writer acknowledges that although he cannot accept the work of the later Toynbee, he is still grateful to Toynbee, for his *Study* provided one of the major stimulants that helped lead to the approach to speech here presented. Especially significant are Parts II, III, and IV.

[3] See *Two Sources of Morality and Religion*, New York, Doubleday & Company, Inc., Anchor Books, 1954, p. 172.

Motivation

Problems are, in the third place, the starting point of human motivation. All motives begin with a need, a desire, or with a lack, a deficiency. But the words *need, desire, lack,* and *deficiency* are merely other words for *problem.* Unless we have a need, a desire, a lack, or a deficiency, and perceive it as such, we cannot be motivated. Just as we are not motivated to eat unless we are hungry, neither can a horse led to water be made to drink until it feels thirsty. Problems are, under certain circumstances, energizing forces that can stimulate activity and drive human beings on to greater achievement.

Creativity

Fourth, problems are the prerequisite for creativity. "Necessity is the mother of invention," rightly runs the adage. Inventions may not always come when they are needed, but they will not likely come at all and will not be adopted until a need for them is perceived. Creativity in art, likewise, springs from a problem, although the problem may be merely the artist's wish to express something in a way different from the current style. Nevertheless, with no problems, there would be no creativity.

Democracy

Fifth, problems are especially important in a democratic state, for only a democratic state has institutionalized the possibility of locating and solving problems. Only a democratic state is persistently responsive to the problems of people, and only such a state offers the possibility of continued growth through perpetual problem solving.

Thus, problems, which often enough are a curse to human beings, still, when responded to with intelligence and vigor, can raise us to a higher level. Nor is there much mystery why, for when something is the starting point for thought, the generating force behind *civilization,* the basis for human *motivation,* and consequently, for human *energy,* the source of *creativity,* and the spark behind *democratic government,* that thing, indeed, could raise us to heights we could not otherwise reach. Problems are, therefore, the great dynamos behind the development of human beings and society.

Speeches that point out the great problems and, in a burst of intellectual vigor, help point to the solution of these problems, are of incalculable value to us. The rest of this book is devoted to helping you speak about problems in such a way that you may convert problems from forces that deprive and plague us to forces that will raise us to a higher level.

THE DANGER OF PROBLEMS

Suffering and degradation

When problems are not responded to with a combination of intelligence and vigor, or when people, because of weakness or lack of knowledge fail so to respond to them, problems do not invigorate, but only enervate. The history of problems is also the history of suffering and degradation. In our rich and free country, it is hard for us to conceive of what life was like for the more than seventy billion people estimated to have lived on earth before us. These people were plagued by disease, stunted by starvation, cursed by flood and famine, only to die an early death and to leave little record of their pains, sorrows, and fears. These people lived in hovels sometimes made of no more than grass and mud and yet were forced to build great palaces and tombs for the tyrants who enslaved them. They died chained to the oars of sinking galleys, or were abandoned to rot on thousands of half-forgotten battlefields, or were strangled by a disease that no one understood. Their survivors drew no welfare checks, and soon followed them to the grave. For billions of people, the problems of war, poverty, caste, tyranny, and disease brought suffering and degradation of a type that we are poorly equipped to imagine. For every person stimulated by problems, perhaps 10,000 or more suffer, weaken, and die.

Destruction of civilizations

In addition to heaping pains and sorrows upon human beings, unsolved problems are the cancers that weaken and destroy civilizations. The unsolved problem of fratricidal wars fought by the city-states of ancient Greece wasted the vigor and wealth of the Greeks, and helped kill, too soon, the first free civilization of the world. In India, caste systems strangled large masses who, had they been more free, might have added strength to the civilization. The problem of disease, virtually unsolved until a hundred years ago, brought plagues that dealt the final death blow to defeated Athens, later smothered dying Rome, and nearly destroyed Europe in the Middle Ages; in each of these cases, a plague put at least a third of the populace in a hastily dug and unmarked grave, and left millions more permanently enfeebled. Declining Rome reminds us that ethical and moral blight can weaken a great culture. The value of the great institutions of Rome was destroyed because these institutions were perverted into devices that filled the vaults of the corrupt with gold, which they used to purchase power over the more deserving. The unsolved problems of war, poverty, caste, disease, political immorality, and tyranny have obliterated every civilization yet created, except as yet, our own, and our culture has done a minimum to bring these destructive problems under control.

CURRENT PROBLEMS

The wealth of our country often leads some of our citizens to feel that these problems are past, but they are not, for problems have caused more intense suffering in our century than in any other era. Poverty in the world at large is as great as ever, and more people are alive to suffer it. The average person in the world, despite the wealth of a few countries, has an income of about

$130 per year. In India, the average income is $75 a year, and annual income is still lower for perhaps a billion people. However low the cost of living is in countries having so low an income, no one can come near to achieving his or her potential on such income. The problem of poverty is with us, and is a constant source of weakness to the world, as well as a source of danger to the wealthy countries.

Nor must we think that only others have these problems. Even in some highly civilized countries, systems of caste and prejudice dangerously weaken large populations so that the total strength of a country that tolerates a caste system (or its milder form, prejudice) is much less than it might have been had the nation developed the strengths of all its people. These problems are not restricted to underdeveloped countries; some of the worst problems are found only in the wealthy countries. Even the richest countries have relegated their women to an inferior caste, thereby losing the potential skills, intelligence, and much of the value of half the population. Especially in the more developed countries, the rate of crime, of suicide, of insanity and of pollution seems to soar each year. And especially only in the most civilized countries is the problem of war one that can bring instant devastation. Only the richest countries can fight expensive, devastating, and mistaken wars. Our many comforts must not blind us to the fact that this century is the bloodiest in history. More have died from war in the twentieth century, and more have been killed in pogroms—particularly in Germany and Russia—than lived on earth in the fifth century, B.C. The destructive power available in the form of atomic fission is such that we could destroy Russia nineteen times—and she could destroy us only twelve times. Enough nuclear power is available to give the equivalent of one-half ton of TNT to every man, woman, and child on earth. No one knows—or, at least, experts disagree about—how much longer our air, land, and water can be polluted and still sustain animal, plant, and human life. The great problems are not from the past, but exist here and now; they are problems for you and me, and will decide much of our destiny. These problems must not be forgotten, for Western civilization seems to have at least started down the same road that has taken all previous cultures to their funeral pyre. A failure to study these problems may not only increase human misery and human degradation, but it could blast the last remaining civilization from the earth, and with it the best creations of civilization: philosophy and wisdom, art and science, freedom, religion, and perhaps even human existence. If, perhaps, our last chance is at hand, it is well that we learn all we can about problems.

SPEAKING AND PROBLEMS

Speaking, one of the great drive-shafts that transmits the power to propel man's civilizations, likewise acts as a rudder that steers. The course and speed are set in part—in large part—by what speakers say. Therefore, *the aim of speaking should be to direct us toward the solution of our problems with the greatest possible speed.* The speaker must awaken those who sleep or who are indifferent, and must help others see the unnoticed danger and understand it. Speakers must direct us away from the false and petty problems that set us off course. The men and women who speak hold the destiny of our civilization at least partly in their hands. For this reason, the rest of this book focuses on problems in the hope that such a focus will help us improve the quality of our civilization and earn for all of us the chance for survival.

Some think one should not speak of a nation's problems, and that to do so is unpatriotic. To such people, we should point out that one of the highest forms of patriotism is to study the problems of one's people so that the problems might be solved; such problem solving can insure the permanence and well-being of a nation, whereas constant super-adoration of the nation cannot. The Golden Age of Augustus was the best attempt to save a nation by praising it: Augustus paid poets, artists, and architects to sing the glory of Rome and greatness of the Roman gods. Such praise did not save Rome, and the Empire grew weak even as the choruses of praise grew louder. In the end, the problems destroyed the Empire and then the city itself.

Among our greatest needs is to develop speakers who can help direct us toward the solution of our problems. No society can move forward—or long exist—when its speakers lull people to sleep, or when "orators" lead people to believe that there are no significant problems, or when lecturers produce no more than interesting but superficial trivia.

In the present age, the task of speaking so as to solve problems is greater than in all previous ages, because the problems themselves are greater in magnitude, if not also in number. Perhaps the results will be more gratifying than in past eras, for we know more about solving the problems of war, poverty, caste, disease, and tyranny than in any previous age. The task is worth the unprecedented effort that will be required, for we can either climb to the threshold of a better world or plunge to destruction.

DISCOVERING PROBLEMS

If our speakers are to direct us to solutions, they must first search for whatever gnaws at the human spirit; they must find the sicknesses of our age, and they must discover the forces that may be weakening the last remaining great culture. Speakers, however, often have not performed these crucial functions. One could cite illustrations from Rome where speakers (as well as poets and dramatists) never discussed the grimy poverty of most Romans, or contemporary Russia where speakers cannot discuss all the Soviet Union's policies, but let us take America for example, for the failure to discuss problems sometimes happens in democracies as well. In 1932, the life savings of millions of Americans were wiped out as banks closed, and the income of millions more was stopped as businesses and industries shut down. Mass starvation was prevented only by setting up bread lines and soup kitchens. Yet in the presidential election of that year, one of the two principle political parties of the country tried to make the issue of the election not the depression, but prohibition. Party speakers insisted that "Prosperity is just around the corner," and proceeded to discuss the evils of Demon Rum. These speakers who tried to divert attention to prohibition failed to grasp the central problem of the people, but the voters did not. The party that ignored the important problem of that day was not returned to the nation's highest office for twenty years. The penalties for failing to treat great problems are often not so mild as this.

Intelligent speaking about problems is not easy, and requires special study. One cannot learn much about attacking the problems of the world by speaking about "How I spent my summer vacation"—unless, perhaps, he was in the Peace Corps—or by speaking about "How to hold a golf club," or about "My most embarrassing moment." Just as bad are those speech topics that are selected to develop confidence (but that do nothing to foster competence and hence do not work) and that aim at making the speaker merely a skillful or even deceitful salesman. Such speaking encourages the least possible growth in both the speaker and his audience.

Criteria for selecting problems

But what *is* a "significant" problem? To offer pontifically a succinct definition might be to omit some problems of importance. We cannot say, for example, that a significant problem is one that influences a large number of people—a national or international problem, for example. For local, even personal problems that occur in the classroom, the college, or the community likewise take their toll and should be recognized and solved. We will, therefore, offer some criteria, and if a problem meets any one of these, it may be worth speaking about:

1. A significant problem may be one that has caused the decline of a previous civilization. The problems of war, poverty, caste, tyranny, and disease are the classic problems of humanity, and wherever one finds civilizations in decline, one or more of these problems is a significant part of the cause.
2. A significant problem is one that has caused or causes human suffering.
3. A significant problem is one that limits human achievement.
4. A significant problem is one that, when solved, releases new energy.
5. A significant problem is one that prevents growth and development.
6. A significant problem is one that forces on us an important choice.
7. A significant problem is one that violates an important value.

In any event, the kinds of problems that are worth solving vary from personal to international from agricultural to zoological, from economic to spiri-

tual, from political to religious. The array is vast, but the rewards for selecting the most significant problems are great, and the penalties for failing to do
so are terrifying.

A classification of these problems will help point out their variety and
thus, perhaps, encourage better choices. Problems may be classified as (1)
timely or timeless, (2) conscious or unconscious, and as (3) survival or growth
problems.

Timely and timeless problems

The kinds of problems one reads about in the newspapers and magazines
are, generally, timely problems—problems of shortages and surpluses, floods
and famines, strikes and lockouts, accidents and wars. These problems are
urgent problems, but they are problems that change, disappear, or increase
and, especially, timely problems are ones that theoretically can be solved. In
1932, for example, the timely problems were how to prevent banks from
closing, how to restore employment, and how to increase purchasing power.
By 1942, the timely problems had changed drastically: They were how to
win the war against Germany and Japan, how to keep prices down, and how
to prevent strikes in defense industries. By 1952, the problems had again
changed: They were how to reduce agricultural surpluses, how to make the
world secure against the aggression of our former ally, the Soviet Union, and
how to win the war in Korea. In 1962, the problems again changed so that
they were how to restore full employment, how to desegregate the schools,
how to get the Soviet missiles out of Cuba, and how to land the first man on
the moon. In 1972 the problems were inflation and unemployment, pollution, corruption in government, crime, civil rights, and military spending. In
1982, they will have changed again. But although these problems change
quickly, there is no reason to disregard them. Nor is there the slightest
reason to think, if we ignored them, that they would go away. Timely problems demand our attention, and unless we give it, these problems can become chronic. By quick recognition, careful diagnosis, and a bit of luck, we
can render these problems short-lived.

Some problems, however, are present now and will be in any age. They
are problems such as "How should one live?" or "What are the potentials
and limitations of the human being?" or "What is a just society?" or "What is
the significance of art?" or "How can a society provide for the individuality of
its members, and yet maintain order?" These are questions each generation
must answer, and does answer, although the answers are usually not carefully thought out. These questions were also asked 2,000 or more years ago;
the Egyptians answered these same questions as did the Greeks and Aztecs
after them, and so must our sons and daughters.

Timeless problems are thought, in our culture, to be "impractical." Timeless questions are ignored by the super-practical person, because like philosophy, "they bake no bread." In other words, they do not tell us what to do in

a specific situation, they do not increase our earning power, nor do they usually contribute to our prestige, at least not until recently. The practical man doesn't know it, but he has already made up his mind about the timeless problems—and has done so without the careful scrutiny he would give a business deal. Although timeless problems have been thought of as unessential in our culture, the relative interest in timely and timeless problems is reversed in a few oriental cultures. In our own culture, the timeless is not studied in school, although bookkeeping is and so, too, is cooking. We emphasize the practical and, hence, Western peoples have more difficulty understanding and discussing timeless problems than do other peoples.

Nevertheless, timeless problems are extremely important. *Underlying each timely problem are one or more timeless problems.* "How much should the city spend on the art museum?" is a timely question. But the answer must—or should, at any rate—depend on an answer to the question, "What is the significance of art in human life?" If art is merely a means for momentary escape, a means for a bit of variety or for amusement only, then perhaps we should not spend so much as if art is a means of symbolizing ideas that cannot be put in words but that can be communicated through color and form. "How much should we tax people to support the schools?" is another practical question, but underlying the various answers is the timeless problem of "What is the significance of education?" "What should our foreign policy be?" is a timely problem, but underlying it are questions such as "What are our responsibilities to the rest of humanity?" and "How may we guarantee the responsibilities of others toward us?"

The timeless problems of living have generally been neglected by our culture. College students will find it easier to prepare a speech on a timely problem, yet these more neglected permanent problems demand that people speak about them. Each age gives new answers and re-examines old answers. A speaker who would speak well in the twentieth century must be informed about timeless questions and the answers given by different ages. If our speakers will impress on our people the significance of these timeless problems, perhaps education will respond by helping our people understand the often unnoticed but, nevertheless, demanding timeless problems; for these, too, determine our successes and failures.

Conscious and unconscious problems

We are relatively aware that war is a problem, that education can be improved, that periodic inflation and deflation pose threats to our economy, that medical care is not always so good nor so universally available as it should be, and that our air and rivers are polluted. We are conscious of these problems, for they are discussed in our newspapers, over radio and television, and sometimes even from the pulpit. They rightly deserve our attention, and we must work toward solutions of them.

Some problems, however, are not so clearly seen as these; they are problems of which humanity does not seem aware. Sometimes it takes centuries to bring one of these problems to consciousness. Slavery did not seem to be a problem to the Greeks; Aristotle avowed that some men were by nature slaves. But by the 1860s in the United States, through the influence of the abolitionists and with the effect of *Uncle Tom's Cabin*, slavery became recognized as a significant enough problem so that thousands enlisted in the Union Army to end the problem. Cruel and inhuman treatment of children seemed no problem early in the nineteenth century, but with the novels of Charles Dickens portraying the plight of the child, legislation was soon enacted to ensure the safety of children.

We are made conscious of problems, not so much, at first, by writers of polemics, but often by artists, sculptors, poets, and novelists. Much later, these problems receive consideration from philosophers, and long after the sensitive artist has tried to symbolize the problem, psychologists, sociologists, and news commentators take up the problem. To take an example, the idea that life is becoming mechanized and therefore somewhat subhuman seems first to have been reflected by cubist painters and musical composers about the turn of the century. (Søren Kierkegaard, the Danish philosopher, had anticipated the problem, but he was largely ignored, suggesting perhaps that unconscious problems are best first depicted by less discursive forms than philosophy until the people have been prepared by poets, artists, musicians, and novelists for discursive consideration.) After 1900, ten or more years elapsed, during which time artists were depicting the mechanization of life through cubist painting; then novelists such as Franz Kafka and H. G. Wells, wrote about how life was becoming more and more meaningless and increasingly more dehumanized, despite our proudly proclaimed progress and, indeed, precisely because of this progress. Still later, by the middle of the century, certain philosophers—usually existentialists and phenomenologists—began to find a growing sense of alienation, loneliness, and futility in modern life. Eventually, psychologists and sociologists brought the skills of their professional orientation to the problem. The hippie movement was a popular reaction against the meaninglessness, mechanicalness and lovelessness of big business, big labor and big education. Today, the problem is well known. Thus, unconscious problems are recognized slowly, and usually noted first by the artist, the poet, the novelist, and only later by politicians, editorial writers, and polemicists.

To discover problems that exist but of which we are unconscious, the speaker must cultivate the study of art, music, and of contemporary writing other than that found in news magazines and even in the best idea magazines. One should try to discover what men and women are trying to reflect or symbolize in art and music; one should read the most advanced contemporary writers, especially those of uncommon sensitivity. Perhaps through these media, we will learn to look at our society more clearly and will be able to keep in mind that there are problems of which we are not yet aware that must, one day, be the subject for discursive discourse.

Survival and growth problems

Certain kinds of problems must be solved in some degree if we are to live at all. The problem of obtaining safe and clean food in adequate amounts to support life is a "survival" problem. The dangers of food contaminated by poor handling and by super-pesticides, the danger of polluted water and air, the dangers of home accidents, and of automobile and industrial accidents constitute survival problems. The classic problems that seem to have destroyed all previous civilizations—war, poverty, caste, disease, and tyranny—are survival problems and are of enormous significance. In our own times, these problems seem to increase in number, and they must be met if we are to survive and to live securely.

Yet even if we were to solve *all* these problems, if we were all to have full—and even overfull—stomachs, and to be as safe as a baby in his crib, we would still find life unsatisfying, for when our survival needs are reasonably well met, a new set of needs arise. We will call these needs *growth* problems, as does A. H. Maslow.[4] These problems are unique to human beings, for no cat or dog, nor even the highest of the apes, seem to encounter them. To human beings, life must offer more than a full stomach, or be unsatisfying and uninteresting. According to Maslow, once one has enough to eat and can live with security, one begins to feel the need for more than food and security; the next step in the ladder of growing needs is that, after experiencing reasonable security in survival needs, one then feels the need for love, for affection, and for admiration from others. But once this need is reasonably well met, still another set of growth needs emerge; one then feels the call of "higher" needs: perhaps we wish to make sense out of our world, or wish to interpret the world in art, music, or literature. At any rate, when certain basic needs are met, we begin to feel the pressure to create, to build, to grow, to understand, to symbolize, to compose; the call of the trinity of Western culture—the good, the true, and the beautiful—is most fully manifest in those whose needs for survival and whose needs for others have been somewhat gratified. The higher, more philosophic needs permit man to rise to new levels, and lead us to evolve in directions impossible for other animals. These growth needs offer the possibility of continuing the transformation of human beings and society beyond any known limit.

But the growth problems of an individual or of a society are not easy to locate. A frustration of growth needs does not cause the same kind of pain that a frustration of the lower needs does. When one is thirsty, the nervous system leaves no doubt in one's consciousness that one needs water. When one is in pain, the nervous system can usually help tell what is wrong. But a frustration of a higher need is often ambiguous, and may result in behavior that does not solve the growth problem. When, for example, one suffers from being misunderstood, or when one suffers from not being accepted and

---

[4] *Motivation and Personality*, New York, Harper and Brothers (now Harper & Row, Publishers, Inc.), 1954, chap. 8.

liked by others, there is no specific set of nerve endings that make this need clear. Even though one's greatest need is for acceptance by others, one may become antisocial and behave as if friends were the last thing one wanted. Higher growth problems are even less possible to feel than these psychological problems, and are harder to diagnose. Yet their call, although vague, is powerful, especially today. Today we have full stomachs, and grow richer every year, but we hunger for a vague something, and life is somehow boring. Our growth needs, today, are at their all-time high. If we locate and gratify them, we can create, build, understand, and thus transform ourselves into something uniquely and grandly human. Despite the press of our survival problems, let us try to locate some of the needs we have that will lead us to new levels of existence.

Education and the location of problems

An intelligent speaker must be on the outlook for significant problems— whether they are timely or timeless, conscious or unconscious, survival or growth problems. Speakers must constantly consult the best thinking of the best minds both in our age and in the past. We must read widely, wisely, and well; we must observe and feel; and we must think about what we have read, observed, and felt. We should study problems in college courses, where we often can find information about economic, political, social, and international problems. We should study literature, at least because it abounds in reactions to problems, particularly to timeless philosophical and ethical problems. We should study history and anthropology to discover how other peoples have responded to their problems or failed to respond. We must learn much, for only if we do will we be able to speak intelligently about the problems that confront us and that might, one day, destroy us.

Thus the starting point of good speaking must be the speaker's own education, and not a search for some magic formula, for some trick that will make people listen, or for some device that will persuade. If speakers, instead, speak from a deep understanding of problems, their speeches will be colored, somewhat unconsciously by the sense of values imparted by this depth, and will earn the speakers a hearing that no bag of tricks nor cheap attention-getting devices can. Rather, the audience will listen because it perceives the significance of the speakers' ideas and not because the speakers have tricked them into listening. Thus the starting point for good speaking springs from intelligent choice of ideas, from careful reading and thought, and from a constant willingness to search for the significant.

PRESENTING PROBLEMS TO AUDIENCES

Once a speaker has decided to speak on a certain problem, he or she must search for ways of leading an audience to grasp the importance of that problem. Certain general ideas will enable an audience to recognize and feel the significance of a problem.[5] The speaker should try to use each of the lines of argument to see which units work best for his speech. Quite obviously he will find that some applications of a particular line of argument will be fruitless, but he will also find those lines of argument that *do* yield usable discourse and that will help him to compose some effective units. The speaker must, however, be selective. One should *use as few of the lines of argument as possible*, because one can gain impact from selecting the best ideas if one supports these intensively with statistics, examples, testimony, and the like. Therefore, the speaker should select the best and most effective methods of leading the audience to accept the problem as important and supply a barrage of support for them.

To locate the one or two lines of argument that are best to use, the speaker should attempt to select those that are *most appropriate to the problem, to the audience, to the occasion on which the speech will be given, and to the speaker*. These four aspects of the speech situation should govern one's choice of the following lines of argument:

1. *Show that the problem is a source of danger, suffering, or degradation to those who experience it.* If your problem is the world food supply, you can help us feel its importance if you illustrate it by showing what it is like to be a member of a starving family in India, or by giving statistics about the shortage of food throughout the world, or by supplying the testimony of experts on the shortage of food. We recognize a problem as important when we know that it is hurting others. *But we recognize the problem even more clearly when we understand that these people who suffer are like ourselves.* Speakers must remind us that the sufferers have some of the same aims, hopes, fears, and troubles that we do, that they are hurt by the same things, or that they make the same mistakes that we do. If then, you can show that the problem causes suffering, and can show that the sufferers' goals, aspirations, and needs are like our own, you may tend to lead the audience to recognize the problem.

2. *Show that the problem, directly or indirectly, injures the audience.* Most of the great problems of other people influence us because our world is tied together by communication, transportation, and commerce. When someone, however anonymous anywhere in the world is poor, that person cannot buy from our industries and thus cannot help keep our own people employed. When someone anywhere in the world is degraded to the extent that his or her abilities cannot function, the world, although it may never be aware of it, has lost those abilities. When we treat minority races, or women, or anyone who suffers some form of caste system as if they were less than

[5] The reader who is rhetorically sophisticated will recognize in these general ideas, a remnant of the idea from ancient rhetoric of *topoi*, which, when used intelligently and in moderation, will help the student direct energy and will suggest ideas one might not otherwise have thought of using.

human, we not only degrade them, but we ourselves have lost the understanding, the compassion, the contribution they might have made. If one
could calculate what percentage of our people are reduced to ineffectiveness
by conscious and unconscious caste systems we might become aware of how
great our loss has been. Roughly half our population are women, who are
generally relegated to inferior status, inferior salary, and inferior feelings.
Other portions of our people are members of a race, religion, national origin,
occupation, sexual orientation, or political belief that renders them ineffective. Even people who are overweight are subject to an unwarranted and
thoughtless prejudice that prevents them from making friends and getting
jobs. All these types of castes prevent those who suffer from caste from making their maximum contribution to us all; they earn less, and hence can buy
less to keep the machines of industry going; because they earn less, they pay
fewer taxes, and others must pay more. When suffering embitters people,
the world loses those who might influence their associates to be more understanding and more compassionate. Sometimes we have not understood our
relatedness to others. In the 1920s some people considered it humorous to
joke about the starving Chinese on the other side of the earth. Some of those
who joked lived to see their sons and grandsons die in Korea and Vietnam
fighting those embittered by starvation.

Intelligent speakers must find support for the idea that the problems of
others are the problems of us all. We must locate the facts and let our imagination work to see the relation between others and our audience. It may not
be easy to show a comfortably seated audience that the pains of others are
the problems of each of us, but it is one of the surest ways to arouse interest
in a problem.

3. *Show that the problem prevents the operation of an ideal and growth
toward it.* In these days of two cars in many garages and a sirloin on every
barbecue grill, we yet sense that something is lacking in our lives. Life is
more than riding in a big car, more than overeating, and more than gratifying the obvious natural urges. We have spoken of these "higher" needs
previously. Life is unsatisfying when we cannot create and feel creative,
when we cannot make sense out of the multiplicity and chaos of the universe, or when contentment with physical comforts begins to breed boredom
and emptiness of soul. The person with the full stomach recognizes, vaguely,
a certain emptiness and if one's stomach is not too full, one will begin the
search anew. But as we have seen, these uniquely human desires are not
easy to recognize because there is no sense organ connected with them to
bring specific pain. The hungry person feels hunger pangs, but the uncrea-
tive person feels no specific pain, and is more like an unfeeling apple that
rots while still hanging on the tree. Yet everywhere, even in the savage
state, human beings will still invent art if it is absent. Those blocked from
creativity in their jobs will find an outlet, however distorted, in their family,
in their sports, or through cruelty and destructiveness, until, when age takes

its toll, their creativity is permanently smothered. Somehow, in the late twentieth century, we begin to realize that we do not live by bread alone. Today books about ideals, philosophy, religion, art, ethics, and values are selling better than ever before; presumably, some of these books are being read. One can notice a hunger in audiences for intelligent consideration of values and ideals. If the speaker can locate the values that have potency in our time and show that a problem prevents the operation of these values, audiences will listen. This process requires maturity and intelligence, but it is an effective one.

4. *Show that the problem is a fundamental one.* If you can show us that the problem is fundamental because it causes other problems, we will listen. Poverty, war, caste, disease, and tyranny have destroyed whole civilizations in the past; yet perhaps these problems are not *fundamental.* A religious leader can insist that they are manifestations of the failure to be our brother's keeper. A scientist may insist that they are all the result of failure to use intelligent sources of investigation to find the facts. A politician may insist that they are the result of the wrong economic system, and a good democrat might insist that if the democratic system were practiced, the people might solve their own problems. All of these are attempts to show that some other formulation is more fundamental. We will listen if we think a particular problem is more fundamental in the sense that it may engender other problems.

5. *Show that the problem is recognized by others.* Many experiments in psychology and sociology show how we are influenced by the opinions of others. Sherif has done some of the most clever work on this matter with what he calls the "auto-kinetic" effect.[6] If you are in a totally dark room, and a tiny light the size of a grain of wheat is turned on, the light will seem to move. The light, of course, is stationary, but the uncontrollably jerky movements of one's eyes make it seem to move. Because the room is so dark, no one can tell how far the light "moves." Now suppose a group of five are put into the room, and four of them are told to say that they believe that the light moves about two feet, but the fifth person is unaware of this deception. Generally, on hearing the responses of the other four, this fifth person will also report that the light moves about two feet. We tend to recognize things in the way that those about us recognize them. Thus if we can show that others recognize a problem, we can be more certain of convincing an audience of its importance.

But there are sound and unsound, ethical and unethical ways of using this technique. Audiences are not influenced by everyone who recognizes a problem. An audience may be influenced, however, if those who recognize

---

[6] Muzaber Sherif, *An Outline of Social Psychology,* New York, Harper and Brothers (now Harper & Row, Publishers, Inc.), 1948, p. 266. This work is cited because it gives a more adequate account of the auto-kinetic effect than Sherif's more recent works.

the problem are highly regarded by that audience. In a famous speech at Cooper Union, Abraham Lincoln argued that the federal government had a right to control slavery in federal territory. Lincoln demonstrated that "our fathers who framed the Constitution" understood the problem as he interpreted it; he did so by showing that the majority of the signers each acted to limit the extension of slavery in some way, and, thus, that those the audience admired disapproved of slavery. Lincoln's appeal was more elaborate and painstaking than the hackneyed appeal to "the founding fathers" by the Fourth-of-July orator or the office seeker. Audiences are not much impressed by an attempt to show that "experts"—unnamed and unqualified—endorse a certain program of action or a certain brand of toothpaste. Use of such techniques merits the cool reception that an intelligent audience will give the sophistic speaker. Thus this method of bringing an audience to recognize what others have recognized, in the hands of the TV announcer or the ward-heeling politician, may not represent the application of intelligence to speaking. Yet men such as Abraham Lincoln could use it intelligently, effectively, and with originality. Try it, but use it well.

6. *Show that the problem makes our society or the institutions in it operate less effectively than they should.* We often recognize the importance of a problem by realizing that it causes our government, educational system, family system, or businesses to function poorly. These kinds of problems are called *dysfunctional* problems because they pervert, render ineffective, or slow down the operation of needed institutions. Thus one can show how corruption in government delivers power to those who should not have power, or how the rising divorce rate threatens children who ought to be free from the neurotic manifestations of insecurity. This method, of course, requires knowledge of how our institutions work. No simple, unsupported assertion that a problem may bring about a malfunction of an institution will be effective. The student must corroborate the assertion with examples, testimony, and other support to show that the problem causes a maladjustment of one or more of our institutions. When carefully substantiated, the method can be convincing, but the student who is unable to develop such support should not use this method.

7. *Other methods.* One can show that a problem interferes with certain goals of the audience, or that the audience itself has once before been harmed by the problem, or that the removal of the problem would produce a better life, or that the problem is increasing. We have not exhausted the methods by which people come to recognize problems, and in the last analysis the speaker must select and tailor the method used so that it fits the *speaker*, the *audience*, the *problem*, and the *situation* in which one gives the speech. An experienced speaker will prefer to avoid formulas, and will select the method of making audiences recognize problems by searching the audience, himself or herself, the problem, and the occasion to find that which fits all four most appropriately.

DEBATING PROBLEMS

A free society probably has the best chance to select the most important problems. Problems, in such a society, are chosen by voters who have heard many speakers on many sides talking about many problems. In such a milieu, we are more likely to make an intelligent selection of the most important problems and to come to recognize the superficial and false problems. Thus a free people can define and select for themselves the problems they feel are the most pressing. Herein lies one of the great strengths of a democratic society over an authoritarian society. But the intelligent choice of problems demand intelligent speakers and intelligent listeners. It demands that speakers occasionally be willing to risk a stand for unpopular causes. It demands an electorate willing to listen even to ideas to which they are opposed. It demands that speakers frequently become teachers rather than mere persuaders. But the rewards are worth it, both in achievement and in one's personal satisfaction.

Problems and the future

We have seen that problems cause suffering, degradation, and decay. But we have also seen that intelligent *solutions* to problems may bring a new burst of energy and a new level of life. If, in our time, speakers can help channel the energy of the people of Western culture behind the solution of these problems, the quality of our civilization may make unprecedented improvements. The great problems of our time would then be met by a people who are rich, powerful, free, and gifted; the problems might not only be removed so that our survival may be ensured, and better ensured than ever before, but it may also be that we shall have created a new society—one, and perhaps the only one in history, that deserved survival. The attempt is worth the effort.

PROBLEM SPEECH ASSIGNMENT

Introduction

Problems cause human suffering, the degradation of human beings, and the stultification and decay of civilizations. But an intelligent and vigorous attempt to solve problems stimulates thought, reduces the threat of a problem, creates new energy, and permits life to begin at a new level. It is imperative that we recognize problems and their importance. We will not solve our problems unless our speakers can help direct our energy toward these problems. The aim of this assignment is to enable a speaker to recognize a significant problem and to lead an audience to understand the importance of that problem.

Assignment

Give a four- to six-minute speech in which you select a significant problem and make the significance of this problem clear and vivid to the audience.

At the conclusion of the speech, there will be a question period. To be sure that there is at least one question for you, arrange with a member of the audience to ask you one, for when one question is asked an audience will often begin asking others.

Note: No solution is required for this speech. The solution should be omitted in most cases. Sometimes, however, the solution may be so obvious that it would be inappropriate to omit stating it. In such cases, you may present a one-sentence solution at the end of the speech. No further development than that involved in a single sentence, however, is acceptable, because most of the time should be spent on the techniques of presenting the problem. Nor should the causes of the problem be discussed. The only objective is to make the problem clear, vivid, and important to the audience.

Technique of presenting problems

You should select those methods of leading an audience to understand the urgency of a problem that are most appropriate to you, to your problem, to your audience, and to the occasion on which you speak. *You should select only a few of the most important methods, and support each intensively.* Among these techniques are the following:

1. Show that the problem is a source of danger, suffering, or degradation to those who experience it.
2. Show that the problem, directly or indirectly, injures the audience.
3. Show that the problem prevents the operation of an ideal and growth toward it.
4. Show that the problem is a fundamental one.
5. Show that the problem is recognized by others.
6. Show that the problem makes society or its institutions operate less effectively than they should.
7. Show that the problem violates an important value.
8. Use whatever other methods are appropriate to the *speaker*, the *audience*, the *problem*, or the *occasion* on which the speech is to be given.

Subjects

One of the functions of a course in speech is to help you make your own decision about which problems are most important. Therefore, no list of subjects is presented. One's judgment of which problems are the most important should be the outcome of intelligent study, of discussion, and of debate. The subjects a speaker considers important should evolve gradually, and as the speaker becomes wiser, should change. Moreover, as the speaker reads and listens to other speakers, he or she will be in a better position to select that which is important and to recognize false or less important problems. Hence, a list of what the authors consider the important problems would defeat this purpose of developing a sense of values in the student.

ALTERNATIVE ASSIGNMENTS

1. Analyze the speaking of a well-known speaker to find answers to the following questions:
   a. What kinds of problems does this person believe are the most important problems?
   b. What reasons are given for their importance?
   c. Do you consider that the speaker has chosen these problems intelligently or unintelligently? Why?
   d. Pick a famous speaker from history who misidentified the problems of the times. Why do you say the wrong problems were selected?
2. What five people in human history were most intelligent in their choice of problems? Why do you say so?
3. Analyze the kinds of problems chosen and the support given for them by the following:
   a. The President of the United States.
   b. Each of the senators from your state.
   c. Your representative in Congress.
   d. Your favorite teacher.
   e. One of your friends.
   Especially answer this question for each of the above: Is that person's choice of problems the best possible? Is that person's support for these problems strong?

11

thinking and speaking about causes[1]

We find out the cause of this effect; Or rather say, the cause of this defect; For this effect defective comes by cause.

WILLIAM SHAKESPEARE

Consider a typical, though hypothetical, suburbanite trying to start his gasoline-powered lawn mower. At first, he thinks causally. After turning the engine over several times without starting it, he uses his knowledge of possible causes by looking into the gasoline tank to see if there is fuel. Then he turns the engine over several more times. He still is causally oriented, for then he checks to see if the wire is attached to the spark plug. It is. He turns the engine over and over again without getting so much as a "pop" from it. But depending on his mental state at the time and the heat of the day, he now begins to abandon good causal analysis and indiscriminately pushes and pulls various levers or adjusts fuel valves in a futile attempt to try anything. But with each failure, his actions become less intelligent. At last, he addresses the machine with special epithets reserved for such situations, but his language has no effect, except on those passing by. Finally, he gives the

[1] This chapter was previously published in a different form by Otis M. Walter in *Today's Speech*, IX (Sept. 1961) pp. 12–14; 31 and (Nov. 1961), pp. 20–21; 29, and is presented here by permission of the editor.

machine a swift kick of exasperation, and surrenders by calling the repair man. The repair man behaves differently; because his living depends on his ability to locate causes, he follows a systematic procedure for doing so until he discovers that the magneto points are corroded and therefore the engine cannot produce a spark. The solution is simple: replace the points, and the engine will start at once. *Solutions often require that one locate the cause; when the cause of a problem is discovered, its solution often becomes obvious.*

Although the analysis of causes is indispensable to problem solving, we often behave toward the problems of our day as does the suburbanite. Instead of using careful causal analysis, we fail to understand the causes of inflation and deflation, or to understand how to help underdeveloped nations make their countries economically strong, or the causes of crime, of riots, of school drop-outs, and similar problems. Legislators fail to grasp the causes of the problems for which they propose bills, teachers forget to analyze the causes of their students' failures, and students, likewise, are likely to respond to a poor grade inappropriately by anger or by feelings of defeat. Too frequently, when the causes of a problem are not understood and removed, the problems stubbornly remain.[2] If we are to solve our problems, we must learn (1) to discover the causes of our problems, (2) to look habitually and automatically for causes, and (3) to lead an audience to understand these causes. Only when we do these things can we speak intelligently about problems. Not without reason did Aristotle avow that the test of one's wisdom is whether or not one can understand the causes of events.

ANALYZING CAUSES

There are two basic approaches to the analysis of causes, and each type can be broken into various subtypes:

1. Explaining *how or why* a cause operates by *describing the conditions that produce an effect.*
2. *Demonstrating that* a cause operates *by showing that a cause and effect are associated.*

One might, for example, explain that insulin causes a reduction of diabetic symptoms by either of the two methods. To use the first method, one might describe the chain of conditions that the injection of insulin produces:

1. The injection of insulin into the blood stream increases the permeability of the body cells to blood sugar.

[2] Sometimes problems can be solved by treating the symptoms of the problem, as we will see in the next chapter. But we can best judge whether we must treat symptoms or the causes of a problem *after* the causes have been discovered. Hence, good problem solving usually requires that we try to locate the causes of the problem.

2. Because more blood sugar can permeate these cells, sugar is removed from the blood stream where it can cause damage.
3. Once the blood sugar is inside the cells, it can be oxidized.
4. When blood sugar is oxidized, it becomes carbon dioxide and water, which the system can remove easily.

Thus we have explained *how* insulin operates to reduce diabetic symptoms by describing the conditions that produce the effect.

We could also use the second method, showing that a cause and effect are associated: we would have to present evidence to show that whenever diabetics take insulin, their symptoms decrease. In so doing, we would not show *why* the symptoms decreased, but we would be certain still, *that* insulin can reduce them. Thus the second method does not tell us *why* the symptoms decreased, but only *that* they did. Either method is convincing, and both together are especially strong.

Let us examine another illustration of these two contrasting methods. In the famous, and perhaps legendary, experiment at the Leaning Tower of Pisa, Galileo refuted the notion that gravity causes bodies to fall with a speed proportional to their weight. Which method of causal analysis was he using? In dropping the weights over the side of the Tower he showed that bodies of different weight *did* hit the ground at the same time, but he did not show *why*. Thus he was clearly using the second method. To understand *why* they fall at the same speed, one must remember that heavy weights have more inertia than light ones—it takes more energy to move a heavy load than a light one. As the heavy weight falls, it has a greater pull of gravity on it, but because it has more inertia, it takes more pull to get it moving. The greater inertia of the heavier body exactly balances the greater pull of gravity. Inasmuch as the heavier body's greater inertia exactly balances its greater pull, it falls no faster than the light weight. We will look at each of these two methods in detail, and as we do, try to discover examples of these methods yourself as you come to understand them better.

METHODS OF DESCRIBING THE CONDITIONS THAT PRODUCE THE EFFECT: CONNECTIONAL METHODS

When one describes the cause or causes that produce an effect, one is *connecting* the cause with the effect by trying to explain why the cause produces the effect. That a connection is established between the cause and the effect will be clear with some examples. In the case of diabetes, we connected the cause to the effect by a chain of causes. The chain of causes is one of two methods of describing the conditions that produce an effect by using connectional methods. Let us illustrate this method some more.

The chain of causes

To explain how carbon monoxide causes death, we can use another chain of causes connecting the first step in the link with the last:

1. Carbon monoxide, when inhaled, reaches the lungs where it forms a stable compound with hemoglobin.
2. This compound keeps hemoglobin from absorbing free oxygen.
3. Because the hemoglobin cannot carry oxygen to the tissues, the organism dies of asphyxia.

Such a chain of reasoning shows how a cause leads to a result by breaking the cause into discrete units that form a series of links connecting the cause with the effect.

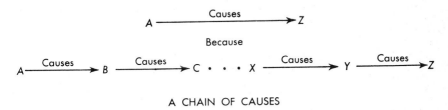

A CHAIN OF CAUSES

Figure 4.

Thus, the chain of causes can show an audience how one factor may cause another in a relatively simple and understandable series of steps.

Listing multiple causes

Not all phenomena in human affairs can be easily explained by a simple chain of causes because in some problems many causes may operate to produce an effect. In describing the downfall of Greek civilization, for example, one cannot single out one supremely important factor because many factors operated to produce downfall. (Figure 5.) Among the forces that led to the weakening of Greek culture are the following: the Greeks persecuted their best thinkers; the Peloponnesian Wars wasted the vitality and manhood of Greece; a plague destroyed at least one third of Athens' population; the soil became depleted; the silver mines at Laurium became exhausted; the Greeks were confronted with a physically more energetic and more unified people; political corruption dissipated Athens' strength; and so on. Thus multiple causes instead of a simple chain produced the result.

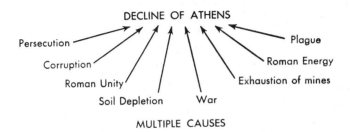

MULTIPLE CAUSES

Figure 5.

Many contemporary problems have multiple causes. Juvenile crime, for example, has several causes, some of which operate in one particular juvenile delinquent, and some of which do not. Thus the tension produced by broken homes or poverty, the lack of socially acceptable ways of finding adventure, the presence of serious psychological maladjustment in the parents or the juvenile, the lack of an acceptable adult model for the juvenile, the influence of the juvenile gang, and the dullness of an unchallenging school environment, may all operate in various ways to encourage delinquent behavior. In such cases, the speaker should be aware of the many factors that produce the effect; *he should mention that there are many* to the audience, but *he need not present each one* and probably *should confine his speech to one or two of the most significant causes.*

After mentioning a cause, the speaker may have to explain it. For example, one might sketch the ways in which the depletion of the silver mines at Laurium contributed to the decline of Athens:

A medium of exchange greatly increases the possibilities for creating wealth. Money is necessary to make money. Several reasons account for this fact: First, the nation without a medium of exchange must do its business by barter; that is, it must trade, for example, grain for wine. When it barters, it must buy and sell *in the same place.* But with a money economy, one may sell where the price is highest and may buy where the price is lowest. Thus nations using a medium of exchange can become richer nations than those who only barter. When Athens exhausted her silver mines, she exhausted her best single source for the coinage of money; money was hard to get and trade suffered.

But a medium of exchange in other ways increases the wealth of a nation. Wealth is not only the value of all goods and services in the country, but is also in part dependent upon the *number of times* the wealth changes hands. It is easier for wealth to change hands in a money economy, and therefore, more people can be employed; the employed people will, themselves, spend more money, which will further increase the turnover of wealth. With the exhaustion of the mines that produced her medium of exchange, the ability of Athens to reap the benefits of a thriving business life were more limited than before. She was not so rich, and she would suffer for it.

Clarity

Whether one is using a chain of causes or listing multiple causes, one must take care to be clear. In order to be clear to an audience, the speaker must first order his or her own thoughts; only then can one clearly explain causes to the audience. This clarity can be achieved, in part, by *stating each causal element in a separate sentence.* Thus, if one is using a chain of causes, or a list of multiple causes, each factor should be stated in a carefully phrased sentence so that the audience can understand that factor with the least effort.

Moreover, while stating the sentence that gives the cause of something, one will be wise to *watch the listeners carefully* for cues showing that the audience does or does not yet understand, or that it fails to grasp the significance of the causal factor presented. If one senses that several listeners have not grasped the idea, one may wish to repeat it or to restate it in different words, or illustrate it further.

Finally, realizing that even strongly motivated, intelligent listeners appreciate occasional reiterations, the speaker who has a complicated chain of causes or a long list of multiple factors should *summarize frequently enough so that the audience will be able to keep the formulations clearly in mind.*

Support of connectional causal statements

Any statement of a cause is a generalization, and generalizations are generally dull. Moreover, generalizations depend for validity on the evidence that can be marshaled to support them. (There are a few exceptions, but they are not very important in speaking.) The mere assertion of a cause is usually not sufficient to convince or interest an audience. Especially when the audience is dubious of an alleged cause, that causal statement must be supported by a barrage of convincing material.

Review the methods of support, as treated in Chapter 3; nearly all these methods can be used to support causal statements. Here are some of them.

The *detailed example* can be used. If you wish to support the idea that psychotherapy can treat alcoholism effectively, you might support this causal idea with an example of an alcoholic who underwent a full course of treatment: tell us of the patient's state before treatment, of the gradually increasing insight into the causes of drinking, of the alcoholic's ability to remove or control these causes as treatment progressed, and of his or her final release from the problem.

Undetailed examples can be used to support causal generalizations. If you wish to refute the idea that socialism causes a country to become communistic, you might use undetailed examples as follows:

If socialism leads to communism, why are the countries that seem the least in danger of becoming communistic Norway, Sweden, Denmark, The Netherlands, Belgium, England, Canada, Australia, and New Zealand? All these countries are socialistic, and not one of them is in danger of becoming communistic.

But most of the nations that have become communistic—Estonia, Latvia, Lithuania, Poland, Czechoslovakia, Hungary, Roumania, Yugoslavia, Bulgaria, and Albania—all were once capitalistic. Only two—Russia and China—were not, and they were feudal states. If so many socialist nations are safe from communism and so many capitalistic nations are now communistic, where do we get the idea that socialism leads to communism?

Sometimes an audience can be led to accept an alleged cause by means of a *hypothetical example.* For instance, one might explain how the lack of a satisfactory adult model could contribute to delinquency:

Consider the kinds of adults that delinquents know. Take Johnny, who is an adolescent in the Hill district. The adults whom Johnny knew were, first, his father who was too tired, too bored, too worried, and too often drunk to serve as a model. The second was his mother, understandably a drudge but too bitter about it to be attractive. In addition, he knew his teachers who were, for the most part, harassed maidenladies whose prime concerns were the prevention of disciplinary problems. Finally, the only other adult he knew was the policeman on the corner whose restrictive arm was a barrier to the boy's antisocial expressions of freedom. These represented the mature adult world to Johnny. He does not want to be like them, and he will not be. And we shall all pay the price.

Hypothetical examples can be found in good drama or good novels, or can be constructed by the speaker himself.

Statistics can also be used to support causal statements. If you assert that more policemen on the beat can cause a reduction of the crime rate, you can use the statistics from an experiment in police protection in New York City.[3]

In a tenement district with a high crime rate, the number of policemen was increased from 248 to 613 for three months. During that time serious crime dropped from 1,102 in the same four months the previous year, to a low of 448—a decrease of 55 per cent. Muggings were nearly stopped, and the tough 25th Precinct became one of the most orderly areas in New York City.

Testimony can, of course, be used to support a cause. Whenever experts know and understand causes, use their testimony. In using testimony, explain exactly why the authority is to be believed, for qualifications help make testimony believable. Wring all the deserved authority possible out of an expert by explaining the experiences a person has had that make him or her an expert.

Both *literal and figurative analogies* can be used to support causes. The literal analogy can be used when the situations are basically similar. If, in England, socialized medicine causes an increase in good health—or doesn't— one may argue that it would do the same here. If a course in speed reading increases the academic ability of thirty college students who took the course, one may argue that it might benefit you. But so can the figurative analogy be used. James Jeans in *Philosophy and Physics* explained why the sky is blue by using an analogy with waves.

When you stand at the shore of an ocean and watch the waves come in, you notice that the small waves, when they hit a post in the water or a large rock, are bounced back, and reflected from the obstacle. The larger ones, on the other hand, roll over the object and continue their course. Light, too, can be thought of as consisting of wave motion. The long waves—those at the red end of the spectrum—"roll" over the obstacles they encounter. But the shorter waves—at the blue end of the spectrum— are reflected by the tiny dust particles that fill the atmosphere. From these dust particles, only the blue light is reflected so that it enters our eyes from every angle of the sky and makes the sky look blue.

[3] Richard Dougherty, "The Case for the Cop," *Harper's*, CCXXVII (Apr. 1964), pp. 129–32.

The method of consequences

One of the more complicated ways of supporting a cause is by the *method of consequences*. The method of consequences requires that one support a given causal statement by finding additional consequences of cause. One looks for signs of the cause operating. Thus one might believe that someone caused the murder of another person, and he would look for signs—additional consequences. The alleged murderer would have to have been present, and would have no alibi that could be supported; moreover clues might be left. The following is a detailed example of the method of consequences. A recent theory of the origin of ice ages, devised by Maurice Ewing and William Donn,[4] leads to the surprising conclusion that ice ages are not caused by an increase in cold weather, but instead by warm weather. The theory first of all involves a chain of causes:

1. As the great glaciers have been melting for 11,000 years, they add more water to the slowly rising oceans.
2. As the oceans rise, the shallow water between Greenland and Europe becomes deeper, permitting the Gulf Stream to flow into the Arctic Ocean. The warm Gulf Stream slowly melts the Arctic ice cap.
3. Once the ice cap is melted, water from the Arctic Ocean can be evaporated into the earth's atmosphere and more precipitation falls all over the earth.
4. Some of this precipitation falls in the form of snow in the Northern Hemisphere where it accumulates faster than it can melt.
5. As snow accumulates, the level of the ocean falls to the point where the Gulf Stream can no longer flow into the Arctic and the Ocean freezes over. Less precipitation falls all over the earth.
6. Because less snow falls than can be melted, the glaciers melt with the result that the level of the oceans slowly begins to rise, and the cycle starts over.

Since the winter of 1977, which in many parts of the world was the coldest in recorded history, we have all become more familiar with the possibility that we are headed for another ice age. Many theories, usually making use of a chain of causes, have been proposed. Since the matter is of current interest, try to find several of these theories and evaluate them, selecting the one you think is best and justifying it.

This particular chain of causes which tries to describe the conditions that produce ice ages connects ice ages with, surprisingly, warm weather. But how is the theory supported? Support for this theory is hard to find because direct observations of what happened in the past several thousand years are not possible. But the theory can be supported by looking for *consequences*

---

[4] An interesting popular account of the theory can be found in "The Coming Ice Age" by Betty Friedan, *Harper's*, CCVII (Dec. 1958), pp. 39–45.

that we would *expect* to find if the theory were correct. If link number one were true, we would expect that the oceans would have been much lower 11,000 years ago than they are now. Geologists tell us that at that time the earth's oceans were 300 to 400 feet below their present level, thus supporting this link. If link number two were correct, we would expect that the ice cap over the Arctic would be getting thinner all the time; measurements, in fact, indicate that the cap is the thinnest it has been since we have begun measuring it. If link number three is correct, we would predict that much more rain would have fallen 11,000 years ago than falls now. What do we find? We find that at that time, *even the Sahara was a grassland*, again supporting the theory. Additional consequences that might be expected are strongly supportive: If the theory is correct, then the snows that cover northern North America, northern Europe, and northern Asia are ancient in origin; little fresh snow has fallen there in recent centuries. In addition, it is clear that the oceans have suddenly become warm, as is indicated by pink layers of tiny warm-water animals—as one would expect if the Arctic became a warm ocean; about 11,000 years ago the oceans entered their present cool cycle.

Such evidence supplied by the method of consequences, strongly supports the theory, but the method is not completely safe. For example, although the oceans became warm 11,000 years ago, nothing in that fact indicates that some other cause, such as an increase in radiation from the sun, might not have produced the effect. As with all other evidence, particularly in human affairs, the results are only probable, and the method of consequences can provide us with only an educated guess that may help us reduce the number of errors we make.

Thus the speaker may support alleged causes with detailed and undetailed examples, hypothetical examples, statistics, testimony, literal or figurative analogies, and by the method of consequences. In addition, the speaker will find the Canons of Causation, to be discussed later in this chapter, of help.

Limiting the number of causes

In a short speech no speaker should present an audience with a long chain of causes or give too many causes that are unsupported. In order to have time to use supporting material, he must limit the number of causes he uses, making each clear and supporting fully those that require support. To give a speech on "the causes of crime" including every conceivable cause in ten minutes would be ineffectual and quite dull. Moreover, the audience will not retain long and complicated iterations of causes. If the speaker covers too many causes, he might as well not have given the speech; indeed, one will have done the audience a disservice, because by boring them on a subject in which their interest should have been increased. On the other hand, to take one factor in the cause of crime and explain it carefully with an abundance of testimony, examples, statistics, and other forms of support would be to perform a genuine service in aiding the audience to understand the significance of at least one causal factor. Therefore, the speaker who is restricted to a short speech should select the fewest number of causes possible, and support each fully.

The causes the speaker selects will depend on the purpose to be served. One may wish to select a cause that is not commonly accepted or one not well understood or one that is considered to be the most important, but one must select the smallest feasible number of causes to present to an audience. In doing so, one should acknowledge the existence of other causes, and perhaps mention them or explain why one has selected those discussed. *Thus by limitation of the number of causes presented, and by careful explanation and support of each, one will give a more effective speech.*

SHOWING THAT A CAUSE AND EFFECT ARE RELATED: ASSOCIATIONAL METHODS

Just as there were variations to the method of connecting a cause with an effect, there are several possible variations of our second method, which shows that a cause and an effect are associated.

The method of agreement

John Stuart Mill, writing in the last century, developed five "Canons of Causation." We shall present a simplified version of Mill's analysis, which will be of help to speakers. The first and easiest is the method of agreement. We might illustrate it by the following:

Suppose seven men living in a dormitory are sick to their stomachs. To locate the cause of their illness, we would try to find something common in their experience that might have caused their difficulty. We would inquire of them where they ate, and would not be surprised to find that they had eaten in the same restaurant. Then we would try to find if they had eaten the same thing, and might be at a loss if we found that some ate hamburger and that some had eaten ham. But we would, probably, have located the cause of their illness when we discover that they had *all* eaten mustard. We might then form a tentative hypothesis that something in the mustard had caused their plight. In forming this hypothesis, we would have found a common element in their experience—something in which their experience *agrees*—that may be the cause of the illness.

The method of agreement may be stated as follows: *Whenever an alleged cause is present, a related effect must occur.*[5] This method requires a speaker to accumulate examples and statistics to show that the cause and effect are *associated* in a convincing number of instances. The method does not explain

[5] Once you become familiar with our simple statement about the Canons of Causation, you may want to read the original by John Stuart Mill in his *A System of Logic, Ratiocinative and Inductive*, New York, 1859, Chapter VII. He states his Canon of Agreement as follows: "If two or more instances of the phenomenon have only one circumstance in common, the circumstance in which alone all the instances agree, is the cause (or effect) of the given phenomenon."

Whiskey + H_2O ⟶ Intoxication
Gin   + H_2O ⟶ Intoxication
Scotch + H_2O ⟶ Intoxication
Rye   + H_2O ⟶ Intoxication
Vodka + H_2O ⟶ Intoxication
Wine   + H_2O ⟶ Intoxication
Brandy + H_2O ⟶ Intoxication

Figure 6.

why a cause produces an effect, but only shows *that* the causes produce an effect by showing an association between the cause and effect. If we used the method of agreement to demonstrate that a certain factor caused crime, we would accumulate cases showing that when the factor was present, crime resulted. If we used the method to show that reducing the work load of teachers resulted in better reaching, we could find examples and compile statistics to show that whenever the teaching load was reduced, measurably better teaching resulted. Or we might support the idea that economic aid to depressed countries reduces the danger of communism by statistics showing that membership in the communist party in these countries was reduced as economic conditions became better. Again, we might try to show that a certain factor caused the decline of civilization by pointing out that whenever that factor was present, civilizations in the past have declined. Thus the method of agreement is one that requires that we accumulate instances and statistics to show that when the alleged cause was present, the expected effect also occurred.

The method has, however, some difficulties. In Figure 6, we might, if we were untutored in such matters, draw the wrong conclusion about the cause.

The method of difference

The method of difference is an attempt to overcome certain difficulties inherent in the method of agreement. We could easily test whether the water is the cause of intoxication by redoing the experiment with one difference: leaving out the water, for example. If, then, intoxication still resulted, we would be convinced that it was not the water that caused the result, but some unnamed common element in the wine, brandy, and gin. It might be stated as follows: *When the cause is not present, the effect should not be; and when the effect is not present, the cause should not be.*[6] The method of difference, which must always be preceded by the method of agreement, is, in

[6] Mill's second Canon of Causation is here combined with his third. His original statement of these two is as follows:

Second Canon: "If an instance in which the phenomenon under investigation occurs, and an instance in which it does not occur, have every circumstance save one in common, that one occurring only in the former; the circumstance in which alone the two instances differ is the effect, or the cause, or a necessary part of the cause, of the phenomenon."

Third Canon: "If two or more instances in which the phenomenon occurs have only one circumstance in common, while two or more instances in which it does not occur have nothing in

effect, a further test of the hypothesis suggested by the method of agreement. Let us take some further illustrations.

At one time, physiologists were convinced by their use of the method of agreement that the cause of hunger was the stomach contractions that occurred when a person was hungry. A tube with a balloon at the end of it was inserted into a subject's stomach and inflated. This tube was attached to a pressure gauge that, whenever the subject felt hungry, showed increased pressure resulting from the contraction of the stomach walls. In every case tested, when the subject reported that he was hungry, contractions were present. If the method of agreement were perfect, we could be sure that these contractions were an indispensable part of the cause of hunger. But there are no "perfect" methods of analyzing causes. Several years later, the method of difference was used to overthrow the older theory. This method requires that we find people who are hungry, but who have no stomach contractions. But where can we find such people? There are at least two kinds: those born without stomachs and those who, for one reason or another, have had their stomachs removed. We have found that people without stomachs—and hence, without stomach contractions—still experience hunger. Therefore, this method has shown us that the conclusion suggested by the method of agreement is wrong.

The method of difference can be used to help establish hypotheses as well as to reject them. In the previous illustration of the people in the dormitory who were ill from eating mustard, we might use the method of difference to confirm our hypothesis. How could this be done? We must supply hamburgers and ham from the same restaurant to several subjects, but not permit them to use mustard. Of course, if these people did not become ill, we would be more certain about the hypothesis that the mustard was the cause of the illness. Better yet, because the following device does not require us to manipulate people, simply inquire among those who ate at the restaurant to see if we find that those who ate there but did not have mustard remained well, we would have strengthened our hypothesis.

Thus the method of difference removes the alleged cause to see what effect is produced. It is the method used by careful experimentalists. If one wishes to test the effects of a given drug on influenza, one will use the method of agreement and give the drug to a number of patients. But one will also give a placebo—a substance known to have no effect—to other patients to rule out psychological effects of receiving treatment and, thus, create a difference in which the alleged cause is not present.

The method of correlation

The method of correlation is not unlike the previous methods and may be stated as follows: *If a large amount of the cause is present, there should be a*

common save the absence of that circumstance; the circumstance in which alone the two sets of instances always differ is the effect, or the cause, or an indispensable part of the cause, of the phenomenon."

large amount of the effect; if a small amount of the cause is present, there should be a small amount of the effect.[7] Thus we might find that when the economic conditions of a European country are very bad, there are also many members of the communist party, but as the economic conditions of that country improve, there are fewer members of the same party, and as conditions become more productive and wealth increases, the number of communists becomes negligible. Or to return to our illustration of the people in the dormitory who were ill: those who ate a large amount of mustard should be very ill whereas those who ate only a small amount should be only slightly ill, and those who ate none should be well. The Canon of Correlation supports the idea that smoking cigarettes is a cause of heart disease, because medical reports demonstrate that the more one smokes, the greater is the danger:

Amount Smoked per Day	Increase in Risk from Heart Disease (In Per Cent)
½ pack	29
1 pack	89
2 packs	115
Over 2 packs	241

With a small bit of smoking, the danger of cancer is increased a small bit; more smoking adds noticeably to the danger of contracting cancer, and with an enormous amount of smoking, the danger is likewise enormous. Note that even the method of Correlation shows only *that* smoking and cancer are associated, and in no way explains *why* the association happens. As is true of all of Mill's Canons, they show an *association* between the cause and the effect, but do not explain the *connection*.

Dangers inherent in the canons of causation

There are dangers in the Canons of Causation just as there are dangers inherent in every other form of reasoning. At least three of these dangers should be noted. First of all, *two things may be closely associated without being related to each other causally* when both things are caused by some

---

[7] Mill's statement of this Canon is as follows: "Whatever phenomenon varies in some particular manner, is either a cause or an effect of that phenomenon, or it is connected with it through some fact of causation." He also included another Canon, which though useful, has too often been misused: "Subtract from any phenomenon such part as is known by previous inductions to be the effect of certain causes, and the residue of the phenomenon is the effect of the remaining causes." In human affairs, it is nearly always impossible to be sure that one has all the causes, and, consequently, this "Method of Residues" is not particularly useful. Nevertheless, the student is urged to read Mill on the subject of the Canons of Causation. He is still the best single source, and although his Canons will not prevent every error that can be made in causal thinking, they will prevent many.

other factor. Two clocks, for example, may be perfectly related in that each moves at the same speed; yet it could not be argued that one causes the other. The two clocks, of course, move together because they both have the same construction.

A second error often made in interpreting correlated phenomena is to *mistake the cause for the effect.* The rooster may think that it brings the sun up when it crows, but, of course, the sun gets the rooster up. In a like manner, some sociologists believe that it is not the comic books that cause a tendency toward socially undesirable behavior, but rather that the tendencies toward such behavior may cause the reading of comic books.

Thirdly, a mistake in the analysis of correlated factors may occur because *the relation may be accidental.* If one takes too seriously the following associations, he would assume that there is something about twenty-year cycles that seem to result in the death of Presidents of the United States. The presidents elected to office in the following years died in office:

1860: Abraham Lincoln
1880: James Garfield
1900: William McKinley
1920: Warren Harding
1940: Franklin Roosevelt
1960: John Kennedy
1980: ?

Accidental associations are difficult to distinguish from causal associations, and one must take care to be as certain as possible.

SUFFICIENT CAUSES

A complicating feature makes the analysis of causes particularly difficult: *Many kinds of causes may produce the same effect.* I may cause myself to be transported across the country by automobile, train, plane, or bus. Any one of these causes is *sufficient* to get me to my destination. In the same sense, there are many sufficient causes of delinquency, each of which can produce, under certain conditions, delinquent behavior. In investigating, however, the relation between broken homes and crime, we will find many cases in which individuals from broken homes have *not* engaged in criminal activity. Could one then assume that divorce is not a partial cause of delinquency? This conclusion might be as unsound as saying that death could hardly be caused by a bullet in the head because so many people have died without such a wound. We must not let the Canons blind us to the fact that there are some causes that will operate under some conditions, but not under others. What we need to do is *to specify the conditions under which a sufficient cause will operate.* Thus our causal statement should take the form, "Broken homes predispose children to juvenile delinquency when. . . ." Until we can make more careful statements of conditions under which certain causal factors operate, we must be careful about permanently abandoning an alleged cause that is not immediately confirmed by the methods of difference or correlation.

There are no sure methods for discovering causes, and in human affairs we must use faulty methods to make decisions. Our decisions will always be based on probable rather than certain evidence. There is no road to certainty, no perfect rule for thought and analysis, and no formula for problem solving that does not have limitations. Our methods are admittedly imperfect, but these methods will help us make fewer errors than we might without them.

The function of these methods is to come as close as possible to demonstrating that an alleged cause produces an effect. The Scotch philosopher, David Hume, pointed out, in the eighteenth century, that causes were never observed, but only inferred. No cause can be seen. All we can see is the conjunction of two events. To use his own illustration, when billiard ball "A" strikes billiard ball "B" and sets "B" in motion, all we can observe is that "A" moves forward until it strikes "B" and stops, and "B" begins motion. The conjunction of these events is as far as we can go in observing a cause. The Canons of Causation help us to analyze such conjunctions. They are not perfect, however, and the intelligent student will always be willing to test his hypotheses about causes further.

LEARNING TO USE CAUSAL REASONING

The student must learn to look for causes habitually. When one faces a problem among the first responses ought to be to look for the cause, and then check carefully to be certain that what one thinks causes the phenomenon really does so. To learn to use causal thinking habitually, we suggest the following procedure:

1. First be certain that you understand the forms of causal reasoning. You should be able to duplicate the following outline of them:
    I. Explaining *how* or *why* a cause operates by *describing the conditions that produce the effect.*
       A. Chain of Causes.
       B. Multiple Causes.
       C. Method of Consequences.
    II. Explaining *that* a cause operates by *showing that a cause and effect are associated.*
       A. Method of Agreement: When an alleged cause is present, a related effect must occur.
       B. Method of Difference: When the cause is not present, the effect should not be; and when the effect is not present, the cause should not be.

C. Method of Correlation: If a large amount of the cause is present, there should be a large amount of the effect; if a small amount of the cause is present, there should be a small amount of the effect.

2. Find your own illustrations of each of these kinds of causes—good and bad—and analyze each illustration. Books on the sciences, psychology, history, and literature abound with illustrations of these causes.

3. You should try to examine the causes of phenomena in your own life and maintain a curiosity about the causes of things you observe daily.

4. Most important, you should try to discover the causes of the problems that confront us locally, nationally, and internationally.

Habitual causal thinking is not common, but it can be valuable when we try to understand and solve our problems.

SPEECH ANALYZING CAUSES

Sometimes societies have been destroyed because they failed to analyze the causes of their problems and failed to provide solutions that removed these causes. Too frequently we try to solve a problem by treating the symptoms of the problem; but when only the symptoms are treated, the original cause of the problem may still operate and the problem may continue. We must learn, in these cases, to find and remove the cause of a problem. Moreover, even when we decide (as sometimes we should) to treat the symptoms of a problem, we cannot make such a choice intelligently unless we first know the causes, and after knowing them, recognize that the causes cannot or should not be removed. Therefore, intelligent problem solving demands that we analyze causes.

Assignment

Prepare a five- to seven-minute speech in which you present a phenomenon of significance and show that one or more causes are responsible for it. In cases where many causes are responsible, select only one cause or very few causes.

Techniques of demonstrating causes

Use any of the following techniques to make your cause clear. See the text to be sure you have used them properly.

I. Describing the conditions that produce an effect:
   A. Chain of causes.
   B. Multiple causes.
   C. Methods of consequence.
II. Showing that a cause and effect are related:
   A. Method of agreement.
   B. Method of difference.
   C. Method of correlation.

Subjects

The cause of any phenomenon in economics, government, psychology science, or other area is acceptable provided the phenomenon is sufficiently *important, and the cause is sufficiently unknown to the audience* to merit a speech.

Analyze the causes (or the most important cause) of any of the following: price changes, inflation, depression, warm or cold fronts, absenteeism, fluctuations in the stock market, forgetting, crime, dreams, evolution of any part of the body, the decline of civilization, disease, prejudice, good grades, safe driving, maladjustment, corrupt government, old age, rapid learning, headaches, monopolies, war, genius, happiness, dope addiction, or any other subject worth the time of the audience.

ALTERNATIVE ASSIGNMENTS

Good causal analysis is rare, even among the best speakers. Select some of the following speakers and describe the extent to which each of them locates the causes of the problems that concern him. Especially note the extent to which he does—or doesn't—support these causes with data that are convincing. You are likely to hear better speeches identifying and supporting causes among your own classmates than you might from some of the following:

1. The President of the United States.
2. The President's opponent in the last election.
3. A candidate of one of the smaller minority parties.
4. One of your senators in the Congress or his leading opponent.
5. A religious speaker you have heard.
6. A teacher who is especially good at causal argument.
7. An article you have read recently that identifies causes of a problem and does so intelligently; or one that identifies causes, but does so unintelligently.
8. After performing some of these studies, what conclusions do you draw about the quality of causal thinking done by those you have examined?
9. Examine conflicting causal assertions to try to determine which has the better support: Why do ice ages happen? Does Vitamin C prevent the common cold? Is IQ inherited? Should medical experiments be performed on human beings? (If they are, the aim of the experiment must be kept secret from the subjects and even from those who gather the data; but the experiment may harm the health of those unknowingly participating.)
10. Explain to the class an analysis of causes that you have discovered elsewhere than in this book—an analysis that you think is a good one; why is it good? Explain an analysis you think is a poor one; explain why.

12 thinking and speaking about solutions

The greatest problem could have been solved when it was small.
LAO TZU

THE IMPORTANCE OF SOLUTIONS

Problems must be solved because each problem represents a source of danger to a civilization. Each problem is like a physical ailment—it weakens, degenerates, or destroys whatever it seizes. On the other hand, each problem solved adds strength, health, and vigor to the culture. Problems must be solved, then, because each of them represents a source of potential weakness and because each problem solved contributes strength.

But in our times, there is a far more important reason for trying to solve problems. The final test of any society is whether or not it can solve its problems. All societies before us have failed that test. The glory of the ancient cultures of Egypt, Greece, Persia, Arabia, Mexico, Peru, China and India has departed. Traces of some of these cultures remain, but their creativity seems largely to have vanished; a few survive, often in part through trying to imitate Western culture. No one doubts that Western culture, the first to surround the whole world, is the strongest. But if Western culture is the strongest, it is also in the greatest danger, for it is experiencing the same problems of war, poverty, caste, tyranny, and disease that destroyed every previous civilization. Oswald Spengler examined Western culture in his famous *Decline of the West* and produced evidence to show that our culture has every characteristic that is found in civilizations as they enter their last period of existence. Albert Schweitzer said:

It is clear now to everyone that the suicide of civilization is in progress. What yet remains of it is no longer safe. It is still standing, indeed . . . but like the rest it is built upon rubble, and the next landslide will very likely carry it away.[1]

Our own survival depends on our ability to solve our problems. Our progress in technology has exceeded that of any previous civilization, but our progress in solving the classical problems that have destroyed previous civilizations is not noteworthy. The problem of war today is more dangerous than ever before. The two greatest nations in the world could now obliterate each other many times over, and there is no foreseeable end to the danger. Now that other countries have the same kinds of weapons, war is so great a danger that it could not only obliterate our country, but could possibly destroy Western civilization, and perhaps, even the human race. The problem of poverty is so great that one billion people have an annual income of less than $100. Caste and prejudice weaken millions in the United States, Africa, and India; these millions might have developed skills and then contributed their skills and strength to the general welfare. Tyranny in this century reached an all-time outrageous peak as Stalin, Hitler, and dozens of lesser dictators poured out their insane venom on their own people and half the world. Except for a few countries, the problem of disease rages the world over. Let not the condition of our two hundred twenty-five million citizens blind us to the danger that for 1,500 times as many people, life is a dangerous misery. Western culture faces the same threats that have annihilated every previous civilization, and the threats we face are at least as great.

But Western culture has some hope. In contrast to all other cultures, we have so great a burst of knowledge that *we may at this moment know enough to solve the problems that have plagued humanity*, or at least *we can find out how to solve them*. The problem of poverty, for example, has been greatly reduced in those countries that have incorporated scientific means of production and intelligent principles of distribution; sometimes in these countries, so much is produced that the supply, for a brief while, exceeds the demand. The same kinds of principles that enabled Europe and North America to produce abundantly can be applied elsewhere, although variations in techniques of production will be necessary, and we must beware of our tendency to export our own techniques without careful study of the other country and

[1] Albert Schweitzer, *The Philosophy of Civilization*, New York, Macmillan Publishing Co., Inc., 1949, p. 2.

corresponding modification of the techniques. You must not forget that you live in the first generation to have a justified hope of solving the great classical problems of war, poverty, caste, tyranny, and disease. Let us exploit our hopes; perhaps we may have some successes where others have failed.

SYMPTOMATIC SOLUTIONS AND CAUSAL SOLUTIONS

Solutions to problems are of two important kinds: *solutions may reduce the causes of a problem.* If a physician, for example, discovers a patient with fever of 107° he or she might try to attack the cause of the problem by first discovering the germ causing the difficulty, and the prescribing of an antibiotic to destroy that particular germ. On the other hand, at 107°, the patient is literally burning up and can live for only a few hours. The physician might feel that the fever is too high to permit time for full diagnosis; proper laboratory tests to discover the bacterium responsible might take several days. The patient's condition nearly forces the physician to give *immediate symptomatic treatment;* therefore the physician may administer a drug known to reduce fever, or in special cases, may place the patient in an ice bath. Although such treatment would be given in ignorance of the causes of the patient's condition, it might work. We may direct solutions either at the causes of a problem or at its symptoms and the speaker must know which direction he or she is taking.

To understand these two kinds of solutions, let us illustrate them further. We might treat the problem of crime by increasing the sentences given those who commit crimes. Such a solution is symptomatic because it does not inquire into the cause of crime, and it can be applied only after the criminal act is committed. Punishment is always a symptomatic solution. To treat crime causally, we would have to find some way of reducing or preventing its causes.

To take another example, is a high protective tariff a symptomatic solution or a causal solution? In order to be sure of the answer we must identify the problem that the tariff is designed to solve. That problem is that foreign countries can produce some goods less expensively than American producers and hence sell them at lower prices. A causal solution would require either the raising of the wages of laborers abroad or reducing costs of production at home, or both. These causal solutions would tend to bring the prices of domestic goods in line with prices of foreign goods. The tariff reduces the symptoms of the problem by adding a certain amount to the price of these goods, but leaves unchanged the two factors that cause the price differences.

Both symptomatic solutions and causal solutions may be effective if they are properly chosen. Each of these solutions, however, has its own limitations and dangers, and when either is inappropriately used, the result may be failure to solve the problem, or even a worsening of the problem. Let us, therefore, see the special characteristics of each of these major types of solutions.

The advantages of symptomatic solutions

Symptomatic solutions have at least two advantages: First, such solutions often may be applied with great ease and rapidity. When, as small children, we overstepped the bounds of propriety, traditional symptomatic treatment may have been administered—the spanking. Often such symptomatic treatment prevented further recurrence of the problem. To uncover the causes of even minor behavior problems could take months; and to treat these causes could consume more months. Just as it is easier to take aspirin for a headache than to find the cause of a headache, so symptomatic treatment usually may be applied faster and more easily than causal solutions.

Secondly, symptomatic treatment may be applied when the causes are either unknown or not agreed upon. Many of the problems about which we speak are so complex that the causes are uncertain. At the time, we were not completely certain about the causes of the Great Depression of the 1930s; at least economists did not then agree on the matter. Yet even though we did not agree on the causes of the depression, we had to treat it. The New Deal attempted many symptomatic solutions. Today most people would agree that the New Deal was relatively successful; at least, few of the reforms of the New Deal have been repealed. But the reforms were almost entirely symptomatic reforms. Thus symptomatic treatment may be valuable because often it can be applied easily and quickly and because it can be applied when we do not know the causes of a problem.

The disadvantages of symptomatic solutions

One danger in attacking the symptoms of a problem is that the symptoms themselves may be of value. For example, sometimes a fever may be useful (although physicians still debate the matter) because it may kill harmful bacteria that have invaded the system; to reduce the fever sometimes permits the bacteria to prosper. A cough may be an unpleasant symptom, but helps clear the bronchial tubes of irritants; to quiet the cough leaves the irritants where they might cause damage. Symptoms may also have value in social problems. The reading of comic books is a symptom that may have unrecognized value; the popularity of these books may be a reaction to the drabness of city life. They may offer a vicarious way of finding adventure and thrills, and may help prevent antisocial and illegal behavior. Similarly, foreign competition that frequently threatens American industries can produce beneficial results. Such competition may spur domestic industries to improve both their products and the means of producing them. The present state of pollution of the land, air, and water may—one day—provide another example. If we are to learn to master the problems of pollution, we may have to change our way of life from a "conquer nature" policy to a "we are all part of nature" way of life, to look on nature so as to cooperate with natural processes, to live so as to be a guardian of nature, a part of nature, a lover of nature, and, above all, a respecter of the balances of nature. Such a change might offer more opportunity for a good life than our present one with smoke-filled cities, poisoned farms, and rivers whose odor spoils the life in them. Symptoms can even lead to new ways of life. Such symptoms, because they can energize, may have more value than we commonly realize.

Another danger in treating symptoms is perhaps more common. Symptomatic treatment may not be effective because the original causes may continue operating. Unless the cause of a fever is finally removed, the disease will persist. If an overweight person is treated only symptomatically by being put on a diet, that person's weight will likely not come down, and if it does, it may not stay down, especially if the cause is psychological or physiological. The cause of overeating may be, for example, that one realizes that if one is overweight, one has a socially acceptable reason for not competing in certain kinds of social situations; in truth, one may feel one is a dull person and unable to compete in such situations, but the weight protects one from recognizing one's "dullness," and thus, being overweight is a temporary palliative. Since the cause of his overeating persists, so does the weight. Thus when only the symptoms are treated, solutions may be ineffective. Just so, however, have we treated many of our problems. We have treated the symptoms of juvenile crime, and juvenile crime continues to increase alarmingly. We have treated the symptoms of poverty, and even in our rich country, one fifth of our people are impoverished. We have treated some of the symptoms of war, and war threatens the extinction of us all. These problems may persist until we can treat them in a more fundamental way of locating their causes and trying to reduce the potency of these causes.

Drug addiction provides an interesting example of the relative effectiveness of symptomatic and causal treatment. In the United States, we have treated the problem symptomatically by trying to enforce the law better and by giving those who deal in narcotics sterner penalties. Yet the problem of drug addiction increases. In contrast, England and Sweden have had greater success in combating the drug problem. Their reasoning is more clearly causal: one usually sells dope to produce money to buy dope. The "pusher" is an addict who must spend up to $75 a day to prevent the withdrawal effects that occur in the absence of narcotics. These effects are so discomforting and painful that one who has not suffered them cannot imagine their severity. A person might, to avoid them, even kill to purchase "a fix." But the habit can hardly be cured. Barely 2 per cent of the addicts who have been taken away from dope stay away from it. Nevertheless, if we could prevent withdrawal symptoms, we could reduce the "pushers" motivation to sell dope so that a pusher would not want to risk the danger of being caught and would stop "pushing." One way to keep this kind of person from feeling withdrawal effects is to administer, under close medical supervision, just enough narcotics each day to present withdrawal symptoms. The cost of such treatment is hardly fifty cents a day. The ex-"pusher" remains a useful citizen who, although he or she should not be permitted to run complicated and dangerous machinery, can perform many tasks that will be of use to others and that will permit the person to retain self-respect. Such a system has been practiced in certain European countries for thirty years, and by reducing the motivation of the "pusher" to sell dope, has greatly reduced the amount of dope addiction. In all of England there are fewer addicts than in any one of America's five largest cities. (A new drug, Methadone, may prove effective in "curing" addicts; its present value is, however, uncertain). Perhaps we should use the European causal solution.

A final limitation to symptomatic solutions is that much symptomatic treatment often results from anger and masks a desire for vengeance. We are sometimes most likely to administer symptomatic treatment to our children when we have become angry with them. We increase the penalties against criminal acts despite evidence that these penalties do not reduce crime. But we fail, in these cases, to attack the causes of the problems, and the problems remain undiminished. Moreover, anger blocks our thinking and reduces our chances for solving our problems. Finally, remember how, when you were treated in a de-humanizing way, you probably became angry; much symptomatic treatment simply masks a desire for vengeance and not only is not a problem solving response, but may even create new problems or worsen old ones. We should be suspicious of symptomatic solutions.

PRESENTING SOLUTIONS TO AUDIENCES

Once the speaker has selected or devised a solution that will help solve the problem, he or she has already gone through a long preparation. If this preparation has been thorough, the speaker has tried to understand the problem and its effects on others and on the audience; the speaker has tried to understand the causes of the problem, studied various solutions, and has selected the one most appropriate. Now the task is to find ways of convincing the audience that the solution merits adoption. There are no invariable rules to follow, but we can offer some general suggestions.

Analogy

One of the best ways to convince an audience that a solution is a good one is to show how a similar solution has worked under similar conditions. This technique requires the use of the analogy. The analogy has two purposes: (1) *The analogy may by used to show that something that was true elsewhere may be true in a similar situation.* When Galileo discovered that Jupiter had moons that revolved around it, he furnished a strong psychological support for the heliocentric theory of the Solar System because people felt that if Jupiter had moons revolving around it, then, perhaps the Sun might also have satellites. (2) *The analogy may be used to show a solution that worked elsewhere might work in a similar situation.* Some have argued, for example, the forced racial integration reduces prejudice because when the merchant marine integrated several years ago, prejudice against blacks seemed to drop proportionally to the number of times men had worked together on ships after segregation ended. Although 54 per cent of the men were opposed to desegregation at first, by the time crews had taken two voyages on an unsegregated basis, only 25 per cent of the men reported dissatisfaction with desegregation and by the fifth voyage, only 9 per cent remained dissatisfied.[2] What worked in the merchant marine to reduce prejudice, one might argue, might work elsewhere. To use another analogy, one might argue that a city should have a city manager form of government instead of a government headed by a mayor, and support this idea by describing how successful the city manager system has been in other cities.

Such use of the analogy requires that the speaker take great care to convince the audience *that the solution worked well elsewhere.* If one is trying to convince the audience of the value of the city manager form of government, one must show that in other cities it reduced the possibility of graft and corruption, or that these cities have maintained or increased the services performed by the city and have done so at less expense to the taxpayer than would have been required under a mayor. If one wishes to convince the audience that the honor system is the solution to student cheating, one must demonstrate that it has worked in other universities. Perhaps the speaker would, for example, tell about the honor system at the University of Virginia, where, for over a hundred years, that system has had the hearty endorsement of students and faculty. One would want to include testimony from faculty and students about how well the system works, studies of the system, and perhaps surveys of opinion about the system. Moreover, one must answer objections by those who are aware of breakdowns in the system that were highly publicized. To take another example, if one wishes to demonstrate that automobile accidents might be reduced by raising the speed limit, one would select statistics from states that had raised their speed limits, and compare these these statistics on accidents before and after the limit was raised. (Surprisingly, the number of accidents sometimes goes down.) But whatever solution the speaker recommends, facts, figures, examples, and testimony must demonstrate that the proposed solution worked well elsewhere.

The speaker must also convince the audience *that the two situations are similar.* If one were arguing for forced integration in the schools and used as support the way integration reduced prejudice in the merchant marine, he would then have to argue that the situation in unsegregated schools is similar in all significant respects to the situation in the merchant marine. An opponent could argue that the situation in which merchant marines are working on a ship away from home is different from that of high school students living with their parents and surrounded by their friends. The students would find it much more difficult to give up their prejudices because such prejudice is sometimes a condition for acceptance by friends and is often approved and

---

[2] Ira N. Brophy, "The Luxury of Anti-Negro Prejudice," *Public Opinion Quarterly,* IX (1946), pp. 425–66.

reinforced by parents. Thus the central task of using the analogy is often to convince the audience that the situation where the solution worked well was similar in all significant respects to the situation for which the solution is recommended. But what are the *significant* respects? As we have emphasized throughout this book, there are no certain and fixed rules that will lead one to correct conclusions, and especially is this lack of certainty true in the use of the analogy. What is significant must be discovered by thorough acquaintance with the two situations and by careful thought. But in analogical thinking, we have a guide: if the causes of prejudices were demolished by the same solution, and no new causes were present in schools, we would have a nearly perfect analogy. But perfect analogies are not always easy to find, although excellent ones do exist. Our guide must be to look for analogies where the solution worked in one place, and the same causal conditions that made it work are present in the case where the solution is proposed.

In some cases the speaker need not find closely similar situations in which a solution has worked. For example, if one is attempting to show that better street lighting reduces crime, one might show that in some areas of New York City crime was reduced by installing more and better street lights. If one can find examples, statistics, and testimony that show that better street lighting also reduces crime in a suburban area, in a country town, in small cities, in cities from various geographical areas, and in poor districts as well as in wealthier areas, one need not show that the situations are similar to that for which one proposes the solution. Here the speaker has shown that the solution works in a *diversity* of situations, and consequently, might be expected to work *anywhere.* In such cases, one need only have a variety of situations, and show with reasonable care that the solution was successful.

Some texts state that the analogy is the weakest form of support. In our opinion, it is no weaker than the example, than statistics, or than any other form of support. As with all forms of support, it is possible to make mistakes and no known system of reasoning or logic guarantees freedom from mistaken conclusions. The analogy is no more subject to error than any other form of support. On the contrary, the analogy has a unique usefulness, for through analogical thinking we can use the experience of people in similar situations. If we find that one system for speeding up the process of education works at one university, we may argue that it might also work at ours. Or if we find that one method of reducing juvenile delinquency worked well in Chicago, we might, by analogy, wish to try it in Los Angeles. If we find one way of discovering how to help an underdeveloped country increase its national wealth, perhaps that way of discovering a solution might be applied to similar countries. If one school system is successful in turning out good students, good citizens, productive scientists, or effective statesmen, perhaps other school systems will find the same methods useful. *Far from being useless, the analogy is indispensable to human thought because it permits us to use the experiences of others.* Without analogical thinking, no man could profit from the success or failure of another. Far from being either weak or useless, the analogy is both necessary and useful. If your friend finds a good dentist, by analogy, the same dentist may be good for you. If you find that a certain professor has profound anesthetic effects on your friends, use analogical reasoning and avoid his class. Thus the analogy is not only useful, but indispensable. Of course, like other forms of support, it is open to error, but inasmuch as it enables us to use the experience of others, we not only can but must use it.

Other methods

Solutions can be supported by means other than the analogy, and frequently these other methods may be appropriate. The speaker should try to use a variety of these methods. Inasmuch as the student already has been introduced to these methods in previous chapters, only a brief treatment of them is necessary here.

1. *Explain that the solution will remove the cause.* If a speaker has chosen a solution that is causal, he or she may wish to use one of the forms of causal argument discussed in Chapter 10. *One must remember that all solutions are causal since a solution is the cause of a better condition.* For this reason, the methods of causal analysis can be used, as described in Chapter 10. Let us restate them:

a. Demonstrating a solution will remove the cause by describing how the cause will be removed.
   (1) Chain of causes.
   (2) Multiple causes.
   (3) Method of consequences.
b. Demonstrating that a solution will remove the cause by showing that it has done so in other cases.
   (1) Method of agreement.
   (2) Method of difference.
   (3) Method of correlation.

Thus causal reasoning may be used to support the idea that your solution could remove the cause of the problem. To illustrate the way in which solutions that remove the cause can be presented, consider the case of India's great western desert, the Rajputana. If this desert could be made productive, India's food problem would be close to solution. What causes this desert? Strangely, the Rajputana should *not* be a desert, because the air above the desert contains more moisture than the air above the Amazon Valley or above the Congo, both which are rain forests.[3] Yet if one were to fly over the desert, he is not likely to see it because of the immense amount

[3] See Reid A. Bryson, "Where Is Science Taking Us?" *Saturday Review* (Apr. 1967), p. 52. Mr. Bryson and his cohort, David A. Baerreis, did the work that led to the discovery described in this illustration.

of dust in the air. This dust accounts for the dryness of the Rajputana because of the following chain of causes: (1) When dust is in the air, the air is heavier and tends to settle; (2) when air settles, it tends to become warmer; and (3) when air is warmer, it can hold more moisture. This chain of causes operates over the Rajputana so that air that would produce a rain forest in a less dusty climate produces a desert over India. But how can one, knowing this cause, devise a solution that will remove the cause? One can't run the air through a filter to take out the dust, nor can one sprinkle the air to wash the dust out. Bryson reasoned that if one could get vegetation to cover the desert, the vegetation itself would hold the dirt in place so that it would not produce dust. But vegetation can't get a foothold because of the traffic from men and wild animals. But suppose one fenced-off large areas of the desert to keep man and other animals out? The Indians have tried such an idea in the desert, and find that with no further attention, in two years the fenced-off areas cover themselves with vegetation. The vegetation holds the dust down. Thus Bryson suggested a solution that removes the known cause of a problem. They further suggest not only fencing, but airplane seeding with specially selected seed that will grow well. Once the air in the desert is clean, the prevailing winds will furnish moisture not only to the Rajputana desert, but to a much larger area of India. But to devise such a solution, one must understand the causes of a problem. And when one has such an understanding, one might be able to see how to hold the dust down, letting the rains pour, making the desert productive as it was in ancient times. Of course, knowledge of the causes does not lead automatically to a good solution, and sometimes it never leads to a solution, but such knowledge sometimes can lead to solutions.

2. *Explain that the solution will prevent the symptoms of a problem from occurring.* One could, for example, recommend reducing juvenile delinquency by imposing a curfew. The explanation of how such a curfew might prevent the symptoms from operating is simple: Most delinquency occurs after ten o'clock at night; if no juveniles were allowed on the streets after this hour, then no juvenile delinquency could occur—on the streets, at any rate. Again, the speaker will be using causal argument, but using it to show that the solution will cause a reduction of symptoms, although this solution is, at best, only a temporary one.

3. *Show that the testimony of well-qualified experts supports the idea.* For instance, the testimony of agricultural experts to the effect that certain kinds of farming would increase the productivity of underdeveloped countries will help convince the audience of the value of your solution to the world food shortage.

4. *Whenever possible, use a combination of ways of supporting solutions.* If the speaker can show that a similar solution has worked elsewhere, that the solution will remove one of the principal causes of the problem, and that experts believe the solution to be a good one, this kind of variety adds logical and psychological strength to the speaker's solution. Because our survival

depends on the quality of our solutions, we do well to expend energy, intelligence, and care in selecting and presenting them to others.

SELECTING CAUSES FOR SOLUTION

One should be careful about the causes he chooses to remove by his solution. As Protagoras, an ancient Greek philosopher and teacher of speech, pointed out, every event has many causes. To use his own illustration, if a javelin thrower at an Olympic game accidentally kills a spectator one may say that the cause of death was that the javelin pierced the heart of the spectator. But someone else could argue that it was the bad aim of the javelin thrower. Perhaps the city council would insist that it was the fault of the manager of the event who permitted spectators to stand too close, whereas a more philosophical mind might allege that without the desire for thrills and spectacles, no crowd would have assembled in the first place. A more hot-headed person would have recommended firing the teacher of javelin-throwing because he failed to produce a student who was both careful and accurate. The causes one selects must depend upon many factors. If one is a doctor, one will choose to treat the wound; if one is a trainer, one will try to prevent future injuries by giving safety precautions to our athletes; the manager of the event may try to erect barricades between the performers and the spectators. The kind of cause treated depends on one's interests, skills, and an analysis of what one believes to be easiest and most desirable. Therefore, when a cause is selected for removal, the speaker should often explain why he or she selected a particular cause.

SUMMARY

To speak intelligently about solutions, we must decide whether or not we will treat the causes or the symptoms of a problem. We know of no general rule that can help us decide which choice to make for knowledge in these matters is slight and much depends on the specific problem. We might remember, however, that symptomatic treatment often is more quickly and more easily applied, and that it can be applied in complex situations where the causes cannot be determined with certainty. But we must also remember that sometimes these symptoms are of benefit, and that when we fail to remove the causes of a problem, the problem itself may remain. Finally, we should remind ourselves that much symptomatic treatment is given in anger and is not a problem-solving response. Within this framework, the speaker must select the best solution.

Analogies that show that a solution worked elsewhere are useful in convincing an audience to accept a solution, and are best when the conditions that made it work are present in the situation in which they are proposed. Since all solutions are causal in the sense that they are supposed to be a cause of a better condition, the methods of causal analysis apply to solutions as well. We can use both the associational and the connectional forms of causation. We can show *that* the solution has worked elsewhere, or *that* it has reduced the symptoms, using the associational methods of Mill. We can use the connectional methods to explain *why* a solution is likely to work by showing *why* it will remove the cause or *why* it will reduce the symptoms. Finally, we can use testimony to show that experts believe the solution is workable.

Most important, whenever possible, we should use a variety of solutions. We should try to show that a similar solution has worked under similar conditions, that the solution will remove a major cause of the problem, or that it has removed the cause in similar places, that it might remove the symptoms and has done so elsewhere, and that experts believe that the solution is a good one. This kind of variety adds both logical and psychological strength to the solution.

Since our survival depends on the quality of our solutions, we can hardly expend too much energy, intelligence, and care in selecting and presenting solutions to others. Yet, when we look at the giant problems humanity faces today, can we have any justifiable hope that we have the necessary energy, intelligence, or commitment to solve these problems? Begin with the problem of war. Seldom has there been a day in human history when there was not somewhere on earth a war in process. Nevertheless, hope is justified because there are ways to tie nations together, especially economically. Germany and France—as well as England, Italy and other nations—are so tied to the European Economic Community that they probably could not fight another war among themselves. Indeed, they may squabble with each other, but squabbling kills no one, destroys no cities, creates no orphans and widows. There is hope even on this old problem. And on the problem of poverty, the World Bank has determined that if only 10 per cent of the world's arms budget were available to supply food, shelter, medicine, and other needs, in ten years the world's poverty would be gone![4]

As far as caste systems are concerned, we are becoming more and more aware of the injustice of racism and we are learning how to alleviate it; we are learning more about sexism, ageism, the caste imposed by wealth, birth, national origin, so that we are beginning to break the bonds that destroy people and their hopes. There is good reason to work for solutions—more reason than ever before in human history.

SOLUTION SPEECH

Once one understands the importance of a problem and tries to analyze its causes, one is in a position to find a solution for it. Finding solutions is of utmost urgency for us. In the past, many societies understood that they had

---

[4] René Dubos, "The Despairing Optimist," *The American Scholar* (Spring 1977), pp. 153–154.

problems, but were unable to meet the problems with the rigorous research and creativity necessary. These societies perished. If our society is to grow, or even to continue to exist, we must solve the problems that beset us. Each problem represents a sign of weakness in our culture; some problems such as war, poverty, disease, immorality, and caste destroyed previous civilizations. In this society, our existence is not assured unless our speakers can diagnose our problems, grasp the causes of these problems, select solutions and make them palatable. In this assignment, you are asked to present a solution to a significant problem.

Assignment

Give a six- to eight-minute speech in which you present a problem of significance and offer a carefully supported solution.

Technique of presenting solutions

Needless to say, you must spend a few minutes making the audience realize the significance and nature of the problem before offering a solution. Your introduction should be short, followed by a short but excellent "problem speech." It may be possible to present a solution to the problem you dealt with in your earlier speech. If so, refer to that speech quickly, remind the audience swiftly but concretely of the significance and nature of the problem, and present a solution. Select from the following methods to show that your solution is a sensible one.

I. Analogy
   A. Show that a similar solution worked elsewhere. Show that the solution removed the problem, or a significant part of it, that its cost in time and effort was not prohibitive, and that it brought with it new problems that were insurmountable.
   B. Then show the audience briefly that the two situations are comparable in significant respects. Significant parallels can often be found in places far removed in time and distance. At all costs, one must avoid an analogy in which the two situations are not similar. If, of course, you choose solutions from a variety of conditions, you need not demonstrate that the situations in which your solution works are similar to the one in which you recommend it because you have shown that it is likely to work whenever tried.
II. Testimony
   Show that qualified experts believe the solution to have merit.
III. Explanation
   A. Explain how the solution will prevent the cause from operating, or reduce the effectiveness of the cause.
   B. Explain how the solution will prevent the symptoms from occurring.

Subjects

No list of solutions is given because the appropriate ones should be arrived at after careful study, discussion, and debate. Through the competition of ideas one can best discover both the problems to be solved and the best solutions to them. Furnishing this competition is one of the most valuable contributions of speakers in a free society.

ALTERNATIVE ASSIGNMENTS

Many people in public life—teaching, religion, politics, journalism, and science—may advocate intelligent solutions without supporting them intelligently. Others may advocate solutions that are unintelligent. A few may both advocate solutions that are intelligent and support them intelligently. Analyze (1) the kinds of solutions the following advocate, (2) the merit of these solutions, and (3) the quality of support given to some of the solutions of some of those listed below:

1. The political party that won the last presidential election.
2. The political party that lost the last presidential election.
3. A small political party that attracts fewer than 20,000,000 votes.
4. The political action committee of a large labor union.
5. Any professional group that offers political advice: a teacher's union, the League of Women Voters, the American Bar Association, the American Medical Association, the National Association of Manufacturers, the American Rifle Association, Nader's Raider's, or any other group that has a lobby or that tries to influence public opinion.
6. After examining a number of such solutions, answer the following questions:
   a. Into what categories do the solutions fall: symptomatic or causal?
   b. What support is given to demonstrate that the solutions will work?
   c. How would you appraise the quality of thinking about solutions from your examination of these?

13

thinking and speaking about meanings: definitions

New truths begin as heresies and end as superstitions.

THOMAS HUXLEY

Not long ago, a painting by Leonardo da Vinci entitled "Ginevra de Benci" sold for $5,800,000—the highest price ever paid at a public sale for a single painting. The price of a painting, however, is not always an index of its greatness. Many a great artist, unable to sell his work, lived and died in poverty. On the other hand, lavish sums were often paid for landscapes and paintings of animals during the nineteenth century; today these paintings are stored in museum attics and basements. If the cost of a painting is not necessarily an index of its greatness, the problem emerges: Is Leonardo's painting a great one? To solve this problem, we must first define *greatness* in painting.

The same kind of problem emerges if we ask, "Is it just to execute a man for murder?" for here, again, if we are to solve the problem, we must begin with a definition—this time, of *justice* and, perhaps of *murder*.

One day, if you have not already done so several times, you will wonder whether or not you are in love. But you cannot solve that perennial and important problem unless you first can carefully define *love*. Definitions, which are mistakenly considered to be dull, are a prerequisite to solving some of the most crucial and most lively problems we face.

THE IMPORTANCE OF DEFINITIONS

Definitions and problem solving

Good definitions are essential to problem solving. Suppose we ask: "Can you increase your intelligence?" The question cannot be answered until one defines *intelligence.* If one means by *intelligence* "the ability to solve problems," one can indeed increase one's intelligence: one can learn to solve problems in mathematics, chemistry, carpentry, and indeed in everything from agriculture to zoology. But if one means by *intelligence* "ultimate capacity for learning," one can never know if intelligence can be increased because all one can measure—and even these measures are poor—is present capacities, whether for learning, strength or whatever; "ultimate" capacities cannot be measured. So to solve the problem of whether or not one can develop intelligence requires a definition.[1] Perhaps now you think you are in love, or in the past you have thought you were, and certainly in the future you will think you are. But are you really? If you are, you will act differently from the way you would if you were merely infatuated or sexually aroused. Whether or not you are in love cannot be determined, however, unless you first are able to discover or devise an intelligent definition of *love.* And, of course, you will want to live a happy life, whether you are in love now or not. But—as you have already guessed—to plan life so as to be happy requires that you first must discover the most useful meaning of *happiness.* And so it is with hundreds of other problems. For some kinds of problems, definitions are not merely useful; definitions are a prerequisite to any solution at all.

Not only is a definition a prerequisite to solving some kinds of problems, but the solution to such problems will be commensurate with the quality of the definition. In the following case the solution can be no better than the definition used to arrive at a solution: If we defined a great painting as "any painting bringing a high price," then, "Ginevra de Benci" would be a great painting, indeed. But, so, too, would be the trite landscapes and romanticized animal scenes from the nineteenth century, because these also once brought a high price. And with such a definition, we would be forced to the untenable conclusion that paintings of Van Gogh were not great while he lived but were great after 1930, and that Landseer's country scenes were great in 1900 but not after 1930. Inasmuch as greatness implies *permanence*

---

[1] The notion that intelligence, or more precisely, IQ, is unchangeable came largely from the "research" of the late Sir Cyril Burt and his followers who studied identical twins and found that when such twins—who have identical heredity—were raised in different environments still have nearly the same IQ scores. Recent study, however, has revealed that the late Sir Cyril seems to have invented his findings, and even, for that matter, his two co-authors, who have been found not to exist. See Jelon J. Kamin, *The Science and Politics of IQ,* New York: Halstead Press, 1974.

of value, a definition implying that greatness can fluctuate wildly is unsatisfactory and leads to a poor solution of the problem. We would have done better to recognize that we arrived at a poor solution because we started with a poor definition. We should have worked to improve the definition rather than to "solve" the problem in a way that is unsatisfactory. Indeed, even if it seems that the problem of defining greatness in art is unsolvable, we would be on safer ground to admit this possibility than to use a poor definition. Such a decision is still an intelligent one, and more to be prized than an untenable "solution."

Definitions and knowledge

Definitions are necessary for certain kinds of knowledge. If one asks, "Does history happen according to certain laws?" the answer cannot be given until one defines *laws.* If, by *laws,* one means inevitably cycles that repeat themselves, then almost surely there are no laws in history. If, on the other hand, one means "general principles of cause and effect based on the examination of historical cases" then, most likely, there are known (and unknown) laws in history, such as "Civilizations sometimes may fall because creative people are persecuted." Moreover, much information requires definitions if the information is to be understood. Certainly, if we are to know whether or not "neurobiotaxis is the cause of learning" we must first know what *neurobiotaxis* is. When the definition tells us it is "neural growth producing interconnections among nerves," we can understand the statement and begin to search for evidence of it. Perhaps the best example of the ways in which definitions lead to knowledge is contained in Euclid's *Geometry,* where, with some axioms, postulates, and definitions, Euclid proves all manner of complicated theorems, showing that these theorems are accurate now, were accurate in the past, will be accurate in the future, here and on Mars, and all without making a single measurement. If we haven't learned to hate geometry in school, we'll admire this proof for its brilliance. But without definitions—which cannot themselves be proved—the *Geometry* could not have been written. Definitions are necessary for knowledge.

Definitions and clarity

Definitions are necessary to assure understanding and to guard against being misunderstood. When one uses a term with which the audience is unfamiliar, or when one wishes to give a precise meaning to a vague word, one must define that word. If one uses the term *socialized medicine,* for example, one must define it; it has meant everything from health insurance to total government employment and management of the medical profession. *Underdeveloped nation* has sometimes meant only those nations with a per capita income of below $50 a year (which would exclude India), all the way to nations such as Mexico whose productivity has increased as much as 14 per cent in a single year and whose wealth ranks her in the upper fifth of nations. "If first you would debate with me, define your terms," said Voltaire, in a frequently quoted, but seldom followed, statement. He knew that speakers should guarantee clarity to listeners by supplying careful definitions, and he was, as we should be, suspicious of those who fail to give careful definitions of their terms. Since definitions are necessary for problem solving, for certain kinds of knowledge and for clarifying certain kinds of terms, you would think that their importance would be recognized and that use of definitions would be taught with care and even inspiration. But such is not the case. Even most experts in logic and communication are not well informed about the use of definitions, and many are misinformed. The lack of accurate information and even interest in definitions is one of the most significant loopholes in modern thinking, and results in all manner of superficiality and many kinds of mistakes in thinking. In the entire English language, there is but one book on definitions, and it is short and often mistaken.[2] Nevertheless, since definitions are important we must study the technique of definition, although such study will lead us into material that will be unfamiliar to many readers. In doing so we will hope to help forge one of the missing links in intelligence.

KINDS OF DEFINITIONS

We will examine three important kinds of definitions, each of which has different uses and limitations. Each of these concepts of definition springs from completely different ideas about the world or about the nature and function of words. Let us begin with that concept of definition that is the oldest and, perhaps, the least understood.

Platonistic definition

Plato believed that certain concepts could transform men and society. These concepts—which today we call *values*—exist as Ideas only. According to Plato, in the World of Ideas are concepts which, if we truly understood them, would change our behavior, our laws, our nations, and our entire culture. Ideas have great power because, according to Plato, every Idea has the following characteristics:

1. *Ideas are the models or archetypes of our popular concepts.* We can clarify the way in which the Ideas serve as archetypes if we apply Plato's Theory of Ideas, for a moment, to chairs (but we must keep in mind that Plato himself was not the least bit interested in objects, but only in values): We can observe many kinds of chairs, some with arms, some made of wood, some beautifully upholstered, some hand-carved and gilded, and others constructed from the cheapest sorts of material. But all these chairs might be conceived of as imitations of the Idea of a chair. All chairs, whatever their dimensions, materials, or qualities, are thus imitations of the Idea of a chair,

[2] See Richard Robinson, *Definition*, Oxford: Oxford University Press, 1954. At least, no other book on definitions is listed in the catalog of the library of Congress or of the British Museum.

and if we had no such Idea, we could not make any chairs at all. Just so, the values in Plato's World of Ideas are the archetypes or models for our concepts. Thus, Plato believed that there is an Idea of Justice, of Courage, of Love, of Patriotism, of Happiness, of Art, and even of the subject you are studying—Rhetoric.[3]

2. *Ideas when understood and applied can transform human beings and society.* True love can transform us remarkably and magnificently into something better; the lack of it, at best, leaves us incomplete, and neurotic love can destroy us. Just so do other Ideas change us. A few examples may illustrate the surprising fact that Ideas transform; geometry, for example, is a system of Ideas. Geometry sets out the properties of circles, triangles, and cones, even though nowhere are there any perfect circles, triangles, or cones, or even anywhere straight lines (because under a microscope all these are most imperfect); and yet, geometry sets out the properties of these Ideas, and does so for *any* triangle, circle, or cone in *any* universe. From the time the Egyptians used geometry to measure the fields, and thereby determine who owned which fields, after the Nile flood (thus creating a more just society) to the present when we use geometry to navigate around the earth and to build fantastic cities, this system of Ideas has transformed us. Presumably Plato got his notions of the World of Ideas from geometry, for he had inscribed above the entrance to The Academy the words, "Let none enter here without a knowledge of geometry."

Perhaps a better example of the ways Ideas transform is Western culture itself. Its differences from other cultures are all traceable to two Ideas: There are no good names for these Ideas, but first Western culture has the Idea of what we might call love of the individual and respect for him, or what we call a dedication to freedom, or what is sometimes called Democracy. Secondly, our culture possesses another Idea that we might label respect for knowledge, or curiosity, or love of learning, of which philosophy and science are the two highest developments. These two Ideas, which, somewhat superficially we can call Democracy and Science, have transformed Western culture in ways that have made it more vigorous, more powerful, and in some ways, more kind, than the ancient Empires of Egypt, China, India, or Mexico. We differ from other cultures in that we are dedicated more or less to the Idea of freedom and the Idea of the search for knowledge. These Ideas have given us our strength and have shaped us. As they are more fully realized, they will shape us further. One can see that Ideas transform: If we knew what Justice is, we could judge others justly; all of us at times must judge, but being ignorant of Justice, we judge poorly. Moreover, we could judge whether a law is just or unjust and either follow that law courageously if it is just or break it, or change it, if it is unjust. Even more important, if we understood justice more perfectly, we could create just laws and create a just society,

[3] Platonistic Ideas are capitalized (Justice, the Good, and so on) to indicate that the writer is referring not to what people generally mean when they use the words *justice* or *good* but to the archetypes of our ideas, and not to imperfect imitations.

and even a just world. Plato was correct; Ideas do transform, and great Ideas can transform greatly.

3. *Most manifestations of Ideas on earth are imperfect imitations of the Idea.* In contrast to the Ideas, our earthly imitations of Justice are hopelessly imperfect, so imperfect that our misconceptions of Justice can work great evil, just as an electric chair or the dunking chairs of Salem's witch-hunting days may be said to be evil imitations of the Idea of a chair, so have men's concept of Justice and other values been evil. Once we thought it just to cut off a man's hand for stealing a loaf of bread, and to sell people into slavery. These practices were evil misconceptions of the Idea of Justice. Had we understood that Idea, we could have acted Justly as individuals, created laws that were truly Just, and built a Just society.

4. *Knowledge of the Ideas is everlasting.* Much of our learning today, rather than being everlasting is ephemeral. By the time an engineer has been out of school ten years, perhaps 50 per cent of the knowledge he or she learned in engineering school will be outmoded. But once one truly understands one of the Ideas—such as Justice—the knowledge is as timeless as knowledge of the theorems of geometry. Thus, if one comes to understand what Justice is, that understanding would have been true in the fifth century, B.C., and would have been true yesterday, just as it would be true for all cultures on earth and on any other planet. A contemporary anthropologist might be tempted to quarrel because societies sometimes seem to have very different ideas of what is just. The Eskimos believe it proper to abandon their aged in the cold and snow when they reach a certain age, whereas we think it best to care for them. Yet even the Eskimos abandon the older person so that he may not endure the pangs of old age; Eskimos feel that they act out of consideration *for the older person himself,* just as our actions are done for the sake of the aged. There may be, therefore, one common idea underlying both kinds of behavior. Plato might reply that if we truly understood Justice, we would all agree on its nature; too frequently we have grasped only another imitation of the real thing, and not Justice itself; hence as time goes on, we change our concepts of Justice, but as we come closer to an understanding of Justice, our ideas will change less and less.

5. *Knowledge of the Ideas is extremely difficult to discern.* One cannot develop perfect and timeless knowledge of the Ideas easily. Plato believed that no one in fifth-century Athens had knowledge of even a single Idea. This lack of knowledge, Plato believed, accounted for the evil that was rampant in the world. Plato himself never offered, in any of his writings, a single definition of an Idea, although he lived until he was past eighty and his *Dialogues* are nearly as long as the *Old Testament.* Perhaps he offered definitions in his lectures, but we have no record of them, and one who reads the *Dialogues* will note that Plato, in those dialogues in which definition is important, overthrows and refutes others' definitions but offers none himself. Nevertheless, if Plato is correct and there are Ideas that are perfect and everlasting by

which we may transform ourselves and our society, it may be possible, 2,500 years later, to discern these Ideas with greater proficiency. The promise that Ideas might fulfill is worth a good try.

Justification for Plato's theory of ideas.   But is such a notion of definitions as Plato's justifiable? Is there, in any sense, a World of Ideas? We can see some utility in the concept of Ideas if we try to operate without it. Suppose, for example, we wanted to make an elaborate study to answer the question, "What are the effects of democracy on people?" To make such a study— which would require large sums of money and several hundred investiga- tors—we would have to study what happens in democracies. In other words, we would have to observe cases of democracy. So we might, for example, decide to study democracy in our own country, in England, Holland, Swit- zerland, France, Spain . . . Ah! But surely someone would say, "Spain is not a democracy; it is ruled by a near-despot." Then we would have to exam- ine the Idea of democracy. We would have to state a definition of democracy and *that definition would serve as a criterion by which we would select the cases that determined the results of our study.* We might find, indeed, that there were no "real" democracies on earth, and that all seemed to be hope- lessly imperfect imitations of the Idea of democracy. We could not proceed without such a definition, and the definition itself would certainly be an Idea. There is merit in Plato, for indeed, we have Ideas, and the use of these Ideas is not only desirable but sometimes inescapable.

Not only are there Ideas, but these Ideas seem to be models, if not arche- types. In some senses, there are countries that have been more closely mod- eled after the Idea of democracy than others and still other countries seem to be the palest imitation of the Idea of democracy. The Idea, moreover, seemed to come prior to the imitation of it, thus supporting another aspect of Platonism.

Moreover, an Idea represents a kind of perfection that is not achieved on earth. We would be more apt, for example, to discern a perfect definition of democracy than we would be to find perfect examples of it. We can, per- haps, after great difficulty, find a good definition of Love, one that rises above the imperfect imitations that are manifest in infatuation, or in neurotic love, and that Idea helps suggest the transforming power of Love that men have felt and have written about through the centuries. Such a definition of Love indeed could help to transform us. Not only do these Ideas exist in some sense of the word, but they also have some power to change men and society.

Plato may have been wrong about whether or not a definition can state the timeless, everlasting nature of some things. Contemporary existentialists, among others, insist that some things are always changing their natures, always growing, always decaying, always altering so that their natures can- not, therefore, be defined as Plato wished. Undoubtedly these existentialists are correct about *things*. But by no means is it certain that they are correct about values and Ideas, even though our notions of certain values and Ideas may change.

At least this much is certain: Working hard to find the perfect, unchanging and transforming meaning of values is stimulating to one who tries it. The process may lead him to new discoveries about the value he is defining, and enable him to speak with greater insight, greater clarity, and greater precision. The promise of Plato's concept exceeds the promise of any other concept of definition, and is worth taking seriously.

Devising a Platonistic definition. Perhaps Plato's theory of definition is of greatest use in defining values. Let us see how one might arrive at a Platonistic definition of a value. The first step in searching for such a definition is to understand thoroughly the characteristics of a Platonistic definition, so that one does not immediately select an inferior one. Thus to define a value, one must search for a definition that expresses the Idea of the Value—the Idea of which all earthly manifestations are but imperfect imitations; the definition, moreover, must be one that if it were completely understood and followed would create a better life: it must be *transforming*. One must attempt, moreover, to define a concept so that the definition will apply always and everywhere. Finally, the Platonistic definition will be difficult to attain. But because the definition does arrive at knowledge that is archetypal, transforming, unchanging, and everlasting, Plato's concept of definition is as worthwhile as it is difficult.

The second step is to learn all one can about the concept to be defined by reading the best works by the best minds on the subject. Third, one should examine *cases* of the Idea to be defined, whether or not these cases are imperfect, for they may jog the mind and stimulate it in such a way as to lead to the best definition. Fourth, to devise a good Platonistic definition, requires especially careful contemplation of the Idea. One must use one's mind, struggling to devise a definition that meets the characteristics of Platonistic definition. Fifth, one must try out, and probably, discard, several definitions until one finds one that seems to be best.

Aristotelian definition

Aristotle had a different conception of the function of definitions. To him, a definition classified a thing into its categories. Plato's concept of definitions is more intriguing and romantic than Aristotle's, but the latter's can be applied more surely and more frequently. *To Aristotle, the act of definition is merely an act of classifying a term; to classify anything one must always use at least two classifications of it: First, one must place the term in a large general class or genus.* If we were defining a circle, we might first put it into the class of "a closed plane curve." But having put the circle into this class does not define it because other figures such as ellipses are also closed plane curves. *Therefore, we must show how the term differs from all other members of that gen-*

eral classification by adding a second class, called the species; the species makes clear how the term differs from other members of the same genus. To define the circle, we might add to the phrase "a closed plane curve" the additional classification, "all points of which are equally distant from a given point." No closed plane curve except the circle fits this definition. Hence, by classifying a circle into a genus and species, we have successfully defined it. Thus, if we were defining a chair, and put it in the genus, "a piece of furniture" and the species "made for sitting on," we would have to add a subspecies to separate chairs from benches inasmuch as both fall into the same genus and species. We could give an adequate definition by saying a chair is "a piece of furniture" (genus) "made for sitting on" (species) "by one person" (subspecies). A definition may have as many subspecies as are necessary, although the speaker should have as few as possible so that the definition is easy to comprehend.

One may be somewhat hesitant to furnish definitions that are Platonistic because of the difficulty of devising them, but it is less difficult to find good examples of Aristotelian definitions. We might try to define *Intelligence*. We would fail if we resorted to the rubric of some psychologists and said that "intelligence is what the intelligence tests measure." This definition not only has no clearly marked genus and species, but it says nearly nothing, for we still must ask, "What do intelligence tests measure?" The obvious answer, "intelligence," does not clarify the matter. We might define it as "Skill in problem solving." Here we would have a clear genus: Intelligence is a *skill;* we would also have a clear species: it is not any skill, but skill in *problem solving.* The definition, so far, seems to meet Aristotle's requirements. But is intelligence only skill in solving problems? Aristotle would not be a guide, for nothing in his theory of definition reminds us that skill in solving problems is not necessarily a sign of intelligence. Skill in solving problems in wood-carving may, for example, be the result of *practice*, not of intelligence. Or it may be the result of excellent instruction. Nevertheless, we may be able to salvage the definition if we add a subspecies and say that intelligence is skill in solving problems *with which one has not previously been confronted.* Here we have, perhaps, an adequate definition of intelligence; Aristotle and perhaps even Plato might have accepted it, since the definition, if adopted in education, could transform.

Combining Platonistic theory and Aristotle's rules of definition

Plato's mode of definition and Aristotle's can often be used in the same definition. We might try to define *Justice*, using both the Aristotelian and Platonistic methods. Plato, even if he did not define Justice, wrote so much about it that, by putting together his writings on the subject from the *Republic* and some other dialogues, such as the *Gorgias*, we can arrive at something like a definition. To Plato, Justice seemed to be "that condition of society in which each person received the most satisfaction possible and gave the most satisfaction possible to others." Here we have a broad genus: Justice, to

Plato, was not merely an action of the courts, as we are apt to think of it, but a condition of a *whole society*. There are two species: This condition of society is one in which the person *receives* the most that he or she needs and *gives* the most that he or she can. Thus we have tried (perhaps vainly) to apply Aristotle's theory of definition to a Platonistic Idea. At any rate, *the two concepts of definition can be used together*. Even though Aristotle did not conceive of definitions as Ideas that can transform as did Plato, and although the former looked on definitions only as means of classifying, the two theories are not necessarily incompatible. One can attempt to define the transforming Idea of something and in so doing, state its genus and species. The two methods work well together, for in searching for the genus and species, one may often hit upon the Idea of the term being defined. The definition of the circle offered earlier, although Aristotelian, still states the Idea of a circle; and it does so although nowhere is there a perfect circle, nor is there likely to be. Yet the Aristotelian definition arrives at the Platonistic statement of the Idea of a circle, of which all our earthly circles are only imperfect imitations! Thus the two methods of definition may work well together. Plato may direct one toward the perfect, the everlasting, and the transforming, but Aristotle furnishes useful *rules for the composition* of precise definitions. The student using Plato's theory should also try to apply Aristotle's rules for defining.

Operational definition

Sometimes it is impossible to state the Idea to be defined as Plato would have us do, or to classify the word in such a way that no one will disagree with our classification. In such situations, operational definition may be of help. For example, take the word *psychology*, the meaning of which has changed through the years. At the beginning of this century, it meant the attempt to analyze the content of one's consciousness. Freud, Adler, Jung, and their followers, however, emphasized that psychology should also analyze those things of which we are *unconscious* but which still influence our reactions. Under Watson, psychology meant the study of human behavior, and to behaviorists, the study of the content of consciousness was considered *not* to be the domain of psychology. Today, educational, clinical, industrial, animal, social, physiological, and phenomenological psychologists have added their own meanings so that the boundaries of psychology have expanded. Presumably the meaning of *psychology* will change further in the future.

Moreover, we cannot state the Platonistic Idea of psychology (because psychology is not a value and Plato was interested only in values), and hence we should avoid a Platonistic definition. Since the meaning of psychology changes, it is difficult to assign the term to precise categories, as Aristotelian definition would require. If we do, we may leave out some aspect of psychology that is under study, or may omit some aspect that someone one day will be studying.

These difficulties have led to the operational definition in which no attempt is made to state the timeless nature of a thing or to place it in categories, but in which an attempt is made to describe a thing *by what it does—the way it behaves, the properties it has, or the things people do when they practice it.* Thus, in defining psychology, operationally, we would attempt to describe what people who call themselves psychologists have done when they study what they call psychology. Or, if we were defining electricity operationally, we would be able to define it only by what it *does*, because we do not yet understand exactly what it *is*. The operational definition contrasts with the Platonistic and Aristotelian concepts, but follows a notion advanced by the pragmatists: *that a thing is what it does and nothing else.* The operational definition is particularly useful to debaters who are arguing a resolution. With most terms that need defining in such debates, neither Platonistic nor Aristotelian definitions are of much use.[4] In the resolution, *Resolved*, that the basic industries should be nationalized, the term *nationalization* must be defined. One doubts that there is a Platonistic Idea of that term, and perhaps Aristotle's system of genus and species is insufficient. Here, we need to know the precise plan of nationalization; would it constitute confiscation of the industries by the government? A forced sale of these industries? What agency of the government would "possess" these industries, and to what end would they be operated? More precisely, in policy debates, the definition of some of the principal terms must be an operational definition of the *plan* implied by the proposition.

Thus, the student who chooses to define things operationally must define the reactions of the thing defined, or what men do when they use it. Operational definitions, therefore, are often longer, more tentative, less pontifical and, under some conditions, more useful than the other two kinds of definition.

SOME DIFFICULTIES WITH THE THREE KINDS OF DEFINITION

The Platonistic and Aristotelian definitions (and sometimes the operational as well) have a special difficulty. When one states what he thinks the Idea of a thing is or classifies it into categories, he is likely to attach too much importance to his own definition and so fail to keep an open mind toward it. For example, those who defined psychology as "the study of the contents of consciousness" circumscribed, limited, and even stultified the thinking of at least some persons so that psychology was not as easily conceived in more useful terms. Such a definition denied that the study of learning, of adjustment, of morale, of groups, of physiological psychology, and of psychotherapy was the province of psychology! Psychology has become enriched by

[4] See the article on the subject, "On Definition in Argument" by Robert P. Newman in *Pennsylvania Speech Annual*, XXIII (Sept. 1966), pp. 30–39. One must agree with the article, provided one is discussing only school debates. In other speeches, however, in which the meaning of a value is crucial, the Platonistic or Aristotelian mode of analysis may be more helpful than an operational definition.

more liberal definitions of it. We must, therefore, whenever we use the Platonistic or Aristotelian definitions, be willing to be skeptical about our own definitions and be willing to permit changes in them. At all odds, we must not look upon them as a kind of dogma to be enforced.

At the same time, much sloppy thinking results from operational definitions. One is restricted by the discipline of stating the transforming nature of a concept or by that of classifying it. Those not so restricted and who define operationally—especially if they are amateurs at such kinds of definitions—may construct overly long, verbose, and fuzzy definitions. The clarity and discipline required by the more ancient approaches to definition would eradicate much of the verbiage of these definitions. Platonistic and Aristotelian definitions, although they may lead to some rigidity in thinking, have clarity, precision, and terseness. These merits are difficult to find in many operational definitions.

For these reasons, often a good way to begin working on a term is to try to state the transforming Idea of the term, as Plato would require, and in so doing to classify it into its genus and species as Aristotle preferred. If, after careful attempts, it seems impossible to use such a combination of methods of definition, the student may wisely make use of an operational definition.

CHARACTERISTICS OF GOOD DEFINITIONS

1. It may seem commonplace to say that a *definition should include all necessary characteristics of a term,* but too often this requirement is overlooked. Particularly is it overlooked with certain kinds of words that "everybody" understands. When "everyone" knows the meaning of a term, it is not uncommon to find that no one understands it. Take the term *history,* for example. Most people would define history as "that which happened in the past." Yet this definition does not contain the slightest suggestion of what some historians are trying to do. To confine the work of a historian merely to noting that certain things happened in the past is not the most useful meaning of what the historian does. Such a "history" would result in a compilation of events and dates. Yet this kind of history, as every school child knows intuitively, is relatively useless, meaningless, and dry. Some historians insist that the purpose of history is to state the *significance* of events in the past. Thus a historian would try to explain the import of the Fench Revolution to the French peasant, to the English noblemen of the time, and to us today. But the significance of history changes. Pearl Harbor meant something different to the American people on December 7, 1941, from what it does today. Inasmuch as meanings shift, history changes with the times so that each age must write its own history. Thus to include all the necessary characteristics of the term *history* requires a search that takes us beyond the obvious.

To find all the salient characteristics of any term requires more than a peek into Webster. It requires thorough knowledge, study of technical works on the subject, painstaking examination of cases of the term, and careful thought. Thus to define a term with something like universal validity, we should, in the case of history, study what historians have said that history is, and what historians seem to have done when they wrote history. None of these kinds of study is easy, but all of them together will result, if not in a perfect definition, at least in one that will stimulate some thinking in both the speaker and the audience.

2. Besides containing all the necessary characteristics of a term, a definition *should not contain what Aristotle called "accidental" properties*. If for example, I defined a chair as a "piece of furniture usually made of wood . . . ," I would have included an unnecessary quality because chairs are made not only of wood, but of metal, plastic, and other materials. There is nothing about "chair" that requires the concept of wood, and hence this part of the definition should be omitted. The inclusion of such unnecessary properties results in cluttered definitions that are unnecessarily verbose and misleading.

3. Finally, *good definitions should not contain words whose meanings are not clear to the audience*. Samuel Johnson wrote the first dictionary of the English language. It was a stupendous feat for one man. He did not, however, always take his task seriously. He humorously defined *net* as "a reticulated fabrication decussated at regular intervals with interstices at the intersections." The definition is brilliant and precise, and displays Johnson's mental and verbal abilities, but it is a poor definition because the term *net* is itself more clear than the definition. Definitions should not include words the audience cannot reasonably be expected to understand nor words whose meanings may be different to different members of the audience. Neither should definitions include the word being defined. If, for example, someone were to define *Buddhism* as "a religion based on the teachings of the Buddha," one would not be answering the most basic problem posed by the term, namely: "What are the teachings of Buddha?" A definition that contains no unclear words may sometimes be difficult to construct (and, occasionally, we must admit, impossible). Yet a definition filled with words of uncertain or fuzzy meanings is often useless. The speaker can, of course, define terms in the definition, although one may sacrifice some interest in doing so. Still better, the careful student will use the greatest care in defining so that the definition will be self-evident.

Whether one is using the Platonistic, Aristotelian, or operational definitions, one must be sure that the definition contains all essential aspects of the term being defined, that it contains no accidental properties, and that the words of the definition are clear to the audience.

DICTIONARIES AND DEFINITIONS

Nowhere in this chapter have we advocated that speakers open that useful tool of scholars and students, the popular dictionary. We have not, because the aim of these dictionaries is not to state the nature of an Idea, as Plato would have us do, nor to classify it as Aristotle suggested, nor to describe its behavior as the operationalists wish. The aim of nontechnical dictionaries, such as *Webster's,* is not necessarily to do any of these things. The popular dictionary tries to state only the ways in which people *have used terms in the past.* (Contrary to popular belief, a dictionary is not a kind of a lawbook of language but only a record of what people have meant by a term. The dictionary is more a history book than one stating the most useful meaning of a term.) The ways in which people have used words may not be the most useful ways of using them. Hence, we do not believe the student will gain much from exploring his collegiate dictionary. On the other hand, *specialized* dictionaries do try to find the most useful meaning of terms, and students who are defining an economic, psychological, philosophical, religious, or other such term should consult several dictionaries in these special subjects. We do recommend the use of *Webster* for the student who wishes to know the common meaning, pronunciation, or spelling of a term; the student should recognize, however, that the purpose for which the popular dictionary is compiled makes it meet some needs but not those we have in mind in this chapter.

SUPPORTING DEFINITIONS

Definitions, although they are valuable tools, are always general statements and tend to be, therefore, somewhat dull and unclear. For this reason, definitions should be supported by an abundance of examples, comparisons, contrasts, and the like. In this respect, the student should review Chapter 3, "Supporting Ideas." We will here examine the kinds of support that are particularly well suited to making definitions clear and interesting.

First of all, *explanation* may often help clarify a definition. Note how explanation may be used to clarify Spinoza's definition of *God:*

Spinoza defined *God* as "That which is the cause of itself." This definition means that God is not created by an outside force; He is not influenced by anything outside Him; only His own nature can change Him; Not even the most cataclysmic crashing together of galaxies can attract His attention, unless His own nature chooses to note the matter. God is that which, alone, of all the items of the universe determines Himself. He can choose, if He wishes, to note the slightest whisper of the wind but what He does, He does only because it is consistent with His own nature or determined by it.

One should be cautious about explanations, however, for explanations can be quite general.

Perhaps a better way of clarifying a definition is by the use of *illustrations* and *contrasts*. For example, if we define *intelligence* as "skill in solving problems not previously encountered," then note how illustrations and contrasts can be used to bring out the definition:

The engineer is intelligent when designing a new bridge, or laying out a highway that will be as nearly accident-proof as possible. The surgeon who develops a new technique of surgery is being intelligent. But the engineer may not be very intelligent in voting, for the skills of engineering do not inform one about who is best and who is least qualified to hold political office. The surgeon may behave quite stupidly when giving an opinion about foreign policy, or even about the way socialized medicine works in England, for skills in making incisions, excising tissues, and suturing do not help one view political or social systems.

Contrasts are a favorite way of clarifying definitions. Robert M. Hutchins, when President of the University of Chicago, borrowed the definition of a *university* from Cardinal Newman and clarified it by contrasting instances:

A university is a community of scholars. It is not a kindergarten; it is not a club; not a reform school; it is not a political party; it is not an agency of propaganda. A university is a community of scholars.

Comparisons likewise may help clarify a definition. We might make clear what the *intellectual* is by comparing him or her with the intelligent person, and then by contrasting the two:

If we agree that the intelligent person is one who can solve problems, the problems he or she solves are usually given by the company employing that person. Intelligent chemists solve the problems the firm gives them; engineers solve the problems their boss ask them to solve. But the most useful meaning of the intellectual is somewhat different: the intellectual *determines* the problems on which he or she will work. Since the intellectual determines the problems he or she will work on such intellectuals often do not fit well into a mold, a firm, or even a society, and when they do so fit, they often do so with friction. But a democratic society can never do without intellectuals, and can never have quite enough of them.

Illustrations, comparisons, and contrasts are the best ways to make definitions meaningful and interesting.

Just as necessary, however, are *repetitions* of the definition. When the speaker gives his definition, he should watch the audience closely to see that they understand it; if the definition is a complex one, he may need to repeat it immediately. Throughout the speech, the speaker would be wise to repeat the definition frequently, not only for clarity, but for emphasis.

Other methods of support are not, as a rule, so interesting as illustrations, comparisons, and contrasts. Nevertheless, with certain definitions they may be appropriate and helpful. The student should however, avoid these methods unless they clearly make a strong contribution to understanding, to clarity, and to the vividness of the definitions:

1. Support the definition by *division*. In defining *psychology*, for example, one might add some clarity to the definition by dividing psychology into its many aspects: educational psychology, abnormal psychology, clinical psychology, general psychology, social psychology, physiological psychology, and others.

2. Support the definition by *synonyms:* To define *ethics*, for example, one might say, "Ethics is best conceived of as being closer to 'fun,' to 'happiness,' to 'enjoyment' than it is to their opposites. When we understand ethics, we find that the ethical person is the one who has the most fun, who is the happiest, and enjoys life the most. Our Victorian ancestors have done us a disservice by equating ethics with 'Don'ts' and 'Thou shalt not's.' "

3. Support the definition with a brief *etymology* (linguistic history) of the term being defined. To define *liberal arts*, it is instructive to discover that the word *liberal* is from the Latin word *liberare*, meaning *to free*. Where etymology illumines a term, use it. But somehow or other, the idea has seeped into the colleges and high schools that etymological considerations are absolutely essential. To the contrary, they are not, for what was originally meant by a root term may have little or no significance for what the descendant of that term means several thousand years later. Therefore, use etymology where it adds interest or where it contributes to understanding but do not use it where it adds nothing.

When a good definition has been made interesting by the use of supporting material, it is more likely to become a compelling value for the audience, and to shape the choices that they make. In so operating, definitions may help enrich our civilization.

The following assignment will help students realize the significance of definitions and techniques by which they may influence the value systems of an audience.

DEFINITION SPEECH

Introduction

If someone wants to know if one is in love, or if a certain painting is beautiful, it is necessary to know, one in the first case, what love is, or in the second, what beauty is. Careful definition is often, therefore, a prerequisite to knowledge. Moreover, one of the ways of clarifying the values that are the basis of our choices is to try to define them. When we can define what we consider to be true or false, good or bad, ugly or beautiful, useful or useless, we are in a better position to understand why we make the choices that we do. We must define these values, because they determine the course of our civilization. A highly developed civilization gathers much of its fire from taking the nature of certain values as problems. The values of art, science, truth, the good life, and the like must be clarified and defined if we are to understand them and to reap whatever rewards they offer. Thus, the act of defining certain kinds of values helps us understand one of the forces that can contribute to our civilization. For these reasons, we should inquire into the nature of some of the ideas that have made our culture the rich, outstanding, and complex culture it is.

Assignment

Give a six- to eight-minute speech in which you present a definition. The objectives of the speech should be to (1) arouse an interest in any of the following concepts; (2) present a carefully phrased and intelligent definition; and (3) make the definition clear and interesting. You may be cross-examined by the class on your definition to test its merit.

Techniques of using definitions

Defining a term.   Use any of the three kinds of definition described in the text.

1. Platonistic definition: Attempt to state the Idea of any of the terms listed in the assignment.
2. Aristotelian definition: Attempt to classify the term by putting it in a large family or genus, and to show how it differs from other members of the same family by putting it in one or more species.
3. Operational definition: Define any term by what it does, or what people do when they create, follow, or practice it.

The definition should contain the following characteristics:

1. It should avoid superficiality by probing deeply into the most important characteristics of what is being defined.
2. It should not contain characteristics that are accidental or irrelevant.
3. It should contain no terms whose meanings are not clear.

Supporting the definition.   One should use the most vivid supporting material possible to clarify the concept and to give the audience a lasting interest in it. The following forms of support are useful: "a," "b," "c," "d," and "e" are especially recommended. The remaining kinds of support should be used with caution and only when they clearly add to our interest in the concept and understanding of it.

a. *Explanation:* Explain the concept clearly and vividly.
b. *Illustration:* Give real or hypothetical, detailed or undetailed, illustrations that are vivid and varied.
c. *Comparisons:* Both literal and figurative comparisons may help the audience understand the concept.
d. *Contrasts:* Tell what the concept is not; give negative examples of it.
e. *Repetition and restatement* of the definition should be used frequently.

f. *Divison:* Often, breaking a concept into its parts helps us understand the concept; division should not be used, however, unless it does clarify the definition or add interest.

g. *Synonym:* Sometimes a synonym will help clarify the concept. Avoid synonyms, however, unless one would work particularly well.

h. *Etymology:* Sometimes a concept may be clarified by giving the original meaning of the word, or by explaining what it means in another language. Often, however, etymology is a poor guide to meaning.

Suggested subjects

Many of the following subjects are values and need the clarity of a good definition to make them understood. Others are not values, but have one or more values as their essential characteristic. In both cases, the clarity furnished by a definition and the support of the definition will help stimulate thought about the value systems of our world and the basis of our choices.

Some of the subjects lend themselves to a Platonistic definition, i.e., stating the most transforming meaning of the term. Others are most suitable for operational definition since what we want to know is what people will follow, for example, pragmatism or Zen do. All, however, can follow Aristotle's directions for composing a definition.

Art, beauty, Buddhism, Christianity, civilization, communism, Confucianism, deduction, dialectic (Hegelian or classical), economics, eloquence, energy, Epicureanism, ethics, evil, freedom, goodness, god, health, history, Hinduism, idea, Islam, induction, idealism, intelligence, Judaism, justice, law, literature, materialism, mathematics, metaphysics, music, normality, mysticism, perfection, personality, phenomenology, philosophy, physics, poetry, psychology, pragmatism, reason, rhetoric, science, socialism, sociology, Stoicism, Taoism, thought, theology, time, transcendentalism, truth, wealth, Zen.

In order to find or devise an acceptable definition, use the following procedure:

1. Consult some general works first such as the *Oxford English Dictionary* (which is the most comprehensive dictionary in the English language and many times the size of *Webster's Unabridged*), *The Synopticon* by Mortimer Adler, and *Encyclopaedia Britannica*. An exception to this suggestion should be made for psychological, sociological, or economic terms; for these words the student should read about the concept in texts and consult several professional dictionaries.

2. Consult works in the specific field of your definition, looking up the concept in the index of a number of recent books.

ALTERNATIVE ASSIGNMENT

Interview a number of people, in person or by telephone, and ask them to define one or more key terms with which they are associated. For example, ask a teacher to define *education*, or a clergyman to define *God*, or *good*, or a politician to define *democracy*, or a psychologist to define *psychology*, or *adjustment*, or a lawyer to define *justice*, or a physician to define *health*.

After you have recorded the definition, ask the persons why they used that particular definition; in other words, appear to question, if not actually attack, the definition. Note whether or not the person defending the definition seems defensive or self-assured. Note especially whether or not the defense seems in your opinion intelligent, and why it does or does not. Explain your reason for concluding that the defense of the definition is intelligent or unintelligent.

14
thinking and speaking about values: consequences

No wind carries those who have no port to sail to.
MONTAIGNE

Light can play strange tricks. In ordinary light, certain kinds of rocks appear gray; but when fluorescent or ultraviolet light is turned on them, the dull grays are replaced by iridescent blues, yellows, greens, and reds. In sunlight, a green sweater appears green, but in pure red light it looks black. Like the light, values and value systems color our world and give it brightness or dullness. By the light of various values civilizations find the unique paths they follow and from that light cultures are given their distinctive hues. The light cast by these values, moreover, either reveals certain problems to us or blinds us to them. But like the light, which is itself invisible until it strikes an object, our values and value systems also remain invisible, until they are reflected in a decision. Even then, values are not always perceived. Because of the pervasive influence of values, we cannot speak intelligently without understanding something of their nature.

THE NATURE OF VALUES

A value is a standard on which, consciously or unconsciously, we base our choices. We may, for example, favor aid to a certain foreign country because we have already promised to help it; in this case, the desire to uphold our public integrity is the value on which we have based our choice. We may be opposed to foreign aid because it will cost a large sum of money, in which case a wish for economy may be the value underlying our choice. *Values may be defined as concepts that express what people believe is right or wrong, important or unimportant, wise or foolish, good or bad, just or unjust, great or mean, beautiful or ugly, and true or false, and that, therefore, underlie all choices.* Intelligent speaking demands that we locate, understand, and analyze the bases for our choices.

THE IMPORTANCE OF VALUES IN CIVILIZATION

High civilizations do not owe their superior development over lower ones entirely to their wealth and power. Their superiority comes in a substantial degree from their commitment to certain kinds of values. Carthage, for example, was wealthier and more powerful than Athens, but never developed a comparable civilization. No other civilization borrowed or imitated Carthaginian ideas, techniques, or culture. Their civilization appears to have been merely rich and powerful and to have lacked the values that have earned for Athens the admiration of all who have known her. The story of Athens, however, is much more than a story of accumulations of wealth and of imperial growth. Greek values shaped Greek greatness. This civilization is worth looking at not only because it is one of the foundations of our own culture, but especially because *it produced more geniuses in proportion to its population than any other civilization, before, during or since, including our own.* One reason for its glory was the sense of values that many of the Greeks accepted.

These values not only were reflected in the origin of Greek philosophy, but were a cause of its development. The first philosopher, Thales, asked, "What is the most fundamental constituent of matter?" Questions about the nature of the world and matter had been asked before by the Egyptians and Persians. The questions, however, produced poor answers because the value system of these peoples permitted explanations involving the gods, demons, and spirits they believed to exist. Thales' contribution was that he posed a question to be answered in the light of a special value: reliance only on that which could be *observed*. This value, which was Thales' conception of the way to arrive at truth, was his most important contribution. Thus the nature of matter was taken *as a problem to be solved,* and the solution required a "natural" and "rational" rather than a superstitious answer; with the choice of such a problem and with the use of such a value system, Greek philosophy could begin, and for better or for worse, the world would never be the same again.[1]

It is not surprising that Thales found the wrong answer to the question, for we cannot, even 2,500 years later, produce a perfect answer. But the example of Thales inspired other philosophers to do as he had done, namely to take the nature of matter as a problem and to search for natural explanations. Heraclitus, Parmenides, and others did so and found, not too surprisingly, contrasting answers. When many people accept the same problem, the same values, and the same method of attack and still find divergent answers, the effect often stimulates further questioning.

The stimulating effect of such questions and values caused the Greeks to wonder about things other than the nature of matter. The same kinds of questions and the same kinds of values were used to explore the nature of mathematics, of political activity, of the good life, and especially of the nature of human beings. One reason Greek culture achieved superiority is that the Greeks valued understanding, valued human reason based on observation, and valued questions about the natures of art, science, life, governments, animals, drama, goodness and the like. In fact, the desire to understand the nature of things became a characteristic value for the Greeks and directed their thinking more than it had that of any previous civilization, and more than that of most subsequent civilizations. Such values produced the memorable things about Greek civilization. The value attached to questions about the nature of Justice and Goodness inspired Plato's *Dialogues.* Moral and religious problems inspired Aeschylus, Sophocles, and Euripides to write plays that can be compared favorably to Shakespeare's. Athenian sculpture, in the fifth century, mirrored the Athenians' concept of the ideal person and thus reflected another of the Greek value systems, a system of values that often excluded women. Greek poetry sharpened the Greeks' perception of humanity's promise and of its dilemmas. Thus Greek civilization arose partly out of a desire to understand the nature of things, and grew because the Greeks' sense of values dictated a unique choice of problems.

Moreover, the values that demanded a rational answer based on observation forced the development of *tools* to solve the problems the Greeks were posing. The Greeks developed dialectic, democracy, induction, deduction, debate, and literary, rhetorical, and artistic criticism. Thus the value systems of the Greeks not only dictated the choice of problems, but also brought forth new tools. The new values and the new tools initiated new or revolutionized old studies that were to change the world: medicine, biology, political science, psychology, logic, ethics, metaphysics, history, physics, music, mathematics, and rhetoric. *The Golden Age arrived, not only because Athens*

---

[1] Thales' answer was that the most fundamental component of the Universe was water. He probably arrived at this conclusion by observing that water fell from the sky, and was presumably, therefore, part of air; that water seeped into holes in the ground making it appear that it was part of earth; that water accumulated on a cold dish held over the fire, making it appear that it was part of flame; and that watery fluids were present in plants and animals.

was rich and powerful, but because she had a value system that was unique among the civilizations of the world.

That civilizations follow the lead of their value systems is illustrated by the differences between Greece and Rome. Roman civilization never quite caught up with Greek civilization, although the Romans admired Greek culture enough to try to adopt it. The Roman was not so concerned with the nature of things as was the Greek; and the practical Roman preferred to accept, rather than refine, the formulations of the Greeks. Consequently, Rome never developed a science, a philosophy, mathematics, or arts that were much above the level of imitation. Moreover, Roman imitations of Greek culture were generally inferior, just as Cicero was inferior as an orator to Demosthenes, and Plautus was inferior to Aristophanes in the art of writing comedies. No Roman philosopher could match Socrates, Plato, or Aristotle; Roman sculptors imitated the Greeks, as did Roman architects and engineers. As one might expect, no new ideas about the nature of human beings and no new formulations about the universe were produced in Rome, for the Roman system of values did not press the Empire's citizens to exceed their Greek teachers.

The Romans, however, had their own values and these, too, had merit. Roman values emphasized order and the techniques for securing it. Roman order gave the world more prosperity, peace, and even more freedom than recent motion pictures would lead us to believe. Rome forged her own tools for securing these values: codes of law, civil service systems, and limited self-government for her provinces. These tools enabled the Empire to operate in spite of insane emperors, incompetent Senates, and vast differences among her peoples. The peace brought about by Rome may have preserved the culture of Greece on which our own culture is based, and without which Western culture would lack much of its richness and variety. Roman values differed from Greek values, but nevertheless preserved Greek culture, and made a contribution of their own.

Thus the kinds of problems a civilization chooses to solve and the means used to solve them determine the richness or poverty of a civilization. In this way also, the value system of a culture determines the nature and the worth of the culture. A few brief illustrations may serve to reinforce the point. The Persians placed little value on the individual and never developed a democracy. The ancient Greeks placed little value on civil order and never developed a nation. The Orientals placed small value on material things; partly for this reason, only recently have Oriental nations begun an industrial revolution. The Americans prized acts and deeds, and passed by the value of comtemplation that is so important to Eastern philosophy and religion. We have each gone down the paths our values lighted for us. Because values underline choices of such magnitude that they determine the nature of our civilization, intelligent speaking demands that we understand and analyze these values.

THE IMPORTANCE OF VALUES IN CHOOSING PROBLEMS

Our value systems determine, in part, which problems we recognize as requiring solution. If we are not interested in art, we shall not try to think about problems of art, and if we are not moved by human beings who suffer, we may not try to understand the causes of poverty. *We recognize a problem because our values give us a generalized picture of an ideal and because the problem at hand represents a marked deviation from that ideal.* Values, therefore, are basic to problem solving.

Because values furnish the light by which problems can be seen, it is often necessary for a speaker to heighten or even inculcate certain values before an audience can perceive a problem. (It would be useless to point out to a savage that his explanations of thunder are not rational explanations, until he first valued such explanations.) Inasmuch as values are the bases of our choices and because they are our idea of what is right, good, true, or beautiful, there is always at least one value that underlies the regognition and acceptance of a problem demanding a solution. Successful speakers will be aware of such values and will attempt to judge the extent to which an audience will require that the value-background of a problem be established or heightened.

THE IMPORTANCE OF VALUES IN SELECTING CAUSES

Causes of problems seem, somehow, less "subjective" than problems; causes are "there" and cannot be subject to human preference, or so it seems. Remember, however, that a given condition, as Protagoras taught, may be caused by many things: Divorce may be caused by lack of sufficient income, by the disregard of one for one's mate, by sexual problems, or all of these and many more. Causes, more often than not, are subject to multiple causation. (See pp. 177–178.) Moreover, in addition to Protagoras' idea of multiple causation, remember that Aristotle taught that each cause has a cause, and that cause has a cause, and so on back to an infinite regress. Therefore, since each cause goes back to infinity and since each event may have multiple causes, the causes we recognize *are* subject to selection. Consider the happy father who is attending the wedding of his daughter: he drinks a bit too much and while driving home, makes a serious mistake in driving, and is killed. Now, one of the causes of automobile accidents, in this case, and undoubtedly in other cases as well, is marriage. We could prevent some deaths from automobiles by preventing marriages, but even though we are against deaths in automobile wrecks, our sense of values does not permit us to think of marriage as a cause worth considering. But since each event has, usually, multiple causes, and since each cause has causes itself running back to infinity, we select the causes we choose, and often our sense of values influences that selection.

THE IMPORTANCE OF VALUES IN SELECTING SOLUTIONS

Our values also influence the solutions we select. We can see, usually, how other people in other times and places were influenced by their values more easily than we can see how we are influenced by our values. Let us begin by looking at some solutions that we have already discussed. Ancient Greece prized freedom and individuality, yet these values, although they helped Greece become the most creative civilization in the history of earth, prevented the Greeks from maintaining peace and order. Ancient Rome prized order, and never developed the brilliant assemblage of philosophers, writers, scientists, and orators that the Greeks did. The values of these ancient lands, curiously, help explain their brilliance, but also explain the weaknesses of each culture.

But rather than simply point out how successful some—or all—other cultures have been, let us see if our own values are not creating problems, limiting our solutions, and preventing us from growth. What are our limitations? Certainly our own world has made no significant progress in the classical problems that have destroyed all previous civilizations: war, poverty, caste, tyranny, and disease; more people suffer these problems today than ever before in the history of the world. Certain values we hold may be blocking us from seeing or adopting solutions to these problems. We invent automatic curtain pullers, automatic lights that turn on at night and out in the morning, and automatic drink mixers. But we haven't invented any solutions to the problems that are most dangerous to us and that have destroyed every known previous civilization. Why? The answer must be sought by you, and not be one you find ready made in a book on public speaking. Search your own soul, your own times, your own peers, your own knowledge, for if enough of us find answers to account for our inadequacies, we may yet save ourselves.

THE NEED FOR ANALYZING VALUES

Most of us would agree that justice is better than injustice, that health is better than sickness, that freedom is better than slavery, and that beauty is better than ugliness. But what precisely, supports our certainty that justice is better than injustice? What makes one value superior to another? How, when we are faced with a conflict of values (such as choosing between peace with slavery or war with the possibility of eventual freedom), do we choose among values? Although defining what we mean by justice, peace, or freedom will help clarify these values, we must do more than merely define them. We must find some further ways of making clear which values are most worth securing.

The Chinese philosopher Mencius once said that if one puts in a heap all of the customs that are somewhere considered good, and then takes from the

heap each that is somewhere considered foolish or evil, nothing would remain. He was saying, in effect, that there is no way of deciding which things
have value and which do not on any intrinsic basis, except insofar as we ourselves assign a value. Thus, a painting has value if someone wants it, and
only if someone does. Values, in other words, are sometimes thought to be
relative to the person. The twentieth century abounds in this kind of relativism and such relativism is an intelligent corrective to earlier dogmatism
and to discussions of value without regard to the circumstances of the person
choosing values. At the same time, however, values do not depend entirely
on one's perception or on one's idea of them. Milk absolutely has a value for
drinking that gasoline does not and could never have, regardless of the subjective feelings of the drinker. It is possible to clarify these values further and
to make clearer the extent to which they should influence our choices. Values are the light by which we see our world; they are the bases of our
choices; they determine which problems, causes, and solutions we believe
are important; they give our civilizations their distinctive hues. Therefore,
we must understand how to analyze values and how to persuade others to accept them if we are to make intelligent speeches.

ANALYZING VALUES: STATING CONSEQUENCES

What makes one value important and another less important? Let us consider an example. A college education may be said to have a certain value,
and an expensive automobile to have another. In these days, both may cost
about the same. Assuming that we could choose one or the other for ourselves, which would be the first choice? The question can be answered intelligently only when we study the *effects* that each will produce. The consequences of an act or a value make it worthless or worthwhile. The
consequences of drinking gasoline make it a poor source of health, and the
consequences of putting milk in the gasoline tank are also not beneficial. Just
so, whether to choose an expensive car or a college education may depend
upon the consequences of each act.

These consequences, however, cannot be easily discovered. One consequence, for example, of choosing a college education may be that you may
(quite without knowing it) influence others to make the same step, just as
choosing an expensive car may influence others to keep up with you. Another consequence of a college education is that you may meet friends and
professors who will influence you the rest of your life, just as the trip you
take in your new car might make lasting impressions on you. You cannot
foretell the effects of a choice or of a value completely. Yet the further you
explore the consequences of selecting a certain value, the more rational your
choices can become. Even if we cannot know all about the effects of any particular value or decision, it does not mean that we shall not have intelligence
in the matter, for even if we are not free of all error, we shall have been
freed of some errors.

Persuading audiences to accept a value

When it is important that an audience accept a value, the speaker can select one of several lines of approach. Following are a number of lines of argument that are particularly useful in persuading an audience.

We have not listed, however, all the possible ways of persuading an audience to see the consequences of a value, and you may find that for your particular audience and value there are more appropriate ways than those described. At the same time, the following lists of methods, when strongly substantiated by examples, testimony, statistics, and similar support, will help an audience accept the value the speaker has in mind.

1. *This value has produced desirable effects in the past.* One might illustrate the use of this idea by explaining that one reason ancient Greek civilization reached such high peaks in so short a time was that the Greeks had a passionate belief, for a brief time, in freedom.

In our country, during World War I, we renamed sauerkraut "Liberty Cabbage," and in World War II we could not see such operas as *Madame Butterfly* or *The Mikado*. The ancient Greeks were in some respects freer than we. *Lysistrata*, for example, was an antiwar play produced in Athens during time of war—and produced at state expense. No one asked if it supported the Greek National aims, or the war effort, but only whether or not it was a good play. As things turned out, it won the prize as the best comedy of the year. It is hard to conceive of such a thing in the United States during any of the wars of the twentieth century. In Greece, freedom stimulated a multitude of ideas about philosophy, politics, man, religion, and nature that could hardly have been uttered, much less debated, had the Greeks not lived in a free atmosphere where ideas could compete. Destroy Greek freedom and Greek thought would die with it—as it did when Athens no longer governed her own destiny, and when Athenians persecuted creative minds.

Several variations of the idea that the value has produced good effects in the past may be applied:

a. Failure to use the value produced harmful consequences.
b. The opposite of the value produced harmful consequences.
c. Where the value was tried and seemed to fail, the conditions were unfavorable for the application of the value; today the conditions are more favorable.

2. *The most admired people accept this value, whereas less admirable ones do not.* One consequence of the soundness of a value is that people who possess good sense (experts, authorities, admirable people, and the like) choose it. This consequence can be used, likewise, to persuade an audience to accept the value. If the value is honored by one whom the audience reveres, they are more likely to accept the value. Thus if the audience is known to think highly of a certain statesman, a philosopher, an industrialist,

or a labor leader, and that person also is devoted to the value in question, the audience is more likely to accept the value. Many of us accepted the values of our teachers—when we liked the teacher—just as we might have rejected some value when we disliked the person advocating it. Thus a value may be reinfored by the example of one who accepts it or by the testimony of such a person.

Moreover, if it can be shown that groups of people worthy of emulation have accepted the value, whereas less admirable ones have not, the speaker can sometimes influence the audience: For example in a section of a speech designed to inculcate a desire for freedom, one could tell of the Greeks, of the struggles of the early settlers in the United States, and of the Hungarian Freedom Fighters, thus making the point that admirable people work for freedom. The theme would be particularly strong if the speech shows that other groups have made greater sacrifices to secure or keep freedom than the audience will need to make.

Some worthwhile variations on this theme may be applicable to the situation facing the speaker:

a. Admirable individuals and groups accept the value.
b. Despicable individuals and groups do not accept the value or despise or fear it.

3. *The value fits the needs of the audience.* We discussed motivation in Chapters 6 and 10. Values must appeal to people, or they cannot be values. If the value does not fit the person and his or her circumstances, it will not exert a strong influence on behavior. The situation can be compared to the soil conditions for a plant. If the soil is too acidic, as clay soils tend to be, the plant cannot make use of the nitrogen, phosphorus, and potash in the soil and will not grow well. In the same way, a value may be desirable because it can produce better conditions for growth of the individual by supplying crucial human needs. These growth needs are difficult to characterize but would include genuine satisfactions instead of momentary pleasures; the possibility of happiness instead of merely gratification; the possibility of transformation of one's self rather than the maintaining of an uneasy neuroticism; and the possibility for inventiveness and creativity rather than of a stolid conformity. In a sense, understanding the nature of these growth needs is the task of the whole of education, and even of the whole of one's life, and can hardly be settled with finality here. Nevertheless some readers will immediately understand these needs and recognize that they are basic, and others, one hopes, will begin the search for goals that bring the deepest and most permanent satisfactions.

4. *The value can be justified by reasoning.* One consequence of a sound value is that it can be subjected to reasoning without being found invalid. Philosophers have invented many kinds of reasoning; one who has studied

the history of philosophy and, particularly of ethics, will best understand the following categories listed here and their significance, if you haven't studied philosophy, you should consider doing so.

a. *The value can be stated as a principle that all people should follow.* Immanuel Kant asserted that one test of the goodness of a thing is whether or not it can be *universalized:* that is, if we believe a value is good, we ought to be able to recommend it to everyone. Thus, for example, we may not like to stop at traffic lights, but we can hardly justify such a dislike because if everyone failed to stop, the resulting chaos would make driving far more dangerous. Therefore, stopping at traffic lights is likely a good thing. Kant's test has some ambiguities, but with it, we can rule out many practices as unethical and can develop some certainty about others. Sometimes the variations of this theme may be quite persuasive: This value can be universalized; its opposite cannot be universalized; the lack of the value cannot be universalized.

b. *The merit of the value is self-evident.* In the sixteenth century, philosophers developed a "new logic," which was the basic logic used by Thomas Jefferson in writing the *Declaration of Independence.*[2] Certain ideas can be seen to be true if one merely gives one's attention to them; argument is not necessary to establish their merit, but only the complete understanding of these ideas. Once we completely understand that value, we will accept it. But the value *itself* must be grasped, not merely words about it or arguments for it.

   We are no longer so certain that there are self-evident truths as were the philosphers of the sixteenth and seventeenth centuries; at least, we know that what seemed self-evident to them does not seem self-evident to us. Despite the ringing words of the *Declaration,* we know that all people are *not* created equal, and if they are endowed by their creator with certain unalienable rights, enough of them are in chains and serfdom to make one question the worth of the "right." Nevertheless, one way to lead others to accept a value is to present it and to present it so completely and so fully in its beauty, its power, and its significance that by the perception of the value itself, people are led to accept it. The last two hundred years have not uncovered self-evident truths, but then there may be self-evident *values.* Indeed, one suspects that a value is either that which, when understood, compels one's belief in it, or it is no value. Far from being a method to be despised, the full and poetic expression of a value may, indeed, be the best "argument" in its favor.

c. *The denial of the value is contradictory and serves to assert the value.* Sometimes to deny a thing logically implies the thing itself. For example,

[2] See Wilbur Samuel Howell, "The Declaration of Independence and Eighteenth-Century Logic," *William and Mary Quarterly*, XVIII (Oct. 1961), p. 478.

if one asserted that "there are no such things as thoughts," one would already have implied that there are thoughts, because the denial of a thought is, itself, a thought. Or if, again, I assert, "Communication cannot occur among people," I have just refuted myself, for I have communicated, and therefore my denial of communication implies communication. This system of logic, known as *noncontradiction*, began with René Descartes. Later philosophers developed the method of noncontradiction more fully than did Descartes, who did not clearly understand it. Perhaps speakers in the twentieth century are more sophisticated in using varieties other than noncontradiction. And, perhaps, values cannot be established by this method. Nevertheless, since the advent of experimental science, this method has not been used with the frequency and intelligence it might have been. William James (who was not only one of the United States' most famous philosophers, but also one of the very best of our psychologists) according to a story that may have been invented about him, was once called to the office of the President of Harvard University. James had been teaching philosophy and psychology at Harvard for many years and was Harvard's most famous professor. The President of Harvard at that time, Charles W. Eliot, had his own theory about what should be taught in a university and decided that James could be brought to use Eliot's theories of education by a scolding. "James," he said. "I hear you are teaching students *ideas*. I want you to stop, and stop now. Ideas have no reality—only facts have; facts—do you understand, James—teach them facts." "Thank you," said William James, "I will consider your idea." Thus the value of ideas was established by denying their value.

Other themes

One could add indefinitely to the list of means for arousing audience acceptance of a value. One could include such approaches as "These values are within the grasp of the audience," or "Where the value produced good effects, the conditions were much the same as in our case," or "This value is easy to attain." Any stereotyped formula, however, will not be so effective as the speaker's selecting and phrasing of ideas so that they fit the unique audience and particular subject with which he is dealing. The speaker must seek ways of convincing an audience that the consequences of adopting a value, whether in the past, in the present, or in the future, are desirable.

Finally, that some values are of supreme importance because unless these values are realized to some degree, no human life, as opposed to animal life, is possible; these values are of such nature, furthermore, that not only are they responsible for our humanness but they can also transform our lives, provided we commit ourselves to them. The identification of these values leads to a standard of values for the speaker.

A STANDARD OF VALUES FOR RHETORIC

The speaker needs a set of values applicable to speaking that will help one to choose ideas, select supporting material, and decide which basic themes are of greatest worth to the audience, aside from their utility as persuasive devices. Such a consideration of values requires an introduction to the ethics of speaking. In addition to the preliminary discussion of ethics in Chapter 1, much of this book has been concerned indirectly with ethics. We have advocated the use of valid and honest supporting material, the choice of subjects involving problems of weight, and choice of solutions most beneficial to humanity. It is now time to grapple more directly with ethics.[3]

The standard of value is to be found in the nature of human beings and in those aspects of our nature that separate us from other animals. The unique nature of the human being seems to originate with two complicated and interlocking processes that generate all capacities that we call *human.* They are, further, of such nature that they can enable us to transform ourselves so that we can achieve the highest success of which humankind is capable. In these two capacities, therefore, should lie the ultimate standard of value. These capacities are our use of symbols and our capacity to be influenced by others in a way that no animals are influenced by their fellows. Let us see how symbols can make us human and can enable us to transform ourselves.

Symbols

Certain peculiarly human performances such as the creation of literature, art, mathematics, and science have their roots in symbols. The function of the human brain itself, according to Suzanne Langer, is to convert the raw data of sense experience into symbols. The brain, therefore, is not to be conceived of as merely a kind of telephone switchboard, but as a powerful transformer:

> The current of experience that passes through it undergoes a change of character, not through the agency of sense by which the perception entered, but by virtue of a primary use which is made of it [the sense experience] immediately: it is sucked into the stream of symbols which constitute the human mind.
>
> Because our brain is only a fairly good transmitter, but a tremendously powerful transformer, we do things that . . . [the cat] would reject as too impractical, if he were able to conceive of them.[4]

Langer traces the origin of dreams, ritual, magic, and speech to the process of transforming the raw data of sense experience into symbols. But the sym-

---

[3] The ideas presented here were first published by Henry Nelson Wieman and Otis M. Walter in "Toward an Analysis of Ethics for Rhetoric," *Quarterly Journal of Speech,* XLIII (Oct. 1957), pp. 266–70, and are reprinted here by permission.

[4] Suzanne Langer, *Philosophy in a New Key,* New York, The New American Library, Inc., 1948, p. 34.

bol itself changes the world into which it is introduced. Ernst Cassirer also emphasizes the power of symbols "not in the sense of mere figures which refer to some reality . . . but in the sense of forces each of which produces and posits a world of its own."[5] Because the brain transforms the raw data of sense experience into symbols, the human being lives in the world of these symbols, which further change this world in a way unknown to animals. Thus the human being will live, fight, and even die for symbols which he or she believes represent supremely important realities. Professor Karl R. Wallace writes:

> This capacity to symbolize abstractly, to combine abstract symbols into patterns, and to employ symbols in referring to past events and to the possible and probable future—symbolism in this way is, so far as we know, uniquely human. . . . The symbol is man's peculiar mode of ordering his experience, extending his experience, and refining his behavior. The growth and development of symbolization is almost synonymous with human growth and development; and learning, problem solving, organizing and evaluating involve high-level symbol behavior.[6]

Clearly, then, the capacity for symbolism is an essential element for the existence of human personality. Without symbols, of course, there can be no language. Without language much that is peculiarly human is impossible, for there can be no extensive thinking or problem solving. Without symbols, we cannot develop into human beings; we can become animals that are only biologically human but psychologically no different from other animals.

Symbolism is also indispensable for the continued growth of human personality. Forming concepts, discovering new concepts, and refining older ones are all impossible without symbols. When the process of growth is interrupted by interference with the process of symbolism, as in aphasia or senescence, the possibilities for refining, ordering, and expressing experience are severely limited.

Finally, symbolism can transform us creatively and progressively. Without symbols, as we have said, there could be no mathematics, no history, no science, no philosophy, no art. Nor could there be any love—that is, the recognizing and appreciating of the needs and interests of other persons and adopting them as our own. Likewise there could be no faith, in the sense of giving one's self in supreme devotion to what one believes to be the guide and goal of life. These human monuments have transformed human life. Symbols, moreover, can extend this kind of transformation beyond any known limit. In this extension lie our greatest possibilities.

Our need for others

But symbols can be used either destructively or creatively. We seek a guiding principle enabling us to use them creatively. The search will lead us to

[5] Ernest Cassirer, *Language and Myth*, New York, Dover Press, 1946, p. 8.

[6] Karl Wallace, "Education and Speech Education Tomorrow," *Quarterly Journal of Speech*, XXXVI (1950), p. 179.

the second peculiarly human quality, which shares with symbolism the responsibility for the origin of human personality, the nurture of personality during its growth, and the capacity to transform it. This quality is *the unique need of human beings for other human beings.* To be sure, animals need other animals for food, for reproduction, and apparently even for companionship—some die when placed in isolation. But this need of animals for each other is not the same as the need of the human being for other human beings, and it must not be confused with mere gregariousness. George H. Mead asserts that human beings need other people in order to generate and develop these uniquely human aspects known as "mind":

Mind arises in the social process only when that process as a whole enters into, or is present in the experience of any one of the individuals involved in that process. When this occurs, the individual becomes self-conscious and has a mind.[7]

Not only is "mind" developed by association with others, but only by *taking the attitude of another person toward one's self* does one form a concept of "self":

The human individual experiences himself as such not directly, but only indirectly, from the particular standpoints of other individual members of the same social group, or from the generalized standpoint of the social group as a whole. . . . For he enters his own experience as a self or individual not directly or immediately, not by becoming a subject to himself but only insofar as he first becomes an object to himself just as other individuals are objects to him . . . and he becomes an object to himself only by taking the attitudes of other individuals toward himself.[8]

Thus taking the role of others generates our mind and self. We may call this need for others, for understanding them, and for being understood by them, the need for *mutual understanding.*

Like symbolism, mutual understanding is essential, not only to the generation of human qualities but to the continued growth of the human being. *Others* frequently provide the motivation for the individual's activity, and make possible shared knowledge and the healthful give-and-take that can stimulate further growth and development. Even the development of language requires the presence of other people, because we create symbols to communicate with others. We can use language to communicate only when we can mutually understand symbols. To understand symbols, we must know something of what is in the mind of the other person; otherwise we could not grasp the meaning of words or use language. Thus symbolism and mutual understanding are inseparable, even if distinguishable, processes, and all growth as a result of language requires at least some degree of mutual

[7] George H. Mead, *Mind, Self and Society,* ed. Charles W. Morris, Chicago, University of Chicago Press, 1934, p. 134.

[8] Ibid., p. 138.

understanding. Without this interchange, one cannot continue to learn from others or increase what one can know, appreciate, and control.

This need for other people also has possibilities of transforming man beyond his present state. On this matter Mead says:

> In the conception of universal neighborliness there is a certain group of attitudes of kindliness in which the response of one calls out in the other . . . the same attitude. Hence the fusion [of interests] . . . which leads to intense emotional experiences. The wider the social process in which this is involved, the greater is the exaltation, the emotional response, which results. . . . This, we feel, is the meaning of life—and one experiences an exalted religious attitude. We get into an attitude in which everyone is at one with each other insofar as all belong to the same community. As long as we can retain that attitude we have for the time being freed ourselves of that sense of control which hangs over us all because of the responsibilities we have to meet . . . but in . . . the religious situation, all seem to be lifted into the attitude of accepting everyone as belonging to the same group. One's interest is the interest of all. There is complete identification of individuals.[9]

The transformation of humanity

The creative transformation of society comes about through the joint operation of symbolism and mutual understanding. When one, by virtue of one's unique individuality, creates some further symbolism, this creation is added to the culture only if that unique individuality is understood by others.

Mutual understanding of the unique individuality of the other does not mean approval of all of his or her thoughts, feelings, and actions. One cannot, however, justly disapprove of anything until after one has first achieved an understanding of it. Therefore, mutual understanding is the necessary prior condition that must be met before disapproval is justified. To be sure, we are caught every day in circumstances that require us to condemn before we achieve any high degree of understanding; but to realize this circumstance is only to realize that human life falls short of perfection. Mutual understanding is, then, the basis on which any judgment must rest, which morally approves or disapproves the conduct of a human being.

Mutual understanding ends in mutual influence. Through this mutuality of concern the purposes of each may be brought to fulfillment even when they are very different. To bring these purposes to fulfillment often requires modification of our purposes and desires, but it does not require that our purposes or desires be the same. On the contrary, in mutual influence, this modification is most profitable when one finds the purposes, needs, and desires of the other interesting and valuable to one's growth and development.

There are, then, two inseparable processes that are distinctively human: the process of symbolism and that of mutual understanding. These two processes are *constitutive needs* of the human being. That is, these processes

[9] Ibid., p. 274.

build the *human* mind and *human* personality, save it from disintegration, sustain it in its growth, and, finally, transform the human being progressively beyond any known limits. These processes, therefore, are the most fundamental of all human values.

If this analysis of the unique qualities of the human being and their significance is correct, it follows that an ethical act is one that enables the organism to meet its constitutive needs for symbolism and mutual understanding; an unethical act is one that destroys, prevents, delays, or otherwise limits the possibilities of meeting these needs. The moral law derived from this ethic might be stated thus: *Always act to provide conditions most favorable for mutual understanding between yourself and all concerned.*

Speaking, if it is to be ethical, must create conditions favorable to the expansion of symbolism and mutual understanding and influence. We define ethical rhetoric *as the discovery of the means of symbolism that lead to the greatest mutual understanding and mutual influence.*

The highest values have the highest consequences. When we use these values in speaking, we may transform ourselves and our society. To this end speaking must commit itself, if it is to serve us best.

VALUE SPEECH

Introduction

When we have studied the problems of our culture, we have gazed upon the cesspools and sore spots of our civilization. Such a view is incomplete without a glimpse of the greater moments of an advanced culture. In addition, more is required of us than that we solve our material problems, for it is not enough to sleep in safety with stomachs filled with food. We need to capture the aspirations and the visions given us by those who made great cultures possible. The solution of our problems may permit us to live, but a keen perception of values will make life worth living and can help to transform us, beyond any known limit, into the best we can become. Let us, then, search out these values and learn what they may hold.

Assignment

Give a six- to eight-minute speech in which you select a single value and build the most powerful case you can for that value. You may, instead, choose to attack a popularly held value that you believe to be false. The speech should aim at changing our ways of thinking and feeling; it should, ideally, change our lives.

Technique of presenting a value

A value must be made clear, perhaps by defining it as suggested in the previous chapter. The value may then be made both interesting and persuasive to the audience. This task may be performed by explaining the consequences of the value, particularly by showing that (1) the value has produced good consequences at other times for other people; (2) the value has been adopted by those the audience admires or rejected by those the audience disparages; (3) the value can fulfill the highest needs of the audience, or (4) the value can be justified by reasoning: (a) the value can be universalized; (b) the merit of the value is self-evident; (c) the denial of the value serves to assert the value. Each of these ideas, however, must be phrased or modified to fit the value selected and the audience. Moreover, it must be undergirded by the best supporting material the speaker can find, for the richness of the supporting material will in part determine whether or not the value gains a wide acceptance among members of the audience.

Subjects

Subjects such as the following should be chosen:

The value of reason, love, music, art, literature, learning, or religion.

A value taken from other cultures, e.g., stoicism, epicureanism, or Taoism.

A value taken from another civilization, e.g., Inca, Aztec, or Chinese.

The value of a specific piece of literature—a poem, play, novel.

The value of a particular period—the romantic, classical, or contemporary.

The value of a particular person—a composer, scientist, teacher, writer, or politician.

The value of an attitude toward life.

The negative values—those that harm, destroy, stultify, or limit human achievement.

ALTERNATIVE ASSIGNMENTS

Try to discover the principal values that govern the life of the following:

1. Each of your parents.
2. A teacher you have disliked.
3. A teacher you have liked.
4. A politician from your district.
5. A religious leader.
6. A relative other than your parents.
7. At least two friends of yours with values different from your own.

Note how hard it is to discern the values a person most respects. How can you be sure the values you ascribe to a person are the ones that are most important to that person? Of course, you can't, but often you can judge by what he or she does and says.

Wherever possible, ask the persons what they believe are the values that most powerfully direct their lives. You will, likely, find a discrepancy in what they say and in what they do.

What values direct you? What values would you like to be most important in your life? Why? How can you order your life so that the values you prefer to live by may be followed? How can you justify these values to be certain that they are the values you should choose?

15

discussing problems and values

Talk to them agreeably and with a flavor of wit, and try to fit your answers to the needs of each.

COLOSSIANS 4:16

People live with others who face situations similar to their own. Few of us can find ways that seem to yield satisfying lives without finding those ways intertwined with the lives of others. In this environment, which does not yield its secrets easily, people must communicate.

Thus far in this book we have concentrated on one form of oral communication, public speaking. Liberally educated citizens in a free society must possess the knowledge, skills, and attitudes that will enable them to conceive ideas and to communicate them purposively to groups of their fellows; but further, the knowledge, skills, and attitudes that are necessary for speaking to audiences will form a useful foundation for other forms of oral communication.

In a free society, men and women share interests, share responsibilities, and share rights. The same sort of problems that prompt individuals to address audiences under various situations may in other circumstances stimulate individuals to speak informally together seeking answers. It is common to call this informal, purposive speaking *discussion*. It is because interests, responsibilities, and rights are shared that we find so much discussion about us. Few of us will go through a week without being involved in talking with others in an attempt to reach some mutual understanding of problems that we face. All of us, whether we know it or not, interpret events that surround us and conduct ourselves according to some set of values. Members of groups share values, and if these groups are to persist and function, the members must recognize these values. This recognition must be constantly renewed. Often the recognition, the renewal, or modification of shared values depends upon discussion.

Undoubtedly the impulses and conditions that lead to discussion are as old as human society. In one of Plato's dialogues, Socrates says, "I think that all of us should vie with each other in the struggle to learn what is true in the matters under discussion, and what is false; for it is to the common good of everyone of us that this should be made clear."[1] Discussion was developed to such a degree of excellence by Socrates and Plato that the results of their thought have persisted throughout the history of Western culture to influence nearly every age. Although we shall be infinitely more elementary than these Greek philosophers in considering the theory of discussion and the practical use of our techniques, we should recognize that we undertake an activity that has proved deeply meaningful in human expression and communication.

A DEFINITION OF DISCUSSION

"I do not deal in definitions. . . ."[2] George Bernard Shaw once wrote. When thinking about defining *discussion*, one is tempted to adopt Shaw's attitude. The word is used in contexts that differ widely. Public speakers, for example, often say, "I want to discuss several issues with you," when obviously they intend to talk while we sit and listen. Although we can define the term in such a way as to exclude these speakers, *discussion* must remain a vague word, that is, there will be many instances in which we cannot confidently assign the term nor clearly justify not assigning it.

First of all, a discussion involves a group (we sometimes speak of *group discussion*). How many? The lower limit is easily stated—two, but the upper limit is more difficult to set. In general the more persons involved, the more difficult it will be to discuss problems informally. Two to six can discuss; six to ten may be able to; if more than ten are involved, discussion is possible, but becomes increasingly unlikely to occur. A group is not simply any aggregate of people; ten people waiting for a bus are probably not a group as we use the term here. A group has some more or less clearly defined purpose for existing—the members share interests, problems, values. They recognize some need for working together.

[1] *Grogias*, trans. W. C. Helmbold, New York, Library of Liberal Arts Press, 1952, 505.

[2] *Quintessence of Ibsenism*, New York, Brentano's, 1910, p. 28.

Sharing some need to work together, the members of the group cooperate; in discussion, they talk together making a situation in which each may address whatever points arise as they arise.

Discussion, then, refers to the effort of a group of individuals who talk informally together in order to solve commonly recognized problems or to arrive at an understanding of values. This definition implies that the desired end product is agreement, that the group intends to arrive at a plan acceptable to all for attacking a problem, or that the members are able to inquire into the meaning of value statements in such a way as to arrive at meanings with which everyone is satisfied. Whereas complete agreement ought to be the goal of those involved, complete disagreement may be the result. There are situations that demand some sort of final group decision. In such a situation, the group may produce a compromise that the members decide represents the most nearly complete agreement they can reach.

Although disagreements in discussion ought not be considered failure, discussions are not as productive of understanding as they ought to be and can be, for a very simple reason. Too many people say to themselves, "I can discuss. I discuss constantly. What is there to learn?" As a matter of fact, a lifetime of learning is necessary, not only for the scholar who may make a career out of studying group processes and interpersonal relations, but also for the man or woman who seeks effectiveness in working with others and who desires to understand himself or herself more deeply.

CONTINUING AND NONCONTINUING GROUPS

The remark that the only constant in life is change is both a very old joke and a very old truth. Given any common definition of the phenomenon "groups," one immediately recognizes that the concept is quite an unstable one. Groups come and groups go. But some groups are relatively stable, that is, they are ongoing as compared to other groups that form for some particular purpose at some particular time with the clear expectation by all involved that the groups will dissolve almost immediately. You undoubtedly have had experience in both sorts of groups.

Continuing groups tend to work out particular ways of dealing with the sorts of functions that give them their identity. These ways, once established, are likely to be valued by the group members who will tend to insist that any new member observe them. The willingness of new members to observe the established ways, and their ability to enact them, may serve as a rather informal initiation rite. Members of continuing groups are likely to feel threatened by outsiders, or by suggestions, made explicitly or implicitly, that different ways of dealing with problems be undertaken.

One reason for a rather strong set of values being built up by members of continuing groups is that the dynamic relationships necessary to make any group function over a long period of time are difficult to evolve and are fragile. The various roles of the members, for example, are likely to have been created in some struggle and are unlikely to be changed without further struggle.

Noncontinuing groups, on the other hand, may be important, but the participants are less likely to feel that they have a strong personal commitment to one another or to the group's function. The members, therefore, will probably be less resistant to having functions and relationships imposed on them by others or by the circumstances. If they participate at all, they will probably accept some external reason as dictating proper conduct for the occasion. After all, they recognize the occasion as limited. Some "director"—a teacher, an employer, a neighbor, or a friend—has called the meeting and, for a limited time, those involved are willing to let that person call the shots.

In most classroom situations, the participants in discussions are more typical of people in the noncontinuing than in the continuing group. By no means is this statement a rule; it is a most tentative prediction.

This chapter is a brief introduction to discussion for students in beginning courses. The student should gain a sharpened awareness of discussion and begin to form some attitudes and learn some techniques that should prove useful in developing effectiveness in discussion. But the student should recognize that these classroom experiences are limited samples of a great variety of situations to which one must adapt.

TASK AND SOCIAL ORIENTATIONS

Just as the ideas of "continuing" and "noncontinuing" groups may be rough approximations that will help people begin to understand groups, the notions of "task" and "social" orientations may serve to clarify personal relationships within groups. The noncontinuing group is very likely to have a task orientation. The "shots" that someone calls in getting the participants started probably will point to doing something that those involved recognize as germane to some interest or function that focuses in a rather immediate problem.

On the other hand, some groups form just because the people happen to be together. Or, in dealing with immediate problems, participants build relationships that tend to persist. These groups have the potential, at least, to continue. Much of the focus of their activity is on the relationships of the people involved. The clarity, strength, and reward of those relationships become quite important.

So potent are our apparent needs for self-definition in terms of our relationships with others that group discussion is being used in a number of situations that may be described in a general way as therapeutic. Group discussion may function to deepen personal understanding and lay the foundation for healthier ways that the individual may relate to others.

Although no group discussion can be free of the social orientation, concentration on this potential is quite beyond the scope of this chapter. We can only mention such things as the sensitivity session. But every discussion that the individual feels has been productive should help him in some small way build up a repertoire of behaviors that will be useful in the future. Most important, of course, will be the person's added insight into his or her own abilities.

ATTITUDE IN DISCUSSION

If anything is the essence of discussion, it is the attitude of those involved. If they have the proper attitudes toward their task and toward one another, they probably cannot fail to have a profitable discussion; if they do not, they probably will be unable to discuss at all.

The key descriptive phrase is easy enough to state and remember, but extremely difficult to learn and practice at a meaningful level; it is *friendly cooperation*. Although this advice sounds simple, let us caution that it's not as simple as it may sound. But perhaps we are a different sort of people from those Plato found in ancient Athens, judging by one remark he puts into the mouth of Socrates:

> I imagine, Gorgias, that you, too, have taken part in many discussions and have discovered in the course of them this peculiar situation arising: people do not find it easy by an exchange of views to arrive at a mutually satisfactory definition for the subjects under discussion, and in this way bring the argument to an agreeable end. Rather, when they disagree on any point, and one declares the other to be guilty of incorrect or vague statements, they grow angry and imagine that everything that is said proceeds from ill will, not from any concern about the matters under discussion. Some of these arguments end most disgracefully, breaking up in mutual vituperation to such an extent that the bystanders are annoyed at themselves for having become auditors of such people.[3]

If we believe that Plato observed the ancestor that still lives in us, we should turn our efforts toward developing an attitude of friendly cooperation. These suggestions may be useful in the development of a productive discussion attitude.

Repress the disposition to take offense

If others do not immediately agree with our sage observations, we should resolve to put firmly aside our disposition to take offense. All too often we quickly assume that others disagree out of bad motives. *Even if, and especially if, we find another's manner distasteful to us or believe that the other person is trying to be irritating, we should make every effort not to be antagonized.* We know that this is difficult advice to follow; each of us has observed and perhaps participated in discussions of religion in which the participants, professing faith in a belief that teaches humility and nonviolence, descend into the bitterest personal denunciations. We should take as our guide Montaigne's statement, "When any one contradicts me, he raises my

[3] *Gorgias*, 457.

attention, not my anger: I advance towards him who controverts, who instructs me; the cause of truth ought to be the common cause of both the one and the other."[4] Too often, however, to use Montaigne's words, "Instead of extending our arms, we thrust out our claws."

What does one gain by taking offense? To answer the question, ask another: Why does one take offense? Probably not simply because one finds another's remarks in and of themselves offensive, but because one supposes that the other *intends* to slight, disparage, or to insult. In short the motivation one *suspects* to lie behind the remarks triggers the offense.

At this point we should repeat one of the most common pieces of good advice uttered (we suspect that it is commonly heard because it is so difficult to heed), that is, that one should always hesitate to attribute bad motives to others. In any case it is better, both more profitable and more pleasant, to attribute good motives to others.

One may suppose a simple disjunction: the other either is or is not motivated by ill will. To take offense when the other is not motivated by ill will is to generate a situation fraught with potential misunderstanding, recrimination, and harm. If the other *is* motivated by ill will, intelligence still dictates repressing one's disposition to take offense because to reply in kind will simply tend to confirm the other's attitude rather than to dispel it. Such an exchange will, further, tend to communicate to any third person the feeling that the ill will is mutual—which, indeed, it will be.

Of course, the realities of the motivations of interpersonal responses are much more complex than our simple *is—is not* analysis pictures. But as we are involved in the complexities of these interactions we ought to come to realize that hesitating to take offense presents more possibilities for conducting amicable discussion than does escalating conflict, no matter how righteous our indignation.

Share disagreements as well as agreements

At first glance, this second piece of advice concerning the attitude one should strive for in discussion may seem contrary to the first. Unfortunately we have learned to take disagreement for offense perhaps because we have so often experienced disagreement that takes on all the shades and tones of being offensive.

Further one might object, "Why this talk about disagreement and the attitude one should take toward it? I thought discussion emphasized agreement." And so it does. Participants should find every possibility for agreeing. Often agreements will be limited but make excellent starting points. Discussion starts with a tacit agreement that the participants share a desire to talk together about mutual interests or problems, that, perhaps, they share responsibilities. And discussion tries to work toward agreement.

[4] "Of the Art of Conference," *The Essays*, ed. W. Carey Hazlitt, trans., Charles Cotton, London, Reeves and Turner, 1892, III, p. 158. This delightful essay, one of the finest ever written on the subject, is, fortunately, widely reprinted in various anthologies.

On the other hand, disagreement is also a prerequisite for discussion, and it may often contribute important junctures during discussion from which the participants can build toward better understanding of problems and solutions. If there is no disagreement, problems are often readily solved or values so self-apparent as to make discussion superfluous. Disagreements represent various interpretations to weigh and choose; potentially, therefore, they provide profitable inquiries to pursue. Failure to share disagreements may be fundamentally dishonest inasfar as a kind of false harmony is generated that may eventuate in a consensus to which the participants are in fact not committed.

Another reason to seek disagreement, and one not to be despised, is that disagreement provides stimulation of interest and activity. Nothing can be so fatal to good discussion as the suppression of disagreement because it may, in fact, mean a suppression of interest and, in substance, a withdrawal from the goals to which supposedly the members of the group are dedicated.

Disagreement, then, forms a basis upon which agreements can be built and a stimulus to get on with the work of so building. Stuart Chase put the matter in these words:

Often it is better to work out varying interests between people than to clamp the lid on them. Reconciliation can be overdone, as in the case of those who would "unite Heaven and Hell by combining the best features of both." Some students go so far as to say that if a serious conference lacks preliminary disagreement and strong discussion, something is wrong. The best solution may be found by fusing several points of view. The fusing process is bound to include some heat.[5]

It is better to risk too much heat than to fall into that attitude described by Montaigne, "They have not the courage to correct, because they have not the courage to suffer themselves to be corrected; and speak with dissimulation in the presence of one another."[6]

Sharing disagreements is far from an easy task. Suppressing the disposition to take offense may make the task more productive.

Disassociate to reduce tensions

Although quite obviously discussion is not a matter of playing at getting along with one another, one can reduce some of the inevitable tensions created by the necessity of working out disagreements. The person who disagrees in the mode of "That's certainly a stupid suggestion, but I expected no better from you!" is not apt to contribute to friendly cooperation. It may be necessary to criticize ideas, to weigh material, to make countersuggestions, but in doing so *concentrate on ideas and materials, not on people.* If you feel

[5] *Roads to Agreement,* New York, Harper and Brothers (now Harper & Row Publishers, Inc.), 1951, pp. 39–40.

[6] "Of the Art of Conference," p. 158.

that an idea is weak, try to talk about the idea without associating it with one of your fellow discussants.

Just as you should take care to disassociate your fellows from ideas that you feel you must view negatively, it is wise to disassociate yourself from the ideas and materials you contribute to the discussion. Don't continually talk about "*my* suggestion"; try "*a* suggestion." If another disagrees, then, the disagreement is with an idea and need not be interpreted as an attack upon you.

Listen carefully

The most irritating tensions are those that arise because the participants just do not listen to one another. "I disagree . . ." we sometimes say, when we do not disagree at all. We have heard only part of what another said. It is often useful to ask another to repeat or to restate an idea, or restate it yourself and ask if the interpretation is correct. Almost everything we considered in Chapter 9 is as relevant to listening in discussion as to listening to speeches. Review the material in that chapter.

If we would develop a healthful attitude toward discussion, we should value the process itself, committing ourselves to the difficult task of sharing materials, ideas, and responsibilities for decisions. We should state disagreements clearly and dispassionately, and should make every effort to reduce tensions. In short, we should seek to foster an attitude of friendly cooperation in the groups in which we discuss.

WHAT TO DISCUSS

In speaking before audiences, you have tried to frame theses as an important step in forming your ideas. Assertions, that is theses, may be the starting points of discussions also. Consider the assertion as being a truth-claim! "Broken homes cause delinquency." A group may bring data and analytical skill together to test the merit of this and other related claims. The discussants may modify or reject it and propose other claims to replace it or to extend its application.

Discussing questions

Most groups, however, and especially those composed of persons who are not experienced in discussion, find it difficult to begin with a thesis. Too often the cooperative quest fails to materialize as persons feel committed to one side or the other. When discussed meaningfully, assertions tend to be restated as questions. Most groups, however, find it more profitable to begin with questions.

Just as an individual may at first be only vaguely aware of the nature of his idea, groups may be bothered by some problem without being able to single out precisely what bothers them. A rather lengthy and thorough discussion may be necessary to state the question satisfactorily. And then the group may find that its statement of a question may need to be modified later.

On the other hand, often groups are formed especially to deal with questions that are quite distinctly formulated: the question exists before the group is brought into being. As a group of employees, as a citizens' committee, as a subcommittee of some larger group, men and women may volunteer or be appointed by their employer, mayor, or fellow committee members to deal with predetermined questions.

"How may we improve the participation of students in decision-making within academic departments?" "What should be the attitude of our group toward a united charity drive?" "How can we increase the incentives of physicians to practice in poor, sparsely populated areas?" "What curriculum will best serve the interests and needs of the students of this college?" These are examples of questions that have been and will be discussed by many groups.

Just as the inexperienced should probably avoid beginning with a thesis, most discussants should probably avoid phrasing a question that can be answered "yes" or "no." As with assertions, the problem is that it may be too difficult for most discussants to keep from committing themselves to a side and failing to think cooperatively. But it is possible, though difficult, to discuss "yes" and "no" questions, and such questions will probably arise as parts of more general discussions.

Discussing cases

Quite often some occurrence, situation, or experience will form the basis for a discussion. We can refer to these generally as *cases*. Sometimes the participants may have been parties to the incident that becomes the case upon which their discussion centers. At other times, discussants are presented with a case. "Here is a letter we received several days ago from a customer," a department manager may begin. "It seems to me to be representative of some difficulties we've been having with increasing frequency. What do you think?" A speech teacher may bring a tape recording to class in order to allow the group to hear a speech that will stimulate creative thinking on some problem or problems relevant to the group's interests.

The participants in a case discussion will inevitably raise questions and, therefore, will ultimately discuss questions; but the case will also provide a shared experience and a real basis from which the participants may start. A group of college students, facing questions of academic honesty, educational values, and personal conduct each day, may be interested in this illustrative case:

One day late in the spring, a student was approached by a close friend. The friend informed him that a small group of students had obtained—"never mind how!"—a copy of the final examination for an economics course in which they were enrolled. The group was more than reasonably certain that they indeed had the test that would be used. There were four students involved, all close friends of the student approached, and they wanted him to join them in preparing for the test.

The student was in the second quarter of his sophomore year. He had a straight "A" average, but was having what was for him a good deal of trouble in economics. He felt that if he received an "A" on the final, that he would receive an "A" in the course, but that an "A minus" would not be good enough. He was in the process of applying for a scholarship, not an ordinary scholarship, but a rather special one, which would be an honor to win as well as highly rewarding financially.

Quite obviously the student had a decision to make.

A group presented with this case would probably immediately ask themselves: What should the student do? Why? In trying to answer these general questions, they may raise a good many more specific questions concerning the conduct of the people involved. Cases such as this one usually prove to be much more complex than they seem at first.

Discussants, like public speakers, will find ideas and materials in their own experience, conversation, and reading that will seem worth working with. They will have to work carefully to phrase the questions they will deal with.

FORM IN DISCUSSION

Discussions have a way of being disorderly. Although we ought to realize that we cannot expect four or five people to think cooperatively in a fashion that will resemble the well-organized speech, disorderliness in discussion may be highly frustrating and may well decrease the potential effectiveness of the group. Participants, therefore, should learn to contribute to an orderly consideration of questions.

Pattern of reflective thinking

Just as in public speaking, both the whole structure and parts of the whole need attention if they are to be ordered in such a way as to make their effective consideration possible. One of the most useful aids to an orderly discussion is the recognition of the general process of reflective thinking. Although many writers have discussed the concept, John Dewey's analysis of reflective thinking has gained wide acceptance by discussion theorists as providing an excellent basis for working through problems in an orderly manner.

As Dewey observes, not all thinking is reflective. We proceed habitually through many problems each day and just let our minds wander much of the time; but from time to time we feel a difficulty in so proceeding, and when we face a "felt difficulty" we are inclined to think reflectively. Dewey has described reflective thinking as consisting typically of five stages: [7]

1. A difficulty (a problem) is experienced.
2. The nature of the problem is defined.

[7] These statements are paraphrases. See John Dewey, *How We Think*, Boston (now Lexington), Mass., D. C. Heath & Company, 1910, p. 107.

3. Possible solutions are suggested.
4. The solutions are examined and compared.
5. The best solution is chosen and verified.

One way of utilizing Dewey's analysis is to apply it to the entire discussion as a general "plan."

Step 1. *Recognizing the problem.* Sometimes the problem is self-evident; sometimes it is not. Usually a participant will find it necessary to review the event or events, the circumstances, the experience, or whatever it is that leads the group to sense or to recognize a problem. The problem will ordinarily be phrased as a question, and the participants will want to exercise care in the phrasing. The terms used in the question will probably need defining to assure that the participants share an understanding of what it is they are discussing.

Step 2. *Describing the nature of the problem.* At this stage the participants will want to inquire further into manifestations of the problem: "What has happened?" "Does the problem have extensive effects?" "Whom does it affect?" and similar questions. The participants will seek the cause or causes of the problem.

Step 3. *Suggesting possible solutions.* At this stage it is especially vital that the participants remember to disassociate persons from suggestions. It may be wise first to set up criteria that acceptable solutions should meet.

Step 4. *Evaluating the possible solutions.* The participants will often deal in comparisons at this stage. The solutions themselves will be compared. The participants will tend to ask of each solution: Has it been tried in other situations? Are the situations comparable? What were the results? What are the comparative advantages and disadvantages of the solutions?

Step 5. *Selecting and acting upon the best solution.* Dewey indicates that solutions should be verified, that is, they should be put into practice to see if indeed they solve or help solve the problem. Often discussion groups are not in a position to put their solutions into action. At other times, groups will be called upon to take some sort of action and should decide what details will be necessary to carry out the plan.

Quite obviously these five steps may constitute an overly ambitious plan in many circumstances. Sometimes a long series of discussions might be necessary for a complete working through of this process. Groups may decide to concentrate on some element of the pattern.

Thinkers discover problems within problems. In concentrating on some particular question that is a part of a larger question, the "plan" of reflective thinking may be usable. A group that has spent days on a question may come to the point of agreement and then ask, "How can we put this plan into operation?" There may be problems to face and describe, solutions to suggest and evaluate, and decisions to make in regard to this question.

We must caution you about using the steps. They should be considered to be a potentially useful guide, not a ritual to be inflexibly adhered to and invariably followed. You may find yourself working in a group in which the participants are not conversant with "the plan" as you know it. You should resist an impulse to insist that the others in the group recognize suddenly and wholly the procedure as you see it. This does not mean that you cannot help guide the group to an orderly discussion; it does mean that you will recognize the rights and responsibilities, the abilities and disabilities, of those with whom you are working. Finally, you should not consider any variation from the sequence of steps to be necessarily an outrage against fruitful procedure. On the contrary, the mind may jump to a solution quickly and then need to backtrack, and this may be stimulating. Thinkers are likely to discover at some late stage that earlier stages need to be reworked. "Each improvement in the idea leads to new observations that yield new facts or data and help the mind judge more accurately the relevancy of the facts already at hand,"[8] Dewey wrote. He considered these steps to be intermeshed, each throwing light on the others, and believed that the thinker would go over and over the "phases, terminals, or functions of thought," as he called them.

The discussant, then, must give attention to both the large outline and the detail of thought. The pattern of relative thinking can be useful in both respects, but should not be looked upon as being an inflexible formula.

Making agendas

Sometimes a group will prepare an agenda to help assure an orderly discussion and guide preparation for discussion. The agenda may reflect a preliminary analysis based on the process of reflective thinking and consist of specific questions based on its stages. Sometimes a group will be presented with an agenda, just as it may be presented with a question or a case to consider.

A group of college students who began with a vague desire "to discuss conformity" composed an agenda for their discussion, that is, a series of interrelated questions, rather than a single discussion question. You will note that the first five questions lead up to the final question that was the chief concern of the discussants.

1. What do we mean by "conformity"?
2. What conformity pressures are placed on us?
3. What conformity pressures do we place on others?
4. In what ways are conformity pressures useful: to individuals? to society?
5. In what ways are conformity pressures harmful: to individuals? to society?
6. Can we state concisely what our attitude as educated young men and women should be toward conformity pressures in our society?

This may seem to be an ambitious agenda, and it was; the group took more than two hours to discuss it. In addition, they spent several sessions in

[8] Ibid., p. 115.

planning the agenda during which they shared initial ideas and sources of material. The agenda served to guide their preparation as well as their discussion.

PREPARING FOR DISCUSSION

Discussion is speaking; almost everything that you have studied in this book is relevant to speaking in discussion, even delivery. Although obviously you are not going to address an audience, you will need to speak directly and vigorously to your fellows. As we pointed out in Chapter 8, lively delivery will be an empty virtue unless one has something of substance to say.

Preparation for discussion is much like preparation for a speech. You need to gather and process information. You need to analyze that information and to formulate ideas. It may be useful to review Chapters 2 and, especially, 3. The result of this preparation process may be an outline as well as a stack of well-ordered note cards. Your outline may utilize the patterns of reflective thinking; it may follow an agenda upon which the group has agreed; or it may, when it is fused with the work of your fellows, become an agenda for the group. The person who understands discussion, who has begun to form a healthful attitude toward the process, will keep individual decisions tentative. You should not expect that others in the group will have made the same preliminary decisions that you have made or that the discussion will follow your outline neatly.

Individuals thinking together cooperatively will analyze problems, causes, solutions, and values; Chapters 10, 11, 12, 13, and 14 deal directly with these concerns and might be reviewed with profit in the context of considering discussion. You can see that you can apply many of the ideas you have already studied and have put into practice in public speaking situations.

Too often discussants do not feel the pressure of having to prepare quite as thoroughly as does the speaker who will stand before an audience. If anything, good discussion is more difficult than good public speaking; not only must discussants develop their own lines of thought, but they must respond to those developed by others. They must be familiar enough with their material to be able to draw upon it as the unfolding discussion situation demands.

THE LIMITS OF TIME IN DISCUSSION

Discussion is likely to be slow work. If a half dozen persons are to express themselves on a complex series of questions, and are to interact with one another, they must take the necessary time. Often time will be limited, and therefore the group will be wise to limit the scope of the questions with which they deal.

Too often groups, especially in classrooms are encouraged to consider difficult and stimulating questions within time limits that are much too narrow.

Whereas time pressure and an impatience "to get things done" may be useful antidotes against indolence and garrulity, little can be done in half an hour. On the other hand, protracted sessions are often wasteful. What is the answer? Many active, productive groups have discovered that a series of short meetings is best. The total time given to the questions is likely to be used more profitably, in that the members have an opportunity for second thoughts—for reconsidering problems and finding fresh data—between meetings.

LEADING DISCUSSIONS

In general, everyone has the responsibilities of preparing for the discussion and of stating as quickly and clearly as possible his ideas and materials relevant to the points under discussion. In general, everyone should try to facilitate participation. There will be in every group the more aggressive and the more submissive, and there will be, therefore, tendencies to overparticipate and underparticipate. Listen, be concise, and be courteous. Question others to gain understanding of their points of view. Remember that frank expression of disagreement is part of discussion; be sure that you really do disagree, then state your objections as dispassionately as possible.

It is common in discussions to designate a leader. The leader, or chairperson, has some special responsibilities. The leader should see to preliminary arrangements: that everyone is seated comfortably (some arrangement that allows each person to see every other person easily is to be highly preferred); that all discussants have been introduced to each other; and that, generally, informality and cordiality are encouraged from the beginning. The chairperson will probably take the initiative in getting the discussion started and will have given some thought to initial questions, or perhaps examples, that will raise questions.

During the discussion, the chairperson will take primary responsibility for seeing that the discussion progresses in an orderly fashion. Taking this responsibility may mean asking participants to restate their ideas; it may involve questioning participants to clarify their contributions; or it may mean being patient and quiet. The chairperson ought to summarize agreements frequently and draw relationships between what has been done and a general plan or agenda. Of course the chairperson should not be arbitrary in trying to keep the discussion orderly, finding agreements that do not exist, or summarizing points that have not been made. The leader must work with the others.

One must not conclude that the chairperson is one set apart, necessarily. A leader should have the rights of participation, of expressing ideas and bringing material to bear on points at hand. The leader should be especially careful in contributing, however, not to seem to be taking undue advantage of a prominent position to force ideas on the group. Some groups like to make the chairperson strictly a traffic director, and there may be some merit in this procedure, but groups should not be too quick to limit the contributions of a potentially valuable group participant.

Although the chairperson may take special responsibility for introducing, restating, questioning, summarizing, and so on, the other participants may well share these functions. No one should be expected to be able to ask all the right questions at the right times, or draw relationships between ideas, or make all the summaries. The progress of the group is the responsibility of each of its members.

SOME FORMS FOR PUBLIC DISCUSSIONS

Sometimes discussions take place before audiences. On these occasions the "discussions" may be either informal, cooperative thinking and speaking, the kind of discussion we have been concerned with in this chapter, or they may be more akin to public speaking in that the participants use the informal groups to communicate ideas as they might in addressing an audience individually even though they may have to be somewhat more flexible. Some public discussions are a mixture of these two types.

Public discussions of either sort may serve the needs of participants and audiences and should, therefore, be of interest to the student of speech. Indeed, it is unlikely that many students are unfamiliar with the various formats that may be used. We shall consider some of the most common arrangements for carrying on public discussions.

The panel

Panels or round tables closely resemble the kind of discussions we have been considering. Often the group members will be genuinely working together toward the solution of problems or the better understanding of values. The public meetings of many boards or committees may be "true discussions." Sometimes, however, the participants will have rather well-defined, predetermined points of view to which they are committed and will probably remain committed. For example, members of congress representing various parties on a radio or television panel are unlikely to participate in cooperative problem solving before their audience. These participants will make short, spontaneous speeches in response to questions as they arise. Probably the group will be conducted informally, often by an impartial chairperson.

The symposium

A series of prepared speeches on a common topic is called a symposium. Usually some division of the topic is agreed upon. Perhaps one speaker will describe a problem; another analyze causes; a third and a fourth may set forth two different solutions. Sometimes the division will be extrinsic to an analysis of the topic itself but bring different points of view to bear. Thus a program at a small, liberal arts college might be headed, "Shall we increase the size of our student body?" and list three speakers charged with presenting "an administrator's view," "a professor's view," and "a student's view." A symposium is sometimes used to begin a panel discussion, that is, after the speakers have finished, they may then discuss the question informally.

The forum

A forum session often follows a symposium, a panel, or a speech. The forum is simply a device for allowing a large group of listeners to become participants. The chair will allow members of the audience to ask questions or to make short speeches, sometimes under predetermined rules as to length and relevancy. The chair may summarize what has occurred in the forum, although often this task is not simply difficult, it is virtually impossible.

CONCLUSION

Good discussions grow from knowledgeable, skillful participants who are stimulated by problems and values. Discussions are not ends in themselves, although we may enjoy participating in them, but are instruments of potentially great utility in contributing to the answers you will seek to many questions that will arise as you interact with others.

About 200 years ago, in fact near the time when the Constitution of the United States was worked out and then ratified through a series of speeches and conferences that entailed nearly unbelievable dedication, skill, and perseverance, a Scotch theologian and teacher put into these words the thought that has been central to this chapter and this book:

One of the most distinguished privileges which Providence has conferred upon mankind is the power of communicating their thoughts one to another. Destitute of this power, reason would be a solitary, and, in some measure, an unavailing principle. Speech is the great instrument by which man becomes beneficial to man; and it is to the intercourse and transmission of thought, by means of speech, that we are chiefly indebted for the improvement of thought itself. Small are the advances which a single unassisted individual can make towards perfecting any of his powers. What we call human reason, is not the effort or ability of one, so much as it is the result of the reasoning of many, arising from lights mutually communicated, in consequence of discourse and writing.[9]

ASSIGNMENTS

A short discussion assignment

1. Your class will be divided into groups.
2. Discuss the case cited in this chapter of the student who was asked to join a group of his fellows in studying an advance copy of a test dishon-

---

[9] Hugh Blair, *Lectures on Rhetoric and Belles Lettres*, London, T. Tegg and Son, 1838. Lect. I, Intro., p. 1. (First edition, 1783.)

estly obtained, or discuss some other case provided by your instructor.
3. The class should then conduct a forum of comments and questions concerning the case.

A longer discussion assignment

1. Your class will be divided into groups.
2. Designate a chairperson or designate a different member as chairperson for each meeting.
3. Hold a preliminary meeting to phrase a question for discussion. Limit the question as much as necessary to make it feasible for the time available. Consider the possibility of a later limitation to a part of the question, to an analysis of the nature of the problems and its causes, for example.
4. Hold a second meeting to compose an agenda and to make whatever modification of the question that seems wise in light of preliminary individual preparation.
5. Discuss the question. Try to reach agreement.
   (If possible, schedule two meetings for covering the agenda. In the second meeting, do not hesitate to reconsider questions.)
6. Evaluate the discussion.
   a. If possible, tape record the discussion so that the group members may evaluate the discussion, especially their own roles.
   b. Each person should listen to and evaluate one other discussion group.

Criteria for evaluating participation in discussion

1. Contributing material.
   a. Does the participant contribute specific material plentifully?
   b. Are these contributions relevant to the points under discussion?
   c. Does this person present material to supplement or test that presented by other participants?
2. Contributing to the orderly progress of the discussion.
   a. Does the participant seem to be working from a sound basis of original reflective thinking, or is this member dominated by a desire to air strong views on some portion of the problem with little regard to the progress of the discussion as a whole?
   b. Does this person suggest ways in which ideas being discussed or materials presented bear on what has been discussed and how they might point toward agreements that will carry the discussion forward?
   c. Does this person ask questions that help clarify ideas and their relationships to the discussion as a whole?

3. Working cooperatively.
   a. Does the participant state ideas and materials as objectively as possible or does this person make strong personal identification with them?
   b. Does this person seem to listen carefully to the ideas and materials presented by others?
   c. Is this person courteous in referring to others?
   d. Does this person help state and clarify disagreements?

Criteria for evaluating the group as a whole

1. Was the question stated clearly? Was it sensible in terms of the time limit?
2. Was the agenda clear and complete? Was it sensible in terms of the time limit?
3. What was the atmosphere of the group? Friendly cooperation? Some antagonism? Marked antagonism? Forced and unspontaneous courtesy?
4. What agreements were reached? Were they real agreements? Were disagreements resolved?

index